God's Glorious Guidance in My Life

The Life Story of Faith Hemmeter as told to Ronald and Anna Smith

ISBN 978-1-934447-05-5

First Printing 2007

Second Printing 2008

Printed by
Country Pines Printing
Shoals, IN
USA

1935

A Life Dedicated to God

2007

Dedication

This book is dedicated to the memory of my parents, Walter and Lillian Hemmeter, and my paternal grandfather, John Hemmeter.

By their examples Daddy and Mama taught me the joy of walking with God, and Grandpa taught me the joy of winning a soul to Jesus. They also taught me the importance of reading and studying God's Word and living by it. The answers they received to their prayers inspired my faith in God. I owe **much** to these soldiers of the cross who showed me the glory of walking with God.

Faith Hemmeter

Content

Foreword

As a young pastor in 1972, I was impressed by the compassionate EFM missionary who tearfully spoke of needy lost souls in faraway Africa. Faith Hemmeter truly made an indelible impression upon me as she shared her burden at the Wesleyan Holiness Church in Peoria, Illinois. That first encounter proved to be the starting point for many diverse and unique relationships that we experienced in the years that followed.

During my pastoral years my wife and I read in the *Missionary Herald* of Faith's adventures in Jinka, Ethiopia, with Carrie Boyer as these brave women took the gospel of the Lord Jesus Christ to pagan people of that primitive region. Our monthly missionary services frequently included reading letters from Faith Hemmeter and praying often in her behalf.

In 1980 I was elected to the Board of Directors of Evangelistic Faith Missions. This allowed me to have greater insight into the sacrificial life of this godly missionary who was then serving in Bolivia, South America, the second mission field to which God had called her.

When I was elected as the president of Evangelistic Faith Missions in 1994, I was able to behold this handmaiden of the Lord in still a different light. It was my privilege to visit Faith on the mission field of Bolivia and see her in the trenches waging holy warfare for the Lord Jesus Christ with the enemy of man's soul, Satan. She served as my able interpreter on several occasions. As her health deteriorated, she was an uncomplaining soldier fighting the good fight until it became necessary for me to give the orders for her to withdraw from the mission field.

The Lord graciously allowed Faith's health to improve after she returned to the States, and my wife and I have been permitted to travel many miles with her in deputation work for the Mission. We have been blessed by the interesting stories of her many experiences on the mission field. God's goodness was always her theme, and answers to prayer were her banner of praise.

9

It became a growing conviction with me that her story had to be placed in print. This life lived for the glory of God had to be preserved for future generations to read, to enjoy, and to be challenged by it. This book shows forth God's glorious guidance in the life of Faith Hemmeter.

Rejoice with this child of God as she walks with the King of kings down life's pathway. Praise God for the many times He answered her prayers. Gasp as she had repeated brushes with death. Be blessed as sinners are converted to the Lord Jesus Christ during the life's journey of this "true missionary."

President J. Stevan Manley, Evangelistic Faith Missions

Acknowledgments

I wish to thank God and the precious people who worked together to make this book possible. The following individuals made significant contributions to its development:

Linda Kelley did intense research and worked on the early phases of the book. She read letters that my mother had saved from my years in Eritrea and articles in previous *Missionary Heralds* searching for material. She also worked on preparing a timeline of events.

Steven Hight continued the work by spending many hours with me reviewing the events of my life and revising some early materials.

Irene Maurer carefully read some of the material, making suggestions and corrections.

Ronald and Anna Smith worked diligently to make this book a reality. They sent me many e-mail messages asking questions, making suggestions, writing, and rewriting the stories and events of my life from birth to the present. There also were numerous phone conversations. On several occasions they traveled to Bedford, Indiana, to review materials, select photos, and make arrangements to get the book printed.

J. Stevan Manley and his wife, Helen, made many helpful suggestions. He is the one who insisted that this book should be written. Helen and I spent many hours together revising each chapter.

Shirley Dye read the manuscript and expressed her observations and suggestions.

Ralph Woodworth and his wife, Erma, worked extensively with the Smiths giving guidance, rewriting, and helping with the final proofing.

I could never have written this book by myself. God knew the desire of my heart to show forth His Glory, so He put it into the hearts of these people to bring this book to completion. Reading over the events that tell what God has done for me has been a real blessing to my heart. I stand amazed at what God has done. What a mighty God we serve!

Part I

My Years of Preparation

Chapter 1

Events in My Early Life
1935-1944

Cleveland, Ohio

The young couple had arrived at the Polyclinic Hospital in Cleveland, Ohio, and was waiting the birth of their second child. Since their first daughter had gone to heaven shortly after she was born, Walter and Lillian Hemmeter were anxiously anticipating the birth of this new baby. They joyfully welcomed me, Faith Eileen, into their family on August 3, 1935.

My mother was born in West Salem, Ohio, and was next to the youngest in a family of eight children consisting of six girls and two boys. Her father was a graduate of Wooster College in Wooster, Ohio. Her parents, Sherman Allen and Dora Luella Rickel, and their children lived on a farm.

Mama never saw her saintly mother walk because of severe arthritis. Her father put wheels on a regular straight-backed chair so that her mother could be more mobile. Mama was sixteen when her mother passed away. At that time her mother called all her children around her bed and asked, "Don't you hear that beautiful music?" Then she sat up and said, "Oh, the angels! They've come to get me!" With that she went home to glory. After she passed away, Pearl, an older daughter, gave up marriage to help take care of her siblings. The family later sold the farm and moved to Cleveland.

My father was born in Cleveland and had an older sister, Pearl, and a younger brother, Virgil. His father, John Hemmeter, graduated from Cleveland Bible Institute and married Ida Mae Haydorn. John was a circuit-riding preacher in Wisconsin

Grandpa John Hemmeter reading his Bible in his favorite rocking chair

and then became an evangelist in the Ohio Yearly Meeting of Friends.

I always thrill to tell the story about the time my father's parents had nothing to eat. It was noon and Grandpa became aware that he heard no sound of food preparation. He entered the kitchen and found Grandma crying. "Why, Ida, what's wrong? Why aren't you getting dinner?"

"John," she said through her tears, "we don't have anything to prepare."

"What happened to the cornmeal we had?"

"You ate the last of it last night." Grandpa suddenly remembered that Grandma had not eaten much the night before. She had said she was not hungry.

"Well, set the table, fill the tea kettle, and put it on the stove," he directed. "Now let's go into the living room and pray." While they were praying, they heard a knock on the door. There stood a black saint of God with a basket on her arm. In the basket she had an entire meal prepared. They thanked her, put it on the table, and sat down to enjoy the dinner that God had provided through His servant.

When Daddy was twenty-one, he started showing attention to Mama by fanning her on hot days during choir practice. At the same time there was a redheaded young man named Bill Ford who told Daddy he was setting his cap for Lillian Rickel. Daddy told me he thought that if Bill was going to beat him, Bill would need to work awfully fast. That spurred Daddy to ask Mama for steady company. Later they learned that they had been praying about each other for two weeks before Daddy asked Mama.

Daddy wanted a small wedding in his parents' home, but Mama wanted a big church wedding. They compromised and planned a small wedding in the Second Friends Church in Cleveland on June 24, 1932. However, the church was in an Italian neighborhood, and when the neighbors realized there was going to be a wedding, they came. Thus nearly two hundred people attended the wedding.

Mama's whole family was very musical. Her father had a good bass voice and taught my father to sing bass after my parents were married. However, when Daddy and Mama sang together in church,

Daddy sang tenor instead of bass. My father often played the mandolin and Mama played the piano.

My parents' first baby was a little girl who was a "blue baby" and lived only twenty-four hours. Ralph Jacket, who had married Daddy's sister, said to Daddy, "I don't feel that God is fair. I am not serving Him, and I have three beautiful daughters. You are and yours died."

Daddy replied, "I still have a daughter. She's in heaven with God." Later Daddy asked God for another girl, and when I was born he said, "Now I have a daughter in heaven and a daughter on earth. It doesn't matter whether I live or die; I have a daughter with me!" My father had read a story in a Sunday school paper about a girl named Faith and decided to give me that name. Years later Faith Dell Ford told me another reason why I was named Faith. She said she knew my mother in Cleveland, and Mama had promised her that if she ever had a little girl, she would name her Faith after her. I became very close to Faith Dell Ford in later years and called her Mama Faith.

At the time of my birth, my parents were attending the Second Friends Church in Cleveland, and that is where they dedicated me to God. On Saturday evenings they frequently took me in a basket to all-night prayer meetings. I believe those prayer meetings had an impact on my life even though I was an infant and slept while the others prayed.

My very first memory is of Daddy playing with me around the house. Sometimes he would get down on all fours and let me ride on his back, or he would put me on his shoulders and run through the house. Also he would race with me to get ready for bed. He would call

"Gotcha"

from his room, saying, "I only have my shirt to take off," or "I have one sock off; what about you?"

When we had family worship, Daddy would ask me what Bible story I wanted, listing several, and I almost always chose "Jonah and the Whale" because he illustrated it with words like "kersplash!" I knew that our water came from Lake Erie, and whenever I was naughty, I would fear that a whale would come after me while I was taking a bath. I could picture it elongating itself to come through the pipes and then swelling out in the tub.

My father was my first theology teacher. He helped me to understand the goodness and justice of God. When I was good, we had much fun together. I enjoyed going places with him and just being with him. When I was bad, I could expect him to correct me. After he corrected me, he would pick me up, set me on his lap, and explain why he had corrected me. He reassured me that he loved me and wanted me to grow up to have friends. Then he would say, "Now give me a hug and a kiss." If I gave him just a little peck, he held me until I gave him a big hug and a big kiss. He then treated me as though I had not done anything wrong.

Standing at the hand pump on the farm near Quakertown, Pennsylvania

Daddy taught me instant obedience and that delayed obedience is disobedience. When I was playing outside and Mama would call me to come home, if I did not answer at the first call, when I got home, Daddy questioned me, "Why didn't you answer Mama the first time?" I quickly learned to drop everything when I heard my mother call and to run home saying, "Coming, Mother, coming, Mother," all the way as I ran. The neighbors thought that I was such a remarkable child. It was not that as much as it was that my father taught me instant obedience.

I credit Daddy for the fact that I can honestly say that the first time the Holy Spirit spoke to me, I answered His call to salvation. That occurred one Sunday morning when I was four years old. I remember it so clearly! I was seated in the Second Friends Church in Cleveland with my mother sitting on my right and my father on my left.

As the minister preached that morning on the crucifixion of Jesus, my child's heart was moved against the cruel men who nailed my Jesus to the cross. I thought, *"Why did wicked men want to kill my Jesus? All He ever did was good. He healed the sick, raised the dead, and fed the hungry. Why then did they want to kill Him?"*

Suddenly the Holy Spirit spoke to me saying, "But, Faith, it was your sins that helped to nail Him to the cross." My heart was broken. Turning to my mother I asked, "Mama, may I go down there?"

"Why? Why do you want to go?"

The tears gushed out as I said, "Why, I want to pray." I knew deep in my heart that if I could just get to the altar and ask Jesus to forgive me, He would.

Mama replied, "Yes, Honey, you may go and I will go with you." As we stepped into the aisle, my father followed us.

Kneeling with my parents I poured out my heart to Jesus, asking His forgiveness. At that moment the Holy Spirit showed me my sin. It was disobedience to my parents, so I asked Jesus to forgive me. He did, but then He said, "Now you need to ask your mama to forgive you." I turned to Mama and asked her forgiveness. Giving

On my fourth birthday with Aunt Naomi Rickel shortly before I was saved

19

me a hug she told me that she forgave me. Then the Spirit said, "Now you need to ask your daddy's forgiveness." Turning to my father I asked him to forgive me for being disobedient. He also hugged me and forgave me. At that moment the assurance came that I was forgiven. Praise God, even a child can know that her sins are forgiven!

Mama was a very cheerful person who laughed and smiled often. She frequently sang hymns in her beautiful soprano voice as she worked around the house. On Christmas mornings her custom was to wake us up by singing, "We wish you a Merry Christmas."

While we still lived in Cleveland, I witnessed to my Catholic girl-friends. One day before I was eight years old, I gathered them in our backyard and told them about the Second Coming. As I talked, we heard beautiful music. I looked up and saw a beautiful sunset and thought Jesus was coming back right then. I said to my friends, "There **He** is right now! Let's go out and meet Him!" As we ran to the front yard, I fully expected to be taken up in the rapture right then, but we saw that it was only a Salvation Army band starting a service about a block away.

Joanne Naroni and her cousin Marlene Naroni lived next door to us with one family downstairs and one upstairs. Their mothers were sisters and their fathers were brothers. Years later the mother of one of them, when told that I was going to Africa as a missionary, said, "I'm not surprised. I always knew Faith would be a missionary." She remembered that I had begun by trying to evangelize her daughter and niece when all three of us were just little girls.

Another time I went from door to door giving out tracts in a Catholic neighborhood. "Here's a tract," I would say. "You can give me however much money you want to give." I returned home with a sum of money.

"Where did you get all that money, Honey?" Mama asked.

"I sold tracts," I said.

"Oh, Honey, you must not sell tracts. Tracts are free. Go back to those houses and give the money back."

I was crying as I went from house to house saying, "My mama said I wasn't supposed to sell tracts." I held out my cupped hands and said, "Take back however much money you gave me."

Most of the people said, "Oh, Honey, that's OK. Keep the money and give it to your church." That left me with some money for God, but it was a very humiliating experience.

A little girl named Joanie Chalupka lived across the street from us in Cleveland, and her Czechoslovakian parents were bakers. The rich people from Shaker Heights came to Mr. Chalupka's bakery to buy their baked goods. Joanie was an only child, the same as I was at that time. Every Sunday morning I would go across the street and call, "Oh, Joanie!" over and over until one parent would open a window. "Can Joanie go to Sunday school with me?"

"No, Honey, not today."

One day Joanie ran home from school without waiting for me. When I got home, I found her sitting on our front steps. "There's a letter in your mailbox," she said. The letter was from Joanie saying, "I will go to church with you next Sunday if you will come to a picnic at my house tomorrow." True to her promise she went with me the next Sunday, but that was the only time she went to Sunday school with me while we were children.

Eight years later I was back in Cleveland in junior high school when the Holy Spirit began dealing with me about speaking to Joanie about her soul. I did not know how I would do it, but finally one night I said, "OK, Lord, I will speak to her tomorrow." I knew that if I made a promise to God, I must keep it. The next day after school I went home with Joanie. We went upstairs to her bedroom and sat on her bed as I told her about the Tribulation and the Second Coming. "Do you want to pray?" I asked her.

"Yes," Joanie said so we knelt by her bed and prayed.

"Will you go to church with me next Sunday?" I asked.

"Yes," she replied. The next Sunday the pastor, Amos Henry, spoke on the crucifixion, and Joanie cried throughout the service. "Oh, Faith," she said later, "I never heard anything like that in all my life!"

A few weeks later Owen Glassburn preached a revival in our church. I invited Joanie to go with me and she accepted. As Owen Glassburn preached, I realized that Joanie was under conviction. I did not say anything to her but I prayed earnestly. During the invitation she stepped out on her own and went to the altar.

After Joanie got saved, she said, "Faith, I'd like to go down to the Ladies' Room and wash off all my makeup. I'm not going to wear lipstick anymore. I'm not going to the dances anymore. I'm not going to the motion pictures anymore." But on the way home that night, she said something that disappointed me, "I don't think I am going to tell my parents." I thought to myself, *I'm going to pray for you.*

The next morning before school Joanie came running out of her house, hugged and kissed me with her face all aglow! "Oh, Faith, how can I ever thank you enough for leading me to Jesus! Do you know what happened to me?"

"What happened?"

"This morning at breakfast Daddy asked, 'Joanie, what's happened to you? You look so happy.' I told him and he said, 'Joanie, you lead the way for three months and we will follow.'" Later I went with her to buy a Bible.

The same night that Joanie was saved, another girlfriend named Yvonne also went to the altar. When she went home and told her parents, they forbade her to go back to that church.

A decade later when I was back in Cleveland en route to Africa to say goodbye to my aunts, Joanie came to see me. "Oh, Faith, I wanted to tell you that Yvonne and her family have become Catholics, and Yvonne says that only Catholics will go to heaven. I said to her, Yvonne, you mean to say you don't think Faith Hemmeter will go to heaven? She said, 'Oh, I think God will make an exception for her.' So I just wanted you to know that according to Yvonne, you're going to be the only person in heaven who is not a Catholic." She laughed as she told me that story. I look back now and think how interesting it is that I lived so many years among Catholics as a little girl and then later worked among Catholics as a missionary in Bolivia.

Daddy had a call to preach before he married Mama. However, he thought that he could not support a wife and perhaps children and still attend Bible college, so he chose to get married. Mama had reasoned with him saying that perhaps he just thought he had to be a preacher because his father was a preacher. What he did not know until years later was that his father had decided that if either of his boys ever felt a call to preach, he would pay his way through Bible college. Evidently my father never told his father about his call.

Daddy continued in his walk with the Lord until I was seven. Then one day he came into the house and told my mother that God had left him. Mama and I both cried and begged him to pray. He replied, "It won't do any good. God has left me."

Mama said, "Pray, Walter, pray! Beg Him to come back. He is a merciful God." So finally Daddy, Mama, and I fell on our knees at the living room couch. Daddy prayed and begged God to come back into his life. After a short time God returned, and then He asked my father, "Now will you preach?"

Daddy said, "Yes, Lord. I will preach every time a door opens for me to do so." Almost immediately the phone rang. It was someone from a little mission in Cleveland asking my father to come and preach for them. He accepted the invitation, and other preaching opportunities soon followed.

Phoenix, Arizona

For some time Daddy had been testifying in church, saying, "The hand of the Lord is upon me for something, but I know not what." During that time my father was having severe sinus problems that resulted in frequent headaches. The doctor told him that he had to get to a hot, dry climate, and a friend of the family strongly suggested Phoenix, Arizona. That was during World War II when both gas and tires were rationed. God wonderfully made it possible for my father to get the ration stamps for gasoline and new tires that he needed in order to make the trip to Arizona in July 1943.

We pulled a small house trailer my paternal grandparents had given us. It took us five days to drive from Cleveland to Phoenix arriving on a Friday night. Saturday morning my father went in search of a church. He could not find a Friends church, but he did find a Nazarene church. Sunday morning found us in church. We visited several Nazarene churches in Phoenix, and eventually my parents became members at the West Side Church of the Nazarene because God's presence was very real in their services.

Shortly after we arrived, Daddy found a trailer court where we parked our small house trailer. We were there about a month when Daddy realized that his headaches were gone.

With a friend in Phoenix, Arizona, when I was 8 years old. I am on the left.

In the fall of that year, Dowie Swarth, who was the superintendent of the Arizona district of the Church of the Nazarene, came to the West Side Church and preached a message on the need for home-mission pastors. My father cried during the message. At the close of his message, Dowie called on my father to dismiss in prayer. He came to Daddy after the service and said to him, "My brother, you have a call to preach, don't you?" Daddy replied that he did.

Dowie then asked where Daddy lived and promised that he and his wife would come to visit us. The very next night they came, and he told my parents about the little Church of the Nazarene home-mission work in Flagstaff, Arizona, that had been started by C. Helen Mooshian. He inquired if they would be willing to pastor that church. My father told him that he had never attended Bible college. He told my Father that he could take the home-study course while he pastored. My father asked for a little time to pray about it, and that was granted.

Flagstaff, Arizona

In November we moved to Flagstaff where my father pastored his first congregation. He started to take the home-study course under the Church of the Nazarene.

When we first moved to Flagstaff, we had a wood stove and Daddy and Mama took turns getting up during the night to put wood on the fire. Finally they were able to get an oil-burning stove. They were so happy! Now they could sleep the entire night without needing to tend to a wood stove. However, one night the wind blew the stovepipe apart, and we were covered with soot. Daddy learned that in Flagstaff you need to put a T-shaped cap on the top of your stovepipe.

After C. Helen Mooshian left Flagstaff, she started another church in Williams, Arizona. She often came to visit us, and I really loved her. She became a friend to me, and our family made a room for her in the attic above our one-room parsonage.

The Lord always let me know when Helen came to visit us though she never told us that she was coming. Often when I was in school, the thought would come to me that Helen was at our house. I would run all the way home, and unfailingly my impression was correct. She was always so much fun and did funny things to make everyone laugh. One time when she was asked to say the blessing at a meal, she said, "Lord, bless this bite, and help us fight. In Jesus' name, Amen."

One year we told Helen that we were going to spend Christmas Day with her. She did not do anything special for Christmas since every day was alike to her. She said, "You're apt to just have slumgullian."

"What's slumgullian?" Mama asked.

"Any leftovers in the refrigerator put together to make a soup."

We went and it was one of the happiest Christmases I can remember. That morning I received a doll from my Aunt Naomi and Aunt Pearl. A few nights earlier when I was lying awake in my bed in our one-room parsonage, Mama said, "Walter, what do you suppose is in that box for Faith? Do you suppose it is a doll? If it's a doll, I'd like to take a peek."

"You'd better not," Daddy said. I thought that if my mother looked, I would look, too, but Daddy did not allow Mama to look.

On a cold, snowy night in 1944, God spoke to me during a service in our little chapel. We actually worshiped in an old barn that had been converted into a chapel. I was nine years old at that time. As Daddy led the singing, the Holy Spirit spoke to him and said, "You can't preach that message you prepared for tonight."

Daddy said, "Lord, what shall I preach? I'm not a seasoned minister. I don't have a barrel of sermons from which to choose." The Holy Spirit told him to preach from Hebrews 12:14. He then wondered about that because there were only two families present—his and one other. He pondered the need for such a message, but he minded God.

As Daddy preached, the Holy Spirit spoke to me saying, "Faith, you have been saved for a long time now. Many times you have had to ask for My forgiveness, but tonight all your sins are under the blood, and if you will ask Me, I'll take the thing out of your heart that made you sin in the first place."

I thought, *Lord, if you can do it, that is what I want!* I stepped out and went to the altar. I did not know all the theology of the experience of heart holiness, but the Holy Spirit, Who is the Spirit of Truth, faithfully led me.

All I knew to do was to ask the Holy Spirit to take out of my heart the thing that made me sin. Then a surprising thing happened. It was not a missionary service, but God showed me many dark-skinned hands reaching out to me. He spoke to me from the missionary song "Dusky Hands" by Haldor Lillenas:

> Dusky hands are reaching for the Bread of Life…
> In the far-off heathen lands…
> Shall they always hungry be?

God then said, "Faith, there are some people in Africa who have never heard of Me. Would you be willing to go and tell them?" That was my point of consecration. He showed me a vision of myself with long hair put up on my head and dressed like a holiness woman, going from hut to hut giving out the message that Jesus came to save the lost.

My reply was, "Yes, Lord." In that instant He sanctified me and I **knew** it! There was no great, immediate feeling. I just knew that the work was done. How thankful I was that Daddy had obeyed the leading of the Holy Spirit.

I returned to my seat, and when my father asked for testimonies, I stood and said, "Jesus sanctified me and called me to Africa as a missionary."

Just then the godly man who was seated right behind me stood and placed his hand on my head and said, "Faith, God really did call you to be a missionary, didn't He?"

The Church of the Nazarene congregation in Flagstaff, Arizona, taken about the time God sanctified and called me to Africa. I am second from the left with Mama behind me.

"Yes," I said as I began to cry. The Holy Spirit then descended on the congregation and everyone knew it was so. After the service when we returned to the parsonage, God suddenly poured out on me such a blessing that I did not know what to do. I began walking around our dining-room table, clapping my hands, saying, "Oh, Mama, Daddy, Jesus sanctified me and called me to Africa as a missionary!" It was **wonderful!** We all do not have the same emotional response, but we can have the inner assurance that God has sanctified us.

Chapter 2

Experiences That Shaped My Life
1945-1954

Winterhaven, California

My brother, John Paul Nelson, was born on February 7, 1945. A few months later, Dowie Swarth, who was now superintendent of the North American Indian work for the Church of the Nazarene,

My brother and I in June 1945

visited our church in Flagstaff and told of the need for missionaries to minister among the North American Indians. Daddy felt that was what God would have him do, so we moved to Winterhaven, California, in June to work with the Yuma or Quechan Indians. At that time I was almost ten, and Johnny was four months old.

I fell in love with the American Indians while living in Winterhaven and really believe that the Lord sent Daddy and Mama there partially for my sake. While we lived there, I preached my first message. I had wanted a desk, and my parents told me to save my money. Finally I had enough to buy an unfinished desk from Sears, and Daddy assembled and stained it. Later the Lord gave me a message from John 3:16 while I was seated at that desk. I asked Daddy if I could preach it, and he told me I could during prayer meeting on Wednesday evening. Of course, he had a message ready, but he allowed me to preach my little sermon that probably took only a few minutes; however, I was satisfied.

One night Daddy was going to take our family to a revival meeting in Yuma, which was just across the Colorado River in Arizona. As we were walking through the kitchen to go out the back door, suddenly I was strongly impressed that we should not go. Immediately I said, "Oh, Daddy, I feel that if we go tonight, something terrible is going to happen to us!"

Daddy wheeled around and asked, "Faith, do you feel that way, too?" I replied that I did and he said, "That settles it. We're not going. I feel the same way." I do not know what would have happened if we had gone, but I believe it would have been something terrible.

While we lived in Winterhaven, we attended the Indian camp meeting in Parker, Arizona. The Friday family, who also attended the camp meeting, were missionaries to the Indians and co-workers with my parents. They had two daughters close to my age who one day got into a heated argument. I told them that was not pleasing to Jesus and suggested we go and have a prayer meeting together. Another missionary child, Richard Timmer, and an Indian boy, Melvin Herbert, joined us.

I read to them from the Bible, and then we went across the road into an open area where we had a **wonderful** prayer meeting! We returned to the mission compound, running and jumping over the little tumbleweeds. Arriving at the Swarths' trailer, I pounded on the door, and Dowie answered. "Oh, Brother Swarth," I exclaimed, "we just had a most **wonderful** prayer meeting! Would you please announce that we are going to have a children's prayer meeting every day at two o'clock?"

"Yes, I will, Faith, and I'll tell you something else. When you grow up, you just come back to me, and I will have a mission station ready and waiting for you." That never materialized because God led me to work with Evangelistic Faith Missions.

We had lived in Winterhaven about a year when my father wrote to Pacific Bible College and inquired about furthering his education. I will never forget the day Daddy drove into our yard honking his car horn. He had been to the post office and received a letter from the college indicating that they were offering him a four-year scholarship.

Huntington Park, California

We moved to Huntington Park, California, the suburb of Los Angeles where the college was located. While there I had fun helping my father teach my baby brother to walk. Sitting on the floor, one of us would let Johnny hold one of our fingers while the other person coaxed him to walk to an outstretched hand. One day my father realized that Johnny was walking on the side of his feet because his ankles were weak. After Daddy bought him shoes with ankle supports, Johnny quickly learned to walk. One day I got into trouble over my love of playing with Johnny. I was going up the steps to our apartment when my girlfriend Emily invited me to go to her house and play. I told her that I would rather play with my baby brother. Poor Emily, an only child, replied, "I wouldn't have a baby brother like that."

My family in Huntington Park, California, in 1946

I should have invited Emily to come and play with us, but instead I took her by the shoulders and shook her. "Don't you dare talk about my baby brother that way," I said. Later God convicted me for my conduct, so I asked Emily to forgive me.

At the end of Daddy's first semester in college, one of his teachers, who was also a friend of the family, advised him to leave the school and finish his ministerial studies through the home-study course. He told Daddy that all the fundamental teachers were leaving the college since the modernists were having a growing influence. My father followed his advice.

La Palma, Arizona

Our family then moved to La Palma, Arizona, where my father pastored the Church of the Nazarene. During our first year my father faithfully spent each morning in his study and completed the home-study course. He was ordained in the Church of the Nazarene at an ordination service conducted in Phoenix, Arizona. It was a joy for our entire family to be present.

At one point during our two years in La Palma, Daddy became very anemic and did not have money to go to a doctor. Mama said, "Honey, what you need is to eat some liver." At that time Daddy did not own a car, but a man in the congregation loaned him a pickup truck that had a leaking radiator. Consequently, Daddy had to take a pail with him to fill the radiator periodically.

One day my father went to the only store and gas station in town, and the attendant asked him, "Would you do me a favor if I put gas in your tank? A man close to town needs gas. Would you take some to him?" Daddy agreed to do so.

The man had run his truck so dry that it was necessary to put gas into the carburetor before they could get the truck started. The man then said to Daddy, "Do you like liver? I just butchered, and I have a whole cow's liver in the truck."

"I sure do."

"Do you have anything in which to put it?"

"Yes, I have a pail here." The liver filled the pail three-quarters full. Daddy joyfully brought it home and set it on the kitchen floor.

"What's that?" Mama asked.

"Why, that's the liver you prayed in," he replied with a twinkle in his eye.

My mother laughed and said, "Walter, I knew you needed liver, but I didn't know you needed so much!" Then ignoring the twinkle, she presented another need. "I don't have any grease in which to fry it."

"Well, let's go into the living room and pray for some grease," and they prayed, trusting God to supply the need.

Daddy went calling in the afternoon and visited in a farmer's home. When he was ready to leave, the wife said, "Oh, by the way, Rev. Hemmeter, I just rendered some lard. Could you use some?"

"I sure could," he eagerly replied, and she gave him a five-quart can of lard.

At the next farmer's home the wife indicated that she had just rendered some lard and offered some to Daddy. She, too, gave him a large container of lard. He went home and put them both on the kitchen counter. "Well, Honey, there's your lard."

We ate liver and more liver for many days. By the time we had eaten all the liver, Daddy was well. My heart and mind were being imprinted with the importance of fully trusting God.

While we were living in La Palma, a man from Italy came to a church in a nearby town and played specials on his violin. He was able to make his violin sound like birds singing and brooks flowing. A desire was created in my heart to play the violin. That finally became a reality when I began violin lessons in September 2002 at the age of sixty-seven.

Casa Grande, Arizona

Two years passed quickly while we lived in La Palma. Then we moved to Casa Grande, Arizona, where my parents began working among the Papago Indians. They were migratory workers who picked cotton for farmers in the area.

Sunday afternoons we took our folding pump organ and went to the camps where the Indians lived. After Daddy set up the organ, Mama played hymns while Daddy and I joined her in singing. When the Indians gathered around to listen, Daddy would preach to them. He always needed an interpreter, and the only person he could find to help him was a man who did not really know the Lord. One time when Daddy finished preaching, the man said to my father, "Boy, I sure told them!" That is how my father learned that his interpreter was not saying exactly what he had said. From that experience I learned how important it is to have a dependable interpreter.

Parker, Arizona

Later when our family went to the district camp for the Indians, Dowie Swarth asked my father to take over the work among the Mojave Indians in Parker, Arizona. I loved living in Parker and became very close to those Indians.

One time, though, I had a terrifying experience. Daddy had gone to take some of the Indians to their home on the reservation. While he was away, my mother, an Indian man, and I were singing while Mama was playing the piano in the church. My brother, who was about three, came into the church crying. I went to see what was wrong. He said that Dolly took her children and went home, but he wanted to play with them. I looked around and saw that her belongings were still on one of the church benches, so I told him that I did not think she had gone. Taking him by the hand, we walked through two rooms that were connected to the church and outside into a courtyard.

Quickly we walked around to the front of the church where we saw Dolly lying on the ground crying. A man was kicking her and saying he was going to knife her. Although she was just below the church window near the piano, our singing had kept us from hearing her cries.

With my heart beating rapidly with fear, I took Johnny back into the building. As we went through each room, I closed the door behind us. When we were safely inside the church, I let go of his hand and ran to the front of the church where Mama and the Indian were still singing. I cried out that someone was trying to kill Dolly. Mama stopped and said, "What?" I repeated what I had said. Then we all started running toward the back of the church.

Just then the door opened and Dolly came inside. She was crying, and blood was dripping from her face onto the floor. Mama took her to an outside faucet and washed her face. I followed, and all the way I was praying in my heart for Jesus to send my father back to the church.

Praise God, just then Daddy drove into the church parking lot. We took Dolly to the government hospital for Indians. On the way she told us that when her husband, the man who was beating her, heard the whole church running to the door, he got scared and left. Although there were only three of us running, God used that to scare him and thus save Dolly's life.

At the hospital Dolly was examined and released. She then asked my father to take her to some relatives who lived at a distance on the reservation. Dolly told my father that her husband was too drunk to walk that far, and she would be safe there for the night. After leaving her with relatives, Daddy told us, "You mark my word; her husband will be back tonight."

Sure enough, Daddy was right. In the middle of the night, Dolly's husband, a much bigger man than my father, pounded on our door. Daddy called out, "Who's there?"

"Dolly's husband."

"She's not here."

"Where is she?"

Daddy told him since he knew that in his condition he could never make it to where she was. Thus God protected all of us that night.

On another occasion Daddy had gone to New Mexico to work on the boys' dormitory at the Church of the Nazarene Indian Bible School. Mama told the Indians that while he was gone, we would come to their place for the Wednesday evening prayer meeting instead of them walking to the mission. As Mama, Johnny, and I walked past the government hospital, a three-legged collie came running and joined us. We had never seen that dog before. While we continued walking, we met a group of drunken Indian men who frightened us. The collie ran toward the men and barked and then came back to us. He repeated that several times until the men gave us a wide berth letting us past them safely. God used that dog to protect us.

Upon arriving at the home of Brother Emmanuel, we were invited inside for the service. Meanwhile the collie lay down outside and waited for us. After the service he joined us as we started for home. On the way we met some friends who offered to take us home in their car. Mama told them how kind the collie had been to us, and they said we could bring the dog with us, but it refused to get into the car. That was the only time that dog ever went anywhere with us, but it was the only time we really needed him. God is so good!

One summer when I was about thirteen, there was an epidemic of tropical dysentery that began claiming many lives. On the average there was a funeral every other week. My parents believed that the funerals provided good opportunities to minister to the unsaved Indians.

The funerals were held over a three-day period after which the Mojave Indians would cremate their dead. They would set up a brush arbor in a large open area. Since they had no electricity, they hung a lantern from one of the beams of the arbor where it cast an eerie light. Under the shelter there was a bench on each side. One of those benches was reserved for the witches who would stand and shake their gourds while chanting.

We would drive to the reservation to attend the funerals, and as we stepped out of the car into the hot desert air, I could feel the demon powers. It felt as if my hair was standing on end. We stood there watching and listening until the witches got tired and sat down. Then our family and our Christian Indians went forward. As soon as Daddy began a song about the blood of Jesus, the demon powers left. What a relief it was to have them gone. My father usually led us in one or two more songs about the blood before bringing a message from the Word of God. We closed with prayer and then left.

That scenario continued for some time. Then one day when I was with my father on the reservation, some of the witches came and told my father that they were very angry with him. They said that not only did the spirits leave when he was at the gathering, but no matter what they did the rest of the night, the spirits would not return. They also indicated that they were going to put a curse on Daddy and tell the Indians not to come to our church anymore. As we drove away, I exclaimed, "Daddy, I'm kinda scared."

"Scared, Faith? Why? Scared of what?"

"Why, Daddy, those witches said they were going to put a curse on you."

Daddy laughed and said, "Faith, they can't touch me as long as I am under the blood!"

I watched for days, weeks, and months, but nothing bad ever happened to my father. Thus it was that I became convinced that there is much power in the blood of Jesus!

La Jolla, California

When I was fourteen, our family moved from Parker, Arizona, to La Jolla, California, in 1949 to work with the Mission Indian tribe. We lived on the Church of the Nazarene mission station that was just below the Palomar Observatory. Our house had no electricity, and our only running water was from a hose that ran from an outside

With Indian girls in La Jolla, California

faucet to one inside at our sink. Our only other facility was an outhouse. I believe God was getting me ready for the mission field.

As I saw Daddy and Mama pray in our needs in Flagstaff, so it was in La Jolla. One time my mother was hungry for bread and butter and asked Jesus to send us money so that we could buy some. She cried when we opened the mail and there was no money. Later we got a letter from a dear Christian asking Mama to forgive her for disobeying God. Mentioning the date, she wrote that God had told her to send some money to us, but she put it off. Now at last she was sending it. It let my mother know that Jesus had not failed her.

Another time the mother of one of my classmates gave us a peck of red tomatoes and a peck of yellow tomatoes. That was all we had to eat for several days. I took tomatoes and a salt shaker to school for my lunch, but I learned that God does provide for His children.

Sometimes when I walked to our mailbox, some children from the Catholic Mission threw stones at me. They never hurt me and probably just wanted to scare me. La Jolla was a beautiful place in the mountains with lovely trails through the wooded areas. I wished my cousins from Cleveland would come to visit us so I could take them for a walk on those trails.

Cleveland, Ohio

The following spring while we were in La Jolla, word reached us that my paternal grandmother was dying of cancer. She was asking for my father so we moved back to Cleveland. My parents and brother lived with Grandpa and Grandma Hemmeter on the West Side. I was in the eighth grade and lived with my Uncle Fred and Aunt Naomi Rowe and Aunt Pearl Rickel on the East Side. While living with them I graduated from Audubon Junior High School in the spring of 1951. After graduation I moved to Medina, Ohio, to live with my family.

Medina, Ohio

After Grandma went to heaven, my father began to get very restless. He knew he needed to be preaching somewhere. At times when God gave him a message, he went to the park and preached. Finally the Lord opened the way for him to become the pastor of the Church of the Nazarene in Medina, Ohio, in the fall of 1950. Only eight people attended the first Sunday night service, but with God's help the congregation grew to about sixty. They eventually erected a new church building.

While in high school I had an experience that greatly increased my faith. My mother was very ill and in the hospital. Daddy was troubled. One evening I saw him go out of the house, get in the car, and drive away without telling us where he was going.

The devil told me that he was leaving us and would not return. I was foolish to listen to him and began to pray, "Oh, Jesus, please send Daddy back. Please send Daddy back home. Please send Daddy back to us."

Mama inside the Church of the Nazarene in Medina, Ohio

Suddenly God spoke to me and said, "Faith, can't you believe me?"

I replied that I wanted to believe. Then I said, "Lord, help my unbelief!"

As soon as I got those words out, I heard the car return and my father walked into the house. That really helped my faith! Later

37

Mama had surgery to stop internal bleeding and soon was able to come home.

Grandfather Hemmeter had moved with us to Medina. He was a godly man who could bring any conversation around in two or three minutes to witnessing to a soul about Jesus. He told me many stories of people whom he had won to the Lord that way. I do not know of anyone who influenced me more to win souls for Jesus than my grandfather.

Graduation from Medina High School on April 27, 1954

Daddy pastored in Medina for nearly eight years. During seven of those years, we had no place to worship except in our house. The church furniture was set up in our dining room and living room. Eventually the group was able to build a church. While we lived in Medina, I graduated from Medina High School and from Olivet Nazarene College.

Wherever my father pastored, the women often came to see Mama. They loved her because she took as much time with them as they wanted. Then she would need to stay up late to get her own work done. Any place Daddy felt called, Mama was ready to accompany him. They sold out repeatedly to go and do what God wanted them to do. Material things were not of primary importance to them. The all-important thing was to mind God, and that was imprinted deeply on my mind.

Chapter 3

Challenges During My Bible School Years
1954-1958

Leaving Home to Attend College

After God called me to be a missionary at the age of nine, I hoped to attend the School of Nursing at the Nazarene College in Nampa, Idaho, and become a missionary nurse. However, by the time I was in high school, the college at Nampa had terminated its nursing program. Before I graduated from high school in Medina, Ohio, in 1954, I began praying and asking God where He wanted me to attend college. During my senior year I considered a nursing school in Cleveland, but I was becoming fearful about nursing. I was afraid that if I became a nurse, I might someday accidentally give someone the wrong medicine. By that time I had learned from working in Vacation Bible Schools that I also enjoyed teaching, and so I was undecided whether I should be a nurse or a teacher.

After discerning that God wanted me to be a teacher, I thought about going to Cleveland Bible College. My paternal grandfather had graduated from Cleveland Bible Institute, which later became Cleveland Bible College and is now Malone College in Canton, Ohio. Since my father was pastor of the Medina Church of the Nazarene, I wrote to Olivet Nazarene College in Kankakee, Illinois, asking if I could receive any financial help toward my schooling. I told the Lord that if Olivet would assist me, I would understand that it was His will for me to attend there. The college replied with a positive answer, so I went to Olivet.

Shortly after my graduation from high school, my mother's sister Pearl called me from Cleveland. She said that since I had a call to be a missionary, she would pay half of my college expenses. Thus God used my Aunt Pearl to help me prepare for Christian service at Olivet.

One September morning in 1954, Mama came into my bedroom and kissed me awake saying, "Honey, this is the day you have been waiting for so long. Today you are going to college." My parents, my brother John, and I made the trip by car to Kankakee. As they helped me move into my room, Mama seemed very happy. She talked about me coming home for Thanksgiving and asked what I would like for Thanksgiving dinner. She did not let me know that her heart was breaking at the thought of our parting.

The morning my family was to return home, we went to a restaurant for breakfast. While we were eating, I noticed that my father had the strained expression that indicated something was bothering him, so I asked him what was wrong. He gulped and admitted, "I guess I was just thinking of the parting." Sometime later he told me that Mama cried all the way back to Medina.

Learning Practical Lessons

During the school revival in the fall of my freshman year, the Lord taught me a valuable lesson. It had to do with a mistaken idea that I had acquired. I had come to believe that one should **never** speak to individuals about going to the altar during an altar call but just pray and ask God to speak to them. I had drawn that conclusion from observing a cousin who never gave his heart to the Lord as far as I know. People would deal with him during revival after revival, and I watched him get increasingly harder to the gospel. I also had the experience of just praying for a girlfriend of mine during an altar call and seeing her yield to the drawing of the Spirit by going to the altar.

During a morning chapel service in that fall revival, an altar call was given. Three times the Holy Spirit spoke to me and said, "Speak to Janette Hanson about going to the altar."

I replied, "No, Lord! I don't want to make her hard. You speak to her." I continued praying, and soon she stepped out and went to the altar. That confirmed to me that my idea was right.

However, God was faithful to me through Janette's testimony when she later said, "I almost didn't go to the altar this morning." She went on to explain that she had been telling the Lord that if He really wanted her to go to the altar, He should have Faith Hemmeter speak to her about doing so. That really scared me and taught me that one should always follow the leading of the blessed Holy Spirit. God knew I needed to learn that lesson before I went to the mission field.

God provided other ways for me to get practical Christian experience. I joined the Missionary Band when I was a freshman and remained a part of that group all four years of college. I also was a part of a student prayer band that met in one of the rooms of the administrative building each day at 7:00 p.m. It was my joy to attend those prayer meetings as often as possible.

Sometimes I joined others on Sunday afternoon when they went to hold services in rest homes and in a hospital in the area. We took turns going to the various places so that everyone

With my roommate Jean DeLong in front of William's Hall, the girls' dorm, at Olivet Nazarene College

enjoyed a variety of experiences. One time it was announced that a song leader was needed for a revival meeting in a nearby Church of the Nazarene. I volunteered and participated in that revival.

At other times I went with various groups to minister on Sunday night to nearby home-mission churches that asked for help with their services. On one occasion a group of us went to a home-mission church for the weekend. We went on a Saturday morning, took sack lunches, and spent the day calling and inviting people to come to church on Sunday. God met with us in our services, and we felt well repaid for our efforts.

Receiving My Call to Bolivia

When I entered college, I did so with the idea of preparing for service in Africa, but during my second year at Olivet, God spoke to me about another mission field. A missionary from Bolivia, South America, spoke in a chapel service. He told how it freezes most nights in the Bolivian highlands, how they have no heat in their houses, and how they must break ice on the ponds in the morning to get water to use. He also told how hot it gets at those altitudes when the sun beats down but that when the sun goes behind a cloud and the wind blows, it gets cold.

The missionary continued by telling of the people's spiritual plight and said, "They need to hear of Jesus. Who will go and tell them?" I began to cry, and in my heart I asked the Lord, *Would you let me go? Would you let me go?*

The blessed Holy Spirit spoke clearly, "You will be there some day." He was so definite that I immediately stopped crying. That calling to a second mission field caused me some confusion for a time, but God fulfilled both calls in His own marvelous way. I am glad that God speaks clearly and definitely to His children. Glory to His name!

Escaping Death

During semester break of my senior year in January 1958, four of us seniors, Janette Hanson (Smith), Bonnie King (Carter), Sandy Lancaster, and I, went home with Lois Rundberg (Hackathron), also a senior, who lived close to Eau Claire, Wisconsin. We drove Bonnie's old Buick, a solid, heavy, two-door car.

Before we left Kankakee, one of the girls suggested that we write our names and addresses on a piece of paper and put it in the glove compartment in case of an accident. Someone else said, "If we do that, I'm not going!" Consequently, the idea was dropped.

Lois' parents, Einor and Evelyn, treated us royally, and we had a wonderful time on the Rundberg farm. Einor took us to a golf course for tobogganing on nice snow-covered hills. What fun! He also took us ice skating. I enjoyed myself even though I was not good at skating. We enjoyed Evelyn's cooking, especially the steaks from beef cattle that had been raised and butchered on the farm.

Sunday morning we attended church with the Rundbergs and came home to a good dinner. Then we loaded the car and began the trip back to Kankakee. We decided to take turns driving as the trip would take several hours. Since snow was falling, Janette, the least experienced driver among us, drove first while it was still daylight.

Bonnie was sitting beside Janette; I was behind Janette, taking advantage of the opportunity to nap and refresh myself for my turn to drive. As we neared Black River Falls, I suddenly realized that we had just hit a patch of ice as we rounded a curve.

"Bonnie! Somebody! Help me!" Janette cried. Bonnie had once been told never to grab the wheel out of the driver's hands so did nothing.

As I looked up, I saw that we were about to collide head-on with another car. At the last second Janette cried, "Jesus, help me!" She hit the brakes, which threw us into a spin and onto the side of the road where the car flipped.

As the car was turning over, a voice kept saying to each of us, "Keep calm and you will get out. Keep calm and you will get out." Later we all witnessed that each of us felt God's hand around us. It must have been so. For although those were the days before seat belts, not one of us had a cut or even a bruise nor did we even bump into each other. We were all held in place.

"Turn off the key," someone said to Jan when the car landed on its top, and she did.

"Is everyone all right?" someone asked. One by one we all answered that we were.

"Hey," Lois cried, "this thing's on fire! We better get out!" Jan tried her door but it was jammed.

"Try the other door!" Praise God it opened!

I was the last to crawl out, and as I exited, I grabbed Bonnie's coat off the front seat knowing she would need it as it was still snowing. I started to go back for my purse, but the man whose car we almost hit screamed, "Get away from there; it's going to explode!" When he repeated it, his words finally got through to me, and I moved away from the burning car. We all crossed the highway to safety.

"Oh, my clothes!" moaned Sandy, who was planning a trip to Europe that summer.

"Girls," I said, "I can't even think of clothes. All I can think of is what if one of us was trapped in that burning car! I think we better pray and thank God we all got out!" No one cried until we began to pray, and then Jan and Bonnie cried as I thanked God for delivering us from possible death.

Some Indians came along and threw snow on the flames to try to put them out, but that only made them blaze higher. A Greyhound bus pulled beside us, and the driver asked, "Is anyone in there?"

"No, we all got out," I said.

"**You** were in there?" he asked in surprise. "Let me take you all to town."

"We had better not leave the scene of the accident until the police come."

"I'll tell the police and the fire department," the bus driver said. Soon both the police and the firemen arrived on the scene. By that time the inside of the car was engulfed in flames and even the chrome on the outside had begun to melt. After extinguishing the fire, the firemen pried the trunk open and retrieved our suitcases. They were amazingly intact. However, when I opened mine, I found that the fire had gone between the lid and the bottom and cut each article of clothing in two just as if it had been done with a knife.

When we had arrived at the Rundberg home earlier, Lois' mother had taken hold of my red and green plaid skirt and said, "I would like to have this to make into a braided rug!" Well, she got it! Of course, she never expected nor wanted us to have an accident.

As the policemen were taking us to Black River Falls, one of them said, "You girls were lucky."

"No," I said, "it was not luck. God was with us."

He thought a moment and then said, "You know, I think you're right!"

When we got to town, Lois called her father to tell him about the accident. At first he did not believe her because she sounded so calm. He came and took us halfway back to school where her married brother, Charles, met us and took us the rest of the way. Every time we hit an icy spot in the road, we all drew in a sharp breath.

"I wish you girls would go to sleep," Charles said.

"I wish we could," I answered. Every time I closed my eyes, I could feel the car rolling over.

Our friends at school were afraid to see us after hearing about the accident. They could not believe that we were not hurt. One girl came up to me as I waited in the registration line the next morning and broke into tears.

I had my little New Testament in the pocket of my suitcase with an envelope containing ten dollars. Both were unharmed, but the New Testament had a terrible odor. I did not know what to do with it. When I got back to the senior house, I put it in a small cedar chest and left it there. When I took it out several months later, I found that the smell of smoke had been replaced with a sweet aroma. Surely God had done something like that to us through that experience!

My good shoes had been ruined in the accident. I was to do my student teaching that semester and would need good shoes, but I did not have much money. All I could afford was a cheap pair that would have to serve for both church and student teaching.

I went home to Medina for Easter. Soon after returning to school, I received a letter and a check from Jim and Helen Chandler. They had noticed that my shoes were quite worn. They said that they had planned to get new shoes for their children, but when they saw mine, they wanted to do something for me. They began their letter by saying something like this: "Now, Faith, you **cannot** refuse this. We noticed your shoes when you were home for Easter. We asked our children if they would be willing to wait for their new shoes so that we could send money for you to buy shoes for graduation. They said yes. Please use this money to get new shoes for yourself."

I cried when I read their letter. I wrote thank-you letters to them and to each of their three children. Then I bought myself a nice pair of shoes for graduation.

Facing Senior Comprehensives

In order to graduate from Olivet, we had to take our senior comprehensive examinations. All the seniors were scared, including me!

We had to take a two-hour written exam and a one-hour oral exam. The oral exam frightened me more since it was in front of three professors. Two professors were chosen by the college, and we had the privilege of choosing the third. They could ask us anything they wanted regarding our last two years of studies.

Of course, I went to the Lord in prayer. He gave me a promise from II Timothy 1:7: "For God hath not given us the spirit of fear, but of power, and of love, and of a **sound mind.**"

Praise God I passed both exams and graduated on May 29, 1958, with a bachelor of science degree in education.

Graduation from Olivet Nazarene College on May 29, 1958. I am on the right.

Chapter 4

Continued Preparation for Missionary Service
1958-1961

Teaching in an Integrated School

When I graduated from college, I asked God to equip me with everything I needed to be an effective missionary. He began leading me through different phases of preparation. The first step came in the form of a class of unruly children in a public school in Columbus, Ohio. I taught a second-grade class that consisted of thirty-two darlings, thirty of them being black and two white. All were students whose intelligence was average or below. Two were emotionally impaired, one was almost deaf, one had an intelligence quotient of fifty-eight, and one was very sickly. During the week I lived with a widow in Columbus. On weekends I went to Roseville near Columbus to help in the church services where my parents were then pastoring the Church of the Nazarene.

I enjoyed arriving at school early and meeting my pupils at the door with a welcoming smile. One little black boy named Thomas came from a dysfunctional home. He would say one of two things each morning when I greeted him. Either he would declare, "Thomas is going to be a good boy today," or "Thomas is baa-aad! Thomas is just baa-aad!" When he said the latter, he **was** bad!

Frequently I tried to praise Thomas and did everything that other teachers suggested, but nothing worked. Every day about an hour before dismissal at noon and again in the afternoon, he would come to me asking for permission to go home. I asked the principal about that, but she said it was not allowed. When I refused to allow him to go, the poor child would go **wild** and run around the room screaming, throwing anything he could get in his hands.

Another student, Leonard, wanted my attention and would show extreme jealousy when I gave time to Thomas. He had learned his methods of manipulation from his mother who used them in the home. Once he misspelled a word in a spelling test and screamed. Later, during a conference with the mother, she admitted that she acted likewise at home. She promised to improve the home situation, and Leonard's conduct in class improved.

A third boy, nearly as tall as I, had been held back several times and was out of place in that classroom. Once he pulled a knife on another pupil, and I barely succeeded in getting it away from him before he injured someone.

One day the first-grade teacher said to me, "Honey Chile, you means to tell me this is your first year teachin' and you have these chilluns? I've been teachin' for years an' they's the worst class I ever had! You gotta sit on 'em, Honey! You just gotta sit on 'em!"

Many times I wanted to quit, but I knew God had called me to be a missionary, and if I gave up in the face of this first challenge, I would never make it on the mission field. Often during my lunch break I went to the women's rest room in a nearby gas station and had a time of pleading with God for help before returning to my afternoon classes. God was teaching me to persevere.

Through these experiences the Lord also opened my eyes to my need of learning to discipline and control my students. I loved every one of them but discovered that love must be tough in the face of unruliness. Although I did not realize it at the time, God knew I would need to keep order in Eritrean classrooms. I resigned at the end of the academic year after having learned the first lessons in God's missionary training school.

Changing My Church Affiliation

The next step in God's school came into focus one evening during the spring of 1959. I was walking down a street in Roseville when the Lord said to me, "It's time for you to get out." I knew what He meant. He wanted me to leave the Church of the Nazarene. My parents also were thinking of leaving that group because of worldliness, but I was planning to go to the mission field under that denomination. However, God now began to lead me in a more conservative way by applying biblical principles to my own heart and helping me to settle my personal convictions.

During that time Earl and Vivian Williams held a revival for my parents in the Roseville Church of the Nazarene. People came from miles around to hear them preach, and the reaction to their messages showed that people wanted the old-fashioned way. Vivian told how God had asked her to let her hair and her daughter's hair grow. At that time I did not see anything wrong with a woman cutting her hair. I trimmed my hair a little, but I did not cut it short because I knew that would break my father's heart. I thought that was just his old-fashioned idea. When Vivian told her story, though, and combined it with Scripture, God witnessed to my heart that it was His will for a woman to let her hair grow.

God spoke directly to me about other issues as well. He knew I needed to have these things settled if I was going to be an effective example on the mission field. I was learning to hear His voice and obey when He applied the precepts of His Word to my life.

One evening as I sat in the dining room grading papers, my father was reading a sermon to my mother in the kitchen while she ironed. We sensed God's presence as he read.

"Oh, Daddy, that's wonderful! Who wrote it?" I asked.

"Glenn Griffith," he answered with a smile.

Glenn Griffith had left the Church of the Nazarene a few years earlier and in 1959 was instrumental in starting the Wesleyan Holiness Association of Churches. Several months later my parents and I joined that association. If I had stayed with the previous denomination, I am sure I would have taken a worldly way. God was showing me a pattern of living that was grounded in His Word, and He led me to a church that would help me to keep His standards and please Him.

Teaching in a Country School

The third step in my apprenticeship came during my second year of teaching when I taught in a country school near Zanesville, Ohio. That meant that I was able to live with my parents in Roseville since it was only about ten miles to Zanesville. A lovely, older schoolteacher lived across the street. I sought her advice about how to control children. One nugget of wisdom she gave me was that I should treat all my students the same, no matter who they were. Some of my pupils were children of school board members and others were related to the principal. I learned not to favor them above the other children. If they disobeyed, they suffered the same consequences.

During that year I learned another valuable lesson. Since it was my responsibility to teach all the subjects in both third and fourth grades, I learned to organize my time and teaching materials to fit in all the subject matter and to give each grade equal time. I would teach a math lesson to the fourth grade and then give them an assignment to do while I gave a reading lesson to the third graders. God knew that my multiple missionary activities in Eritrea would require organization if I was to accomplish my tasks effectively.

I loved the children I was teaching and they loved me. One of my students, Mikie, was starved for affection because both of his parents worked. Knowing that, I gave him extra attention whenever I could. On Valentine's Day he came to me and said, "Miss Hemmeter, I love you so much I want to give you **all** my valentines."

"I love you, too, Mikie, but I have lots of valentines. You need to keep yours," I replied as I gave him a hug and a kiss.

A new girl named Lessie was brought to the school by her grandmother. Her parents were divorced, and she lived with her father's mother. After she and her grandmother had met the principal and me, the grandmother said to Lessie, "Now I hope you won't come home from school crying like you did at the other school." The principal and I both noticed that Lessie's eyes filled with tears at her grandmother's words.

In the classroom I introduced Lessie. "We have a new little girl in our class today, and I want all of you to make her welcome." At my words the children turned to look at Lessie, and I saw that she was about to cry, so I immediately drew the other pupils' attention back to the front of the classroom.

Later I took one of the girls aside and said, "Joyce, I would like you to be Lessie's special friend. I would like you to show her where the girls' rest room is and to play with her at recess."

"OK," she said.

At recess time Joyce, whose mother taught first grade, went to Lessie and asked her to go outside and play with her. Lessie declined. Joyce went to her own desk and brought out scissors and a new book of paper dolls and took them to Lessie.

"Look," Joyce said, "I have a new book of paper dolls, Lessie. You can cut them out." Then Joyce left her to play alone while she went for recess. Lessie looked at the book with interest but cut out nothing.

At the noon recess Joyce again went to Lessie and invited her to go outside to play. Once more Lessie declined, but that time Joyce took both of Lessie's hands and pulled her to her feet, laughing and urging her to come out with her and play, and Lessie did.

Sometime later Lessie happily said to me, "This is the best school I have ever attended!"

At the end of the school year I could share Lessie's sentiments. For her that had been the best school she had attended, and for me that school year was as good as the first year had been baa-aad!

Visiting the Tri-State Holiness Association Camp

The next step of preparation took me in an unexpected direction. I wrote to Glenn Griffith, general superintendent of the Wesleyan Holiness Association of Churches, telling him of my call to the mission field. In his letter he invited me to come to the Tri-State Holiness Association Camp, better known as Clinton Camp, in Clinton, Pennsylvania, in July 1960. "Victor Glenn, president of Evangelistic Faith Missions, will be there, and I will introduce you to him," he wrote. I accepted his invitation.

One day at camp while I was in the women's prayer room, I had this conversation with my heavenly Father: "Father, I'm a little confused. First you called me so definitely to go as a missionary to Africa. Then you also called me to Bolivia. Lord, You know they are a long way from each other, whole continents away, divided by an ocean. Now I am not sure just what You want me to do."

My doubts and fears evaporated as God lovingly assured me, "The gifts and calling of God are without repentance" (Romans 11:29). Through my meeting with Victor Glenn at the camp, the Lord definitely led me to go first to Africa with Evangelistic Faith Missions, which I did the following year. I served sixteen glorious years in Eritrea and Ethiopia before going to Bolivia in 1979.

While we were at Clinton Camp, Margaret Cook spoke to my mother. "We need a teacher to start a Christian day school for Richard Boynton in Milan, Illinois. Would you speak to Faith about starting this school for us?"

When Mama spoke to me about it, my first response was, "No, I have signed a three-year contract to teach in the public school system

51

of Zanesville. Besides, God has called me to be a missionary, and I don't want to get sidetracked." I was afraid that if I became involved in Christian education at home, I might not follow through with my missionary call.

The next morning as I was on my way to breakfast, Glenn Griffith came out of the workers' door of the dining hall, and a preacher walking toward the dining hall called to him saying, "Did you know Faith Hemmeter is going to start a Christian day school for Brother Boynton?"

"She'll mind God," Glenn Griffith responded.

His words comforted me and made me think that he had been praying for me. After I joined the breakfast line, I heard the voice of the blessed Holy Spirit entreatingly say, "Aren't you even going to ask Me?" My heart melted, and I lost all desire to eat. Suddenly I realized that perhaps God **did** want me to help start the new school.

Quickly I went to the women's prayer room and fell on my knees. "Lord," I prayed, "if this is what You want, then it is what I want, too." Still not certain how God would lead, but determined to mind Him, I decided to leave everything in His hands.

I told God that I would not make an appointment with the superintendent of schools but would just go to his office. If he was there, then I would know it was God's will for me to see him. Upon our return to Zanesville, I went to his office and found him present.

"I hope you're not coming here to tell me you're leaving us." he said.

My heart sank to my feet. "I know I signed a contract for three years," I said, "and if you will not release me, I will stay and fulfill it. However, God has called me to the mission field, and I now have an offer to start a Christian day school."

"Well, if that is the way you feel," he said, "I suppose the quicker you get into that kind of work, the happier you will be. I'll talk to the school board and see what they say, but look at these applications! We have only three, and none of the applicants is fully qualified." Thus it seemed unlikely that they would release me from my contract. However, in a few days I received a letter saying that the board was releasing me. I was now free to follow God's will for my life. That experience taught me the importance of asking God for leadership before making any decision on my own. I was learning to rely upon Him and not on my own understanding.

Moving to Milan, Illinois

The fifth step in my preparation came with my move to Milan to help start a Christian day school. I wanted the school to be recognized by the superintendent of public schools so that our students would not have a problem in attending public school again if they moved and found that necessary. Richard Boynton, president of Francis Asbury Bible College; Margaret Cook, music teacher; and I went to see the superintendent. I explained to him what we wanted.

"I don't suppose you have your transcript from college with you?" he asked.

"Yes, here it is," I said, handing it to him, "and this is my state teacher's license for Illinois and here is the one for Ohio. I also have a letter from the school board at the last school where I taught."

The superintendent smiled and said, "There is no reason why you cannot start a Christian day school."

As we continued our conversation, a complication arose when Richard Boynton asked about our school including ninth grade along with grades one through eight. We had two boys who were ready to begin ninth grade, and we all believed that it was important for them to be in a Christian school setting. Although the superintendent felt very strongly against us having ninth grade, he asked me to give him copies of our curriculum and school calendar.

"Prepare those for him," Richard Boynton instructed me later. "We will pray, and when I present them to him, I will ask again to be allowed to include ninth grade in our school."

We prayed earnestly about the matter. When we presented the material to the superintendent, he said, "I can see having a Christian day school on the elementary level but not for high school!"

We just stood there praying silently. Suddenly the superintendent threw up his hands and said, "All right. You may do it." His next move surprised us for he loaded our car with free textbooks. Praise God! That was a boost to my faith! I saw that the best way to change a man's mind was to pray and let God do the convincing. That lesson bore fruit many years later during my missionary labors.

The superintendent also told us where to go to learn about the curriculum being used in the public schools. We examined it and decided what portions we wanted to use. We also purchased textbooks for classes we wanted to offer that were not on the public school list.

Before I arrived in Milan, the church had purchased a one-story building to house the Christian day school and the Francis Asbury Bible College, which they also started at that time. It was painted a lovely shade of aqua and was trimmed in white. The classroom for my one-room school was already clean and ready with a nice blackboard and desks for the students.

My students included two first graders, one third grader, one fifth grader, one eighth grader, and two ninth graders. I had the responsibility of teaching all the subjects on five grade levels. During that school year I learned new methods of praying. I believe that one of the main reasons God led me to Milan was that I might learn how to pray more effectively. In the frequent times of fasting at the school, I learned to use Scripture and Bible incidents which showed that God was in favor of doing things in a certain way or that He was pleased to honor particular requests.

Learning to Live by Faith

God used various ways to teach me to live by faith as the final preparatory step before my going to the mission field. Before I went to Milan, Richard Boynton told me that he could not offer me a fixed salary. I told him that was all right because I was sensing the need of trusting God for my livelihood. As a teacher in public school, I had been receiving good wages and felt that having that much money was starting to get a grip on me. He told me that each student's parents would pay a certain amount each month for their child's education. "Some months they might not be able to pay," he added.

"All right," I replied. "I will be happy to live by faith."

I also was responsible to be dorm mother for young women in the Bible college. The four of us lived together in a rented house. We fasted frequently and got by with a minimal amount of food. Once when we had very little food in the house, a couple in the church invited us to their home for supper. We happily accepted the invitation and were even more excited when they sent four grocery bags of food home with us. As I recall, the groceries consisted mostly of meat. God had supplied our needs.

What a happy year I had in His service! God was working out His purpose in my life, and on January 17, 1961, I wrote to my parents: "I have been placed under appointment to Eritrea. The Lord willing, I will be going sometime this summer since I am to be there when school starts in September. In April I will begin my shots, and it will take about two months to get all of them. I will also get my passport in April."

One day Margaret Cook and I went to the nearby city of Rock Island. She had a dental appointment, and I needed to have my picture taken for my passport. When Margaret went for her appointment, I walked to the dime store to have my picture taken for twenty-five cents in one of those little photo booths that were popular at that time. That quarter was all the money I had to my name at the moment.

After getting my picture I was standing in the store waiting for Margaret who had promised to meet me there. I happened to be standing near the candy counter, and the chocolate smelled so good! I thought, *If only I had a nickel, I would buy some candy!*

Just then two women walked by carrying what looked like dress boxes under their arms. The enemy said to me, "It's been a long time since you've had a new dress."

Quickly Jesus whispered, "But you have something **so much better!**" My heart instantly overflowed with joy, and I just about shouted right there near the candy counter. I was so happy in Jesus, and the desire for chocolate candy left me.

Jesus had some surprises in store for me. Just a few days later someone sent me a big box of chocolates. Later Aunt Pearl Rickel sent me money to buy material for a new dress. My needs were supplied, my wants granted, and I experienced a blessing that money could not buy!

On another occasion Rosella Knuth came to me and asked what size dress I wore. When I told her, she said, "That is the same size I wear. I just made myself three new dresses, but God told me I couldn't keep them. He told me to give them to you."

I almost told her that I did not need them, but then the thought came to me that if God told her to give them to me, I should accept them. He was supplying when I did not even realize my need. I had worn most of my clothes through high school and college, and they were well worn. Neither did I realize that the tropical sun in Eritrea would cause my clothes to fade and rot. But God knew and was looking out for me. Praise His name!

Traveling for Deputation Services

The spring and summer of 1961, I spent making preparations for going to Eritrea and traveling for deputation services to raise my missionary support. Victor Glenn arranged for me to travel with Pauline Keith, who was on furlough after her first term in Eritrea. We traveled together for nearly three months, visiting Wesleyan Holiness churches from California to Pennsylvania. Glenn Griffith had asked Victor Glenn to allow us to visit all the churches in the group since we were both from that association.

Victor Glenn told us that we were to take our traveling expenses from the offerings. Since the churches usually gave us the offerings in cash, we had a lot of change on hand. Our schedule was too tight to permit us to go to a bank and have the change converted into bills. Pauline had asked me to take charge of both the offerings and our expenses.

Once, as we were traveling near dinnertime, we saw a sign advertising a restaurant that served chicken-in-a-basket. We thought that sounded good and stopped to eat. Pauline finished her meal before I did and went to the ladies' room. After I finished eating, I started to get the money ready to pay our bill.

At first I thought I would just empty the change out on the table to count it, but then I was not sure that would be wise. So I decided to pour some of it into my lap under the table and count it by feeling the coins. As I counted, I realized that if people saw what I was doing, they would think I was acting strangely. I started to laugh quietly. Then it occurred to me that if they saw me sitting alone and laughing as I counted money under the table, they really would think I was crazy. That thought caused me to laugh even more. When Pauline returned, I laughed out loud and said, "Please don't ever leave me alone like this again." Then I explained what had happened.

We were driving a 1958 two-tone green American Rambler that God had provided for me the summer I graduated from college. Daddy had told me to buy a new car because he did not want me to have problems. "If you buy a used car," he said, "you just purchase someone else's problems." I did not want to go into debt for a new car because I wanted to be free to go to the mission field when that time came.

One of Daddy's friends sold cars, and one day we went to his car lot to see what he had. The man showed us a Rambler and told me to take it for a drive. After I came back, he asked if I liked it. Of course I did! Daddy told me that we would put the car in his name so that the debt would be his, and when I went to the mission field, he would take over both the debt and the car. Then the car dealer told me I could have it without making the usual down payment. It was a lovely little car and just to my liking. I accepted the deal.

The car was the right size for Pauline and me, but when we reached Ponca City, Oklahoma, we added a third lady, Mary Macy, who traveled with us for about two weeks. She was a schoolteacher also and interested in the mission field. We had hung a clothes rod over the back seat so that whoever sat back there was rather cut off from the other two by the clothes hanging from the rod. Whenever Pauline or I sat back there, we used the time and privacy to pray and prepare ourselves for upcoming services. When Mary had her turn in the back seat, we jokingly told her that she was "in her closet" and to pray about a call to the mission field.

When Pauline and I reached California, we had a service in the Wesleyan Holiness Church in Pasadena where Robert and Birdie Fleming pastored. They had announced our missionary service, and I felt sure that since Pauline had already spent five years as a missionary in Eritrea, everyone would come expecting to hear her speak. After all, what can one say who has never seen the place of her calling? However, it was my turn to speak that night, and although I felt inadequate, I took my place behind the pulpit. I read my chosen Scripture and prayed, but sensing my need for God's help, I asked the congregation to pray again. God came to my rescue and gave us a good service. Praise His dear name!

One Sunday evening we were in Cheyenne, Wyoming, when we realized that we needed to be at Clinton Camp near Pittsburgh, Pennsylvania, by Tuesday afternoon. Because of a tight schedule we went to a gas station just after midnight and filled our gas tank and started toward Pennsylvania.

We took turns driving. I am a morning person, so during the first part of the trip, I was sleeping in the back seat. Something awakened me and I thought, *If Pauline is as tired as I am, it isn't right for me to be sleeping and letting her drive.* I suggested that we exchange places, so she stopped and I moved into the driver's seat.

I was so sleepy. We had some ice with us, and I took a piece and rubbed it on my face to help me stay awake. I sang silently to myself. Finally I began to pinch my face as I struggled to stay awake. Suddenly I opened my eyes and realized that I had dozed for a second or two. That frightened me, and I decided that I needed a cup of coffee.

When I pulled into the gravel parking lot of a small restaurant, Pauline awoke and asked if something was wrong. When I told her, she also became frightened. Then she told me that when I offered to drive, she was not sleepy but turned the wheel over to me because it was my car. We went into the restaurant and drank coffee and then went on our way thanking God for His hand of protection over us and for the coffee. The rest of the trip to Pennsylvania was made with minimal stops for gas. Arriving in the early hours of Tuesday morning, we stopped at a motel and got some much-needed sleep before going to the afternoon service at Clinton Camp where we spoke. That was the last service we had before we sailed for Eritrea.

After Clinton Camp I returned to Zanesville to spend time with my family. My last weekend in the States, I was privileged to attend the Zanesville Wesleyan Holiness Church where Daddy was pastoring.

The photo for my prayer card before going to Eritrea in 1961

58

Part II

My Years in Ethiopia
The Country of God's First Calling

Chapter 5

Adjusting to Missionary Life
1961-1962

Journey Across the Atlantic

God's marvelous hand had been directing my life, and the glorious day finally came when I boarded the *Concordia Foss* in New York City on August 26, 1961. I cannot explain the thrill I felt when I saw the ship that would take me to Africa. Mama said she thought I was going to get out of the car even before Daddy parked. God had called me when I was nine, and I was now twenty-six and ready to sail to the first land of God's calling. I was sailing with Pauline Keith, who was returning to Eritrea for her second term.

The *Concordia Foss*, the ship on which I sailed to Eritrea in 1961

As my father and brother unloaded my things, I began to feel a little embarrassed by thinking that I was taking so much. I had one suitcase, an accordion, and two footlockers. One footlocker contained books for the missionary children's school.

My parents and brother came on board the ship and helped me to get settled in my room. As they looked over the accommodations on the ship, my father noticed a woman wearing a lot of jewelry. "She

On deck with Mama and John

looks like a walking jewelry store," he said with his usual humor. Shortly after my family disembarked, we were on our way. At last I was going to Africa!

The *Concordia Foss*, which means "Concordia Waterfalls," was a freighter that had staterooms for a dozen passengers. Freighters travel slower than ocean liners since they make stops at various ports to unload and load cargo and passengers, but they provide a relatively inexpensive way to cross the ocean. There was a nice lounge for the passengers where we could read and visit. We ate our meals together with the captain and the chief engineer. During the voyage, which lasted almost a month, we had many opportunities to get acquainted.

I wrote the following to my parents the day after leaving New York City:

> We had a good night's rest, at least as good as can be expected on one's first night on the ocean. You can hear the water from the room. This morning when I looked out and saw all the water, it gave me a funny feeling. But praise the Lord, Jesus is ever near! I do feel His sweet presence. I can never thank Him enough for all His mercies.
>
> I have not been seasick yet.

I had a good time in prayer this morning. I plan to spend some more time with Jesus. There is plenty of time for devotions here. I like it.

Later I read four chapters of *Sweet Smelling Myrrh* and wrote to my parents that it was excellent. I also remarked that Betty, "the walking jewelry store," is from Persia and speaks broken English. Her mother is traveling with her.

Later during the voyage Betty wore a sleeveless dress. As she rubbed one arm, she said, "Me mother no like." She rubbed the other bare arm, saying, "Me husband no like." Then she added, "But me like."

"Oh, Betty, you shouldn't," I replied.

"But it so hot!"

"But I have on long sleeves."

"But you holy woman. Me not."

I wrote to my parents on September 5:

I trust you got my letters that were sent from Las Palmas in the Canary Islands. Our next stop is in Namours, Africa. It will be my first glimpse of "the land of His choice. ..."

I must tell you a little bit of what it is like to sight land after you have been on the water for days. Saturday evening after supper we all went out on the deck to see if we could see any land. Way off in the distance we saw a search light. That, of course, told us that land was near. From time to time we went out on the deck, and each time we could see more lights than we had seen the time before. It really was pretty. It made me think of how Columbus and his men must have felt after so many days on the water. ... It really was interesting to watch the harbor pilot come on board. In fact, it gave me a secure feeling to know that he was at the helm. One could draw an illustration from this of how Christ brings peace when He comes on board the ship of our life. Truly He knows the harbor very well for He has sailed the way before us. ...

We passed through the Strait of Gibraltar this morning, but it was so foggy that we caught only a very fleeting glimpse of it. ...

I trust you are all well and happy as I am. I am anxious to get to work for the Master, but I know I will need your prayers.

Soon after I wrote the above letter, we made our first landing in Africa at the port of Namours, Algeria. From that port I sent my parents a postcard exclaiming, "I can't express the joy of seeing the land that I promised God I would go to when I was nine years old. Truly Jesus is wonderful!"

There were two women on board who claimed to be sisters. With them was Conrad, a boy who was four and a half years old. Although the women said they were U.S. citizens, they were very negative about our country and praised Russia. The captain of the *Concordia Foss* was suspicious of them and asked us to give him our passports for safekeeping.

A retired U.S. naval officer traveling with us also thought the women were strange. Several times he tried to take their pictures, but each time they turned away or covered their faces. They even refused to be photographed with other passengers.

I told Bible stories to Conrad. I also told him that any time he had a problem or was afraid, he could talk to Jesus, and He would hear his prayer and help him. I have often thought of Conrad and wondered what his life was like.

I wrote the following on September 8:

This is Friday and tomorrow makes just exactly two weeks at sea. … We had thought we would arrive in Massawa about the 15th of September, but now it looks as if we will not get there until about the 25th. …

Last night after we went to bed . . . some of the passengers got into a drunken brawl. It was terrible! The mother of the little four-and-a-half year old boy started to yell something terrible. I was afraid at first that someone was doing her bodily harm, but it wasn't long before she began to bark like a dog. …They awakened me about 12:30, and it went on until about 2:30 or 3:00. They used the Lord's name in vain, and I have decided that my Jesus has been ill spoken of too much on this ship. … The Lord helping me, I must say something to them about it. …

I'm so happy that I have wonderful praying parents! Thank you again and again for your wonderful guidance and watchful care. Most of all, thank you for accepting Jesus yourselves and then teaching me the way, first by example and then by word. My heart bleeds for this little boy I mentioned. He has asked me to tell him stories, so I have told him several Bible stories. He had never heard any of them. He is the sweetest little fellow! When I told him the story of how Jesus walked on the water and Peter went to meet Him, he really sat up in interest. Then he wanted to know if Jesus were here now and walking on the water and if we kept our eyes on Him, could we walk on the water, too? Bless his heart; I am afraid he has an awful life ahead of him unless the Lord intervenes. I could wish him in little Jeff's place, for then he would be sure to go to heaven.

By the way, how is little Jeff? Have you been able to talk to his parents much about the Lord yet?

Jeff, who was about four years old, was the son of our neighbors in Zanesville. He had leukemia, and things did not look hopeful for him physically.

At the port after the brawl, the strange sisters and Conrad disembarked. I think the captain of the ship put the women off for causing so much trouble. They were to have traveled farther with us.

The following day I wrote to my family about our visit to Pompeii:

We are in Naples or Napoli as the Italians would say it. It, of course, is in Italy. This morning we hired a tourist car to take us to Pompeii and around the city of Naples. There were four of us who went: the Persian lady, an Egyptian lady, Pauline, and me. That way it was much cheaper and we could afford the trip.

The thing that made it so very interesting was this—it was a city that was inhabited during the Apostle Paul's day. It was built about sixty-two years before Christ was born. A volcano erupted and destroyed the city. They have a museum there in which they even have the bodies preserved that were destroyed at the time of the eruption. The archaeologist located the bodies and then poured plaster over them to preserve them in the very position in which they fell.

The ship stayed in Naples for only one day and then sailed to Genoa where we spent a week. Since we arrived on Sunday, that evening Pauline and I tried to find a church to attend. We located a Scottish minister who preached in English, but when we talked to him by phone from the ship, we understood very little of what he said. Taking a taxi to the address that he gave to us, we found a British seaman's mission comparable to the YMCA. It was in a very large building, and the first floor housed a recreation center. I guess he knew we would not be interested in that, so he took us upstairs to his apartment and told us that we would have a service when and if enough people came.

Pauline Keith, with whom I sailed, on the deck of the *Concordia Foss*

While we waited, the pastor served us tea. Since no one else came, I asked if he would play some hymns on his piano. He consented and we sang along with him, but it was not really what we wanted. When we returned to the ship, we had a service in our room.

In the old section of Genoa, the streets were very narrow. In fact, they looked like alleys. There were no department stores in that part of the city and only one huge dime store. On Tuesday we took the other two passengers, Betty and the Egyptian woman, with us and went shopping in the newer part of the city, which was much nicer but not as picturesque. One afternoon we went to see the famous Genoa cemetery, which had many beautiful marble lifelike statues.

Before we left Genoa, five new passengers joined our group: a young woman who was a Seventh-day Adventist missionary, two Catholic nuns, and an Italian mother and her daughter. We had a good time trying to teach the mother and daughter how to play Chinese checkers. We played with the help of a dictionary and enjoyed a lot of laughter.

Later in September I wrote to my parents:

I suppose this will be my last letter to you from the *Foss* since, the Lord willing, we will be in Eritrea either Saturday or Sunday. There are several things I have wanted to tell you, and if I don't do it now, I am afraid that in the excitement of reaching the field, I will forget to do so. …

One night most of us had gone to our rooms when we heard seven blasts on the ship's horn. That is supposed to be the signal for all the passengers to go out on the deck with their life jackets on. You should have seen me! I had my hair down ready to wash. I put on my raincoat and a headscarf. I had on my bedroom slippers and life jacket and had my Bible under one arm and my purse in the other hand. However, I did not go all the way out on the deck but waited by the room to see if we had interpreted the signal correctly. Soon I heard everyone laughing, so I went back into the room and washed my hair. When Pauline returned to our room, she said they were blowing at another ship that was coming right toward us. Evidently the navigator was sleeping, and they had blown the whistle several times to awaken him. Well, we all had a good laugh anyway. …

Last night they showed a movie downstairs and, of course, Pauline, Evelyn (the Seventh-day Adventist), and I did not go, nor did the Catholic sisters. The sisters told us that we were sisters because we didn't go. Of course, they speak only broken English and were trying to commend us. … Pauline, Evelyn, and I went out on the deck. We decided to sing and soon discovered several church songs we all knew. It wasn't long before the Italian woman and her daughter came out and hummed along with us. Then we decided to sing Christmas carols. We were doing that when the sisters came so we all sang together. We had a good time even though it was a rather odd situation.

The atmosphere certainly is different since we changed some of our passengers. It is much more relaxed now.

I have had several long talks with Evelyn about our beliefs. She is a little stricter than some of the Adventists and seems to have an experience of salvation but, of course, not sanctification. I am praying that the Lord will somehow speak to these souls and make them conscious of their need of Him.

It took us eight days to cross the Atlantic Ocean, and then we spent about two weeks in the Mediterranean Sea exchanging cargo in various ports including a week in Genoa. Our ship then eased through the locks of the Suez Canal over a two-day period so that we could begin our three-day journey down the Red Sea to the Eritrean port of Massawa.

The captain called Pauline and me out on the deck as we sailed down the Red Sea. He allowed us to look through his binoculars at Mount Sinai where Moses had received the Ten Commandments. That was exciting! The Bible was beginning to come alive as we entered that part of the Middle East.

Historical note: When I sailed for Africa, the place of my destination was Eritrea. However, the following year Eritrea became a province of Ethiopia. That will explain the change in names from Eritrea to Ethiopia as my story unfolds.

Arrival in Eritrea

As we approached the harbor of Massawa, the captain again called Pauline and me on deck and handed us his binoculars. Looking intently around the harbor area, we saw a Volkswagen near the lighthouse. Beside the car were Mark Budensiek and his precious wife, Nancy, along with their two-year-old son, Philip, and their second son, Peter, who was in a stroller. As we watched, they got into the car and headed for the dock.

It was Saturday morning, September 23, 1961, and I was finally arriving at the first country to which God had called me. The Fred Cromer family also was waiting to welcome us. At that time Fred was the field chairman. Standing with him on the dock were his wife, Marilyn, and their two-year-old daughter, Karen. Freddie, their seven-year-old son, had stayed in Decamere.

My eye doctor in America had told me that Massawa was the hottest port in the world. He knew that firsthand because he had been stationed in Eritrea while in the U.S. military. As we stood on the deck observing everything, we quickly realized that Massawa was indeed a hot place. Many days the temperature reached well over 100 degrees.

Pauline and I disembarked, cleared immigration, and Fred Cromer made arrangements for us to return the following week to get our belongings out of customs. The Cromers and the Budensieks then took us to the U.S. Navy restaurant for dinner. After that we headed to the highland town of Decamere where Pauline and I would live.

By the time we started over the flat desert plains toward the mountains, nighttime was upon us. Here and there we saw the tiny fires of the nomads who sometimes grazed their flocks in that area. Soon we were climbing the steep mountains on what appeared to be the wrong side of the road. You see, at that time Eritrea was under the influence of the British, having become a British protectorate after the Second World War. That is why people drove on the left side of the road.

In Decamere I met the rest of our missionary family: Roy O. and Esther Norton and their children Glenda Ruth, John, Daniel, and Donald; Leroy and Myrtle Adams with their young children Marie and Melvin; and the three single ladies—Carrie Boyer, Zettie Finch, and Barbara Tierney.

That evening when I was taken to my apartment on the high-school compound, I was struck by the fact that it was clean but starkly furnished. Noticing that the towels in the bathroom had E.F.M. embroidered on them, I tried to figure out to which missionary they belonged. Then I had to chuckle to myself when I realized that the initials stood for Evangelistic Faith Missions.

First Sunday in Eritrea

The next morning, Sunday, Freddie Cromer came to call Pauline, who lived across the hall, and me for breakfast. It was my first time to meet Freddie, and I noticed that he had a large sore on his neck near his shoulder. He told me that some sort of bug had walked on him during the night and that the creature leaves a blister everywhere its feet touch you.

Marilyn Cromer had prepared a good breakfast of fried eggs, toast, and cocoa. Later the Adams family came in the mission jeep to take me to the service in the marketplace of Decamere. The community building where we met had a tin roof. Someone tried to disturb the service by throwing stones onto it. Although it made a terrible racket, he did not succeed in stopping the service. We continued without further incident as Leroy Adams preached.

That evening I went with Fred and Marilyn Cromer to Asmara, the capital city. Services there were conducted in a rented store building. Fred preached with great anointing, and Mesgun Tedla interpreted with the same help of the Spirit. At one point a man entered and dragged a young man out of the building and proceeded to beat him. I learned later that he was the young man's father and was beating him because he left the Coptic Church and became an evangelical believer.

The next morning the Cromers took Pauline and me to Massawa to get our belongings out of customs. Carrie Boyer went with us for the day. In a letter to my parents I wrote, "We surely had a good time going down the mountain. We all sang between Carrie's accounts of the lowlands. I trust that if possible you will be able to have her speak in your church there. She is a real pioneer missionary!"

Excursions to the Capital City

I had been in Eritrea only a short time when I decided I would like to go shopping in Asmara. Esther Norton chose to join me on my Saturday shopping trip. When the Cromers, who also lived in Decamere, learned that we were interested in going shopping, they invited us to accompany them. He drove the Volkswagen that belonged to the Mission and was used to visit our various mission stations.

Neither Esther, who was almost as new to Eritrea as I was, nor I could speak any Tigrinya nor did we know much Italian. Since Eritrea had been an Italian colony for many years before the British liberated it at the beginning of World War II, many of the shopkeepers were Italian and had Tigrinya-speaking people working for them.

Because Esther and I did not know either language, we had to resort to sign language. I wanted to buy some yeast for making

The main street in the capital city of Asmara, Eritrea

bread. With my hands I tried to make the motion of bread rising and at the same time said one of the few Italian words I had learned, *pane*, which means bread. Thus saying *pane* I held my left hand still and placed my right hand above it, then slowly raised my right hand as I repeated *pane*. The older Italian man smiled and turned to pick up a can of baking powder and held it out to me. I shook my head and said *pane* again repeating my sign language. There was a young Tigrinya-speaking man behind the counter. He stepped forward and, to my amazement, showed me that the yeast was in a glassed-in portion of the counter directly in front of me. I laughed and said, "*Sí, sí!*" I had expected the yeast to come in little packets like we have in the United States. That was quite an eye opener to me.

Later two women came up to us as we were walking to another store and tried to sell us large wicker baskets. At first we refused but then decided that they might make good clothes baskets. We each bought one and then began to think about the small Volkswagen in which we had come to town and wondered if there would be room for us to take the baskets to Decamere. We also wondered what Fred's reaction would be. He was very nice about it and just put one basket inside the other and tied them securely to the luggage rack on the car. Everything else fit inside the trunk. After we finished shopping, we returned to Decamere, thus ending our first shopping trip to Asmara.

A short time later Fred called me from the capital and told me that I was to come by bus to take care of my legal papers since I needed an identity card in order to stay in the country. He promised that his family would meet me at the bus station. I boarded the 1:30 p.m. bus in Decamere after being escorted to the bus station by two tenth-grade girls. On the bus I read mail from home and watched the sights until drowsiness overcame me. Rain coming through the open windows awakened me.

Every time the bus stopped to let people on or off, a man behind me would tap me on the shoulder and speak to me in Tigrinya. I would shrug my shoulders since I did not understand any Tigrinya. After doing this several times, I tried some Italian on him. It did not seem to faze him, so I said, "Only English." Following another tap I said, "Bus stop." He smiled and pointed straight ahead.

When I disembarked, I could not see any sign of an American waiting to meet me. However, in no time I was surrounded by a group of African boys. "Taxi?" inquired one.

"*La. La!*" I answered, meaning "No. No!"

The boys spotted a car with Americans in it before I did, and they ran to me again shouting, "*Americanos!*"

"They really take care of strangers here," I wrote to my parents.

Facing New Horizons

A letter to my parents on October 2, 1961, detailed my new life in Africa:

I have just finished my first day of teaching in Africa. The Lord truly helped! However, when four o'clock came, I found myself with just a twinge of loneliness so thought I should like to have a little chat with you. …

Last night I had my first opportunity to preach to the dear African people. We had the service in the marketplace here in Decamere. All the high-school students were there plus several people from the village. The blessed Holy Spirit truly helped as I endeavored to deliver a message on the crucifixion of Jesus, telling all He suffered for us that we might have life eternal. During the message several stones were thrown onto the roof and a man stood up and began to talk, but several of our students spoke to him and he left. Praise the Lord! Jesus helped us, and in the end a holy hush settled down and several lifted their hands for prayer.

Continuing the letter I described my living quarters—living room, kitchen, bathroom, a nice-sized bedroom, and a small bedroom for visitors. The apartment was very nice, but at first it seemed rather big to me, perhaps because of the high ceilings. I also told them that there was no hot, running water and that it was necessary to heat my water on a small gas stove.

The apartment building on the high-school compound in Decamere. My first residence was on the ground floor in the front of this building.

During November I wrote again to my family and told them that it was getting colder and damp due to the fog from the Red Sea, and I needed to wear my heavier coat to my Tigrinya language classes held at our orphanage. Although it was cold and damp, it did not freeze and flowers continued to bloom. I told them that Carrie was visiting again and of the many long talks and times of prayer that we had together. "How I do love her. She is a wonderful soldier of the cross," I wrote.

The harvest season, which began in November, was the time for weddings. One day I heard the beating of drums and ran outside to see what was happening. I arrived in time to see a crowd of people preceded by a man who was carrying a sword. He was leaping and whirling his sword while another man behind him was beating a drum. Others in the group were beating drums also. I learned that this was a common practice in their culture.

A few nights later I again heard the sound of drums, which most likely signified the drinking and dancing for another wedding. I was sitting on my bed preparing for chapel service the next day when I heard a student whistling "What a Friend We Have in Jesus." Oh, how it did bless me to recognize the contrast between light and darkness. All these strikingly different cultural occurrences were making a strong impact on me and did not allow me for a single moment to think that I was in my comfortable home in the States.

It was field-committee meeting time. Since Pauline was on the committee and would be in the sessions, she asked me to give tests to her students in three classes. It really kept me busy covering my own duties and giving her tests. I would meet with the missionary children whom I was teaching for about an hour and a half in the morning. Then giving them plenty to do, I put Glenda Ruth Norton in charge and went to one of Pauline's classes. It was the same in the afternoon.

My first graders: Karen Cromer, Marie Adams, and Donald Norton

A typical Sunday began with devotions at 6:00 and breakfast at 7:00 followed by church at 10:00. The afternoon was spent in teaching a Sunday school class at 2:00 and community visitation from 3:00 to

5:00. After supper there was group prayer with the high-school girls before the evening service at 7:00. The day often ended in physical weariness but joy in being able to serve the One I love.

In one of my letters I wrote to my mother and explained about an Eritrean custom following childbirth.

> The third day after the baby is born, many of the ladies in the village come to the mother's house and eat a thick porridge with sour cream around it. Since the porridge was eaten with a hand, our eating was preceded and followed by a routine of hand washing that interested me greatly. One person came to each participant with a basin of water and had a towel hanging over one arm. Each attendee would dip the hand she would use for eating into the water and then dry it on the towel. Following the meal the basin was brought again. This time a second maid accompanied the first carrying a pitcher of warm water. Water was poured over the diner's hand as she washed, using the soap provided.

Experiences in the Classroom

My first year in Eritrea, I taught English and Bible to the seventh graders along with all the classes for the missionary children. One morning during Bible class, God visited us in a special way. One student raised his hand and asked, "May I have permission to go and ask forgiveness of my friend?"

"Certainly."

"May I, too?"

"May I, also?"

Soon many of those students were asking forgiveness of one another. Then a student asked permission to go to another class-room. In a short time students were going throughout the school and asking forgiveness of one another. It was not long until they went outside the compound and witnessed to neighbors. Praise God! He had come and made Himself known to those young people in a real way. Many of them had been brought up in the Faith Mission orphanage, and the missionaries were the only parents some of them had ever known. How thrilling to see them, now in their teens, minding God and starting on the path that leads to heaven.

I had often told the Lord I knew that He was no respecter of persons. "Surely as You met with us in America, You can meet with us in Africa," I had prayed, and now, so soon, He was proving Himself true.

My heart reached out to my students who had difficulties academically. One day a student remained in his seat after the others had gone, so I asked him if he wanted to ask me something. Looking up rather shyly he said, "Yes." Then he came to my desk with a piece of paper in his hand on which he had written a sentence. I was happy to help him with the punctuation.

Another time a boy came to me and said, "You know, it is easy for those who have been in the orphanage, but for those of us who _____ ____ ____ _____, it is not." As I filled in the blanks with, "come from the villages," he nodded yes. I told him that I understood and would try to help them all I could. It was evident that they did not have the same educational advantages as those who had lived in the orphanage.

One of my seventh-grade students was Josephina, whose father was an Italian and her mother an Eritrean witch doctor. When her father returned to Italy, he did not want to leave Josephina with her mother, so he brought her to the Mission. She still loved her mother and spent many hours in prayer for her.

In December I again wrote to my parents, telling them of my students in seventh-grade English who were studying a poem about a sage who had a pigtail. They were worried because it hung behind him. Poor students! They thought he had a real pig's tail, and I had quite a bit of explaining to do before they could enjoy the poem.

Grappling with the Tigrinya Language

When I arrived in Eritrea and heard the Tigrinya language, it tickled me immensely. I found it difficult to keep from laughing at its strange sounds. When I was a teenager, my father and his father had sometimes pretended that they were speaking a foreign language while making only nonsensical sounds. They made inflections in their voices as if they were asking and answering questions just to make the family laugh. Now when I heard the Eritreans speaking and could not even tell where one word ended and another began, I had an awful urge to laugh as I had at Daddy and Grandpa.

I developed a strong desire to be able to understand and communicate in the Tigrinya language. On Sundays as the congregation sang, I studied the characters in their songbook and longed to read and understand them. Each day right after lunch I would ask the high-school girl who was working in my house to help me study Tigrinya. There were no Tigrinya textbooks to aid the foreign student; neither were there any Tigrinya/English dictionaries. Our only aid was the primer the children in the orphanage used to learn to read.

Some of the other missionaries also were having difficulty trying to make the unfamiliar sounds. Sebhat our teacher, who taught in the school at the orphanage, at times laughed at our efforts. Sometimes he turned his face to the blackboard, laughing so hard that he almost cried. "In order to say some sounds," he would tell us, "you almost have to spit."

At the same time I was struggling to learn to pronounce those difficult sounds, I was trying to teach the difficult English sounds to my students. The "th" sound was one of the hardest for them. One student, trying very hard, could not help but say, "I tink tho," for "I think so," forcing the "th" sound and putting it in the wrong place.

Like Arabic and Hebrew, Tigrinya is not written with English letters. I eventually discovered that Tigrinya has 33 families of characters with 7 characters in each family, making 231 characters. Each character is a syllable that includes both vowel and consonant sounds. In addition there are 4 families of diphthongs with 5 characters in each family and 17 other characters making a total of 268 plus 20 more for numbers. In Tigrinya punctuation a comma is two dots in a vertical pattern like a colon, a period is four dots in a square, and a question mark is three dots in a vertical column. I found that to be very interesting if not rather daunting.

Since I had no textbook, it took me until the end of my first five-year term to begin catching on to the grammar. Consequently, the Mission decided that when I returned for my second term, I would be given the afternoons for language study. I finally learned enough to carry on conversations and to use Tigrinya in teaching

English to my students, but I never learned the language well enough to preach in it.

Like missionaries everywhere I must admit to some funny mistakes. One time in a native home I tried to tell them that their bread for breakfast was very tasty. I meant to say, *"Taum kicha,"* but it came out, *"Taum chica."* I actually said, "Good mud."

One day while walking home I was concentrating intently on learning my Tigrinya. When I reached the door of my apartment, I knocked, not realizing where I was. I stood there waiting until the house girl came and opened the door. We were both surprised and just stood there and laughed.

The Tigrinya alphabet

First Christmas in Africa

As my first Christmas in Eritrea was approaching, I bought a card for my brother, Johnny, with a camel on it and one for my parents with three darling African children pictured on the front. I sent these on December 15 and made a Christmas tryst with them at the throne of grace for their Christmas Eve and the morning of my Christmas Day since there was an eight-hour difference in time.

On the American Christmas of December 25, Pauline and I were awakened by Leroy Adams and some students singing Christmas carols near our apartments. As soon as we had eaten breakfast, we began preparing food and wrapping gifts for the Christmas gath-

78

ering at the Cromers' house where the Budensiek and Adams families along with Pauline, Barbara Tierney, and I would celebrate our Savior's birth. One special item on the menu was canned ham from America. The Budensieks and the Cromers each had a canned ham that had been given to them, which they saved for that special occasion.

The Eritrean Christmas is celebrated on January 7, and since I was teaching in the high school as well as in the missionary children's school, my vacation did not begin until January. During that time I attended my first Eritrean wedding and made my first visit to the lowland town of Tessenie and the village of Ducumbia.

A Problem with Paramecia

The Saturday before New Year's Day, which came on Monday, I was sitting by the fireplace in Pauline's apartment when a spark popped out from the fire and landed on my arm. It stung. I thought the pain would pass but it did not.

After applying some salve I saw to my surprise that little red dots appeared in a line going up my arm. When I showed Pauline what had happened, it scared her, and she immediately sent a high-school boy to tell the Cromers.

"Teacher Hemmeter cut off her arm!" was the message the boy gave the Cromers, and you can imagine how they came on the run from the orphanage to Pauline's apartment a block away. I explained to them what actually happened, showing them how each time I put salve on the burn, red dots appeared. Sometimes the dots went under the skin and then reappeared as if they were living things.

"Do you have a knife?" Fred asked Pauline. In view of the earlier mistranslation, I wondered what was going to happen as Pauline brought a small paring knife. Fred also asked for a microscope and slides from the science lab. Scraping off one of the red dots, he mounted it on the slide. When he looked at the dot under the microscope, he recognized that it was a paramecium. It had the exact shape of the sole of a foot with the little hairs coming out from it and a uvula on it. As Fred watched it on the slide, it divided. We stayed up until 3:00 a.m. Pauline poured alcohol on my arm causing the paramecium to appear, and then they scraped them off my arm. The next day I had a temperature of 102 degrees. Fred was afraid it was caused by a tick because he had read about an elephant that had died of tick fever. He called the missionaries together, and they prayed for me.

The day after New Year's Day the Cromers took me to a doctor who said that I was very anemic. Later our own doctor confirmed that diagnosis. He also said that I had a parasite in my blood and prescribed six weeks of shots to treat that problem. The spark from the fire somehow exposed the paramecia I already had, but I had no idea how I contracted them.

Attending My First Eritrean Wedding

Hagos Michael, one of our preachers, and Hiwan Beraki were married in our high-school chapel during the Eritrean Christmas vacation in January 1962. Carrie Boyer and Zettie Finch along with the Nortons, who were visiting them, came from the lowlands for the wedding. Leroy Adams performed the ceremony with Mesgun Tedla interpreting. Following an Eritrean wedding the families of the bride and the groom each hold a feast in their respective villages to celebrate the marriage.

We all attended the bride's feast held that evening at her home in Asmara. That was my first time to attend a wedding feast in Eritrea. It was held in a tent-like structure that was rather dark inside. We were served the best *zigganey*, which was made with chicken. *Zigganey* is a soup made with tomatoes, onions, garlic, hot peppers, spices, and some kind of meat such as chicken, goat, sheep, or ox and is eaten with *tita*, one of their native breads. The *zigganey* was very tasty but as we ate, our eyes watered, our noses ran, and our mouths burned.

Food for a special occasion—*zigganey* (meat in center) and *alachi* (vegetables) eaten with *tita* (the native bread under the meat and vegetables). Eight people eat from this serving of food simultaneously.

Some of the people were going to a corner of the tent and dipping up something that looked like hot chocolate. Since I was thirsty, I wanted some but was not sure how to ask for it so decided to endure my thirst. Later I was glad I had made that decision. I learned that not everyone at the wedding feast was a Christian and that the brown concoction was a native beer.

The next day we traveled about eight hours to attend the groom's feast in the lowland town of Tessenie near the Sudan border. Following that meal we went by Land Rover to the village of Ducumbia where Carrie and Zettie lived.

Visiting the Lowlands

It was a delight for me to visit Ducumbia after having heard Carrie tell stories about the work there. It was a village located in the midst of a heathen tribe in the hot lowlands of Eritrea where the Mission was endeavoring to establish a church. From Ducumbia a group of us went to the outlying village of Antaray, a typical African village with *tukuls*, one-room round huts made of grass or palm branches. There we met Kuno, a little black boy about seven years old who was the grandson of the chief. Like many of the children, Kuno did not wear any clothes. He was very interested in the gospel and was always happy when Carrie came to share the Word of God in his village, which she did regularly.

A *tukul*—a typical lowland house with stick and mud walls and a grass roof

Kuno's mother brought out a rope bed and placed two brightly colored straw mats on it for us to sit on as we visited. I thought that from their perspective that was like Kuno's mother giving us the best seats in the living room, only we were seated outside under the burning African sun. The first time Carrie went to Antaray, Kuno worried about the Land Rover, which he thought was an animal. "Why don't you take your animal to the river and let him drink on such a hot day?" he asked.

The people in Antaray served us hot, spicy tea in small glasses. It was very sweet, and I learned to say *Hama*, which in Kunama means it is sweet. I will never forget the thrill of giving them the gospel later that day! That was my purpose in coming to Africa.

"I wish you could have seen the little children," I wrote home. "They have no clothing, and almost all of them have distended stomachs from malnutrition. Oh, how they love to sing and listen to our stories." Kuno was from the Kunama tribe. Carrie prayed that his tribe would move across the Setit River so that she could give them the gospel. The Setit River marked the boundary between Eritrea and Ethiopia before they became one country. After Kuno's people moved across the river, Carrie was able to take the gospel to them.

Carrie, Zettie, Christina, Abraha Haile, and I stayed in Antaray several days, sleeping outside and cooking with a little camp stove. We got sunburned in January. Imagine! That was truly the Africa I had pictured in my mind—the heat and the little mud-and-grass huts. They told us that the elephants were just across the river and that lions had come and killed five camels in a village not far from there. We chased monkeys, saw wild goats, heard hyenas in the night, and even saw a hyena one morning.

After we returned to the larger village of Ducumbia, Carrie told us stories about the early days of the work. During those talks a strong desire was created in my heart to work with Carrie in pioneer missionary work among those who had never heard the gospel. A few days later in my home in the highlands, I went into my bedroom to talk to Jesus, the One who had called me. "O Lord, if it be your will, please make it possible for me to help Carrie open a new work some day." When I wrote to my parents about that, Daddy wrote back saying, "No good thing will He withhold from them that walk uprightly" (Psalm 84:11). About fourteen years would elapse before Carrie and I went to open a new work in Jinka in Gemu Gofa province in southern Ethiopia.

Sharing News with My Family

Shortly after my return to the highlands, it was time for the yearly convention, which was always held in Decamere. That year Victor Glenn and Harold E. Schmul came and preached, which was a blessing to the missionaries, national workers and their families, other believers who were able to attend, and our students from the orphanage and high school. Pauline and I felt honored to offer our bedrooms to the guest speakers and to the missionaries who came from other stations. On Sunday afternoon Victor Glenn preached a wonderful message on dedicating your life to Christ. Several of our students prayed fervently and received definite calls to full-time service, two of whom were in my seventh-grade class. I shared the highlights of the convention in my letters.

On another occasion I wrote to my family telling them about Zettie taking a tiny, premature baby who weighed four pounds at birth. His mother died when he was three days old, and he lost a pound before the Moslem father, a policeman, persuaded Zettie to take him. She asked the father's permission to give the baby a Christian name, and they decided on Musie. "He sure is cute," I wrote to my parents. "I don't think I have ever seen cuter."

Zettie placed Musie in a box padded with blankets and then set the box on more blankets on a metal table. Then she placed a small kerosene-burning stove under the table to provide warmth. About every hour she fed him with an eye-dropper. Musie was taken to our orphanage when he was old enough to walk.

Zettie Finch with Musie

I wrote the following on March 21:

Did you get a calendar from the Mission? They are really nice this year. Of course, they mean more to me than usual. If you got one, please notice the picture for this month. It was taken right outside our front door. The two little fellows are from the orphanage, and their names are Twaldae and Esau. Zettie raised Twaldae until last spring when she went to the lowlands to be with Carrie. He still calls her Mommy. All of the little ones at the orphanage call all of us missionary ladies Mommy. They have a lot of Mommies. All the MKs call us Auntie. As the Lord promised, He has given me the desires of my heart. I am both Mommy and Auntie.

The other day I was standing and talking with the Budensieks. Everyone else was seated. Little Philip Budensiek went into the other room and got a chair for me and said, "Sit down, Aunt Faith!" He is only two! I sure do love all my nieces and nephews and all our native babies, too.

I am sending you your birthday presents in Carrie's trunk. I want her to stop and see you. She is a wonderful missionary and not hard to entertain. She has lived in a mud *tukul* (hut). She loves to talk of spiritual things, and she loves to pray. We have had some wonderful prayer times together. My desire to work with her grows and grows.

Shortly thereafter some of us went to a highland village near our high school to hold a service. A Coptic priest, upset at our teaching, disrupted our service and told us to leave and never come back. However, a week later I wrote to my family:

Sunday afternoon Esther Norton, Nancy Budensiek, Ababa, and I went back to the village where the priest told us not to return. We held a good service in the home of Ogbazghi, one of our orphanage workers. It started to rain real hard and then turned into hail. They were preparing coffee beans to make coffee, and thus we had a good reason to stay. The girl who was pounding the beans jumped up and ran outside to get some charcoal. She came back and pounded until she remembered the little goats. She ran out and chased them into the mud house. When she started to cook the coffee, she realized one little goat was missing and ran out to find it. The poor girl was soaked to her skin by that time. We had our coffee, and it was real cozy with the door closed, the charcoal fire burning, sitting on an animal skin on some bed springs, talking, listening to the rain, and watching the little goats playing around us. Little children who had gathered in began to sing *Amlach Ficreyu* (God is Love).

When Victor Glenn and Harold Schmul were here, Rev. Schmul did not eat the first course of the meal (goat stomach), but he did eat *zigganey*. The best part was the natives going around the table sharing a sop that is a sign of friendship. Rev. Schmul almost crawled on top of Rev. Glenn in his haste to get over to the opposite side of the table from the sop. We really teased him about it. He said his wife had told him to stick close to Victor and he did.

The practice of offering a sop was done like this: A person who wanted to express his Christian love and friendship for another would tear off a piece of the native flat bread. Dipping the bread into the soup and picking up a piece of meat or vegetable, he then reached out and placed his left hand under the person's chin. When the honoree opened his mouth, the person would stuff the food into it. Often they gave one another large bites that were hard to chew and threatened to overflow.

Daddy, you asked if this work is anything like the Indian work. Yes and no. The setting is so different, and the language barrier is greater. The customs are very different. For example, young couples do not usually go together at all before getting married. Their courtship is all by letter and through a third person. The wife keeps her own name. The children take their father's first name for their surname.

Living in Decamere

While Pauline and I lived in Decamere, the mice in our apartments caused us much excitement. One day we found a dead mouse in Pauline's stove. Later we called the high-school boys to help us hunt them. When the boys mentioned that they thought they saw a snake, we declared, "We'll just move out!" Moving out was not our answer; learning to cope with such experiences was, and with God's help we did.

Stephanos and Solomon, two of my students, were baptized along with others in May. The following Sunday night heavy conviction fell, and I was burdened for two days. The Holy Spirit met with us in Tuesday's English class. Afterward Isaiah Aroda asked to speak with me alone. He told me that he was under such conviction that he had not slept for two nights, so we prayed together.

Isaiah, from the Kunama tribe, told how the Italians had come to his village and sinned along with the tribesmen. Later when three of our missionaries went to his village, they witnessed about God and told about a school they had started in Ducumbia that the village children could attend.

"Why didn't the Italians tell us about this God?" the villagers asked one another after the missionaries left. They decided to dismiss the new idea, but Isaiah could not toss it off. A desire grew in him to attend the mission school. He asked his parents for permission to fulfill that longing, but they told him that he would never be allowed to go. Isaiah could not accept that decision, so he pretended to go to the forest with some shepherds but instead found his way to the Mission in Ducumbia and started attending classes.

In two days Isaiah's parents came and took him home. He waited a week and then secretly left again. Isaiah told me, "That time my parents did not follow me because I was disobedient to them and was unworthy of their searching for me. When summer vacation came, I returned to my village a different boy because I had met God. The blood of His own Son was applied to my heart. I talked to my friends, and when school opened in September, a number of them went with me."

Carrie told me that Isaiah had been such a beautiful, healthy baby that his people were going to offer him as a sacrifice to appease the gods during one of their plagues. However, one of the men in the village begged for his life, telling the people that if they did not spare the baby, he would report them to the police. Thus God spared his life. At the time of this writing, Isaiah is still pastoring in Eritrea, and one of his daughters is teaching in a Faith Missions school.

Carrie left for a short furlough in April of 1962, and the Cromers went to Ducumbia to fill in for her. After Freddie Cromer completed his school work that spring, he went to live with his parents. Since I no longer had to teach him during the week and care for him on the weekends, I had some free time and began reading *The Kneeling Christian*.

Zettie and Musie came to spend the last weeks of school with Pauline and me. By then Musie weighed twelve pounds, a big contrast from the wrinkled little three-pounder Zettie had put in a makeshift incubator soon after his birth.

During the last week of classes, I was too busy to even write to my parents. In addition to finishing my teaching responsibilities, I returned to Sorona for Sunday services. It blessed my heart to hear those people sing "Jesus Saves" in their own language. Oh, how they could sing!

Chapter 6

Adventures on the Mission Field
1962-1966

Happenings in Ducumbia

During the summer of 1962, I had the joy of serving in Ducumbia. While there I had an impression that Grandpa John Hemmeter was allowed to look down from heaven and see me walking across the mission compound in Ducumbia and that he was very pleased.

It was very hot, and we had no fans. If we walked close to the walls around our compound, we could feel the heat radiating from them. The only relief we had was drinks chilled with ice from the kerosene refrigerator. Cold lemonade or limeade really hit the spot after visits in village homes or walks to the open-air market.

After two weeks for settling in and learning the ropes, I began Daily Vacation Bible School, usually having more than twenty children in attendance. Each story had to be told through two interpreters. Kubra Waldamariam, a girl who had studied in our high school, interpreted into Kunama while Josephina, the girl whose mother was a witch doctor, interpreted into Tigrinya. The children learned choruses in both of those languages as well as in English.

After arriving in Ducumbia I immediately began Sunday visitation, and by the third Sunday I had visited twice in the home of Asha, a young Moslem woman. Asha had refused to marry the rich, old man to whom she had been promised from early childhood. Even as a child she warned her parents that she would not marry him. By the time she was fifteen, the man had spent much money buying clothes for her and last of all, paying for the wedding feast. Moslem custom decrees that on the wedding day the bride sits on a bed behind a curtain unseen by the guests.

Asha had other plans. Wearing her beautiful wedding dress she ran from the village, climbed a thorn tree, and refused to come down. Her house was crowded with guests, and her parents were greatly ashamed, but their pleading did not bring her down. Others pled, but she did not budge. Finally her parents asked her, "Who will pay

Asha and I

back all the money he has spent on you all these years if you do not marry him?"

"I will pay him back myself," Asha declared. "I will make and sell fancy work until I get him all paid back if you do not force me to marry him."

Asha sat in the tree until late that night. When she was sure that everyone was asleep, she climbed down the tree and ran to the government offices in Barentu about fifteen miles away. Next morning she asked the authorities there if her family could force her to marry a man she did not want to wed, and they said, "No."

The young Moslem woman worked faithfully and repaid the man whom she had spurned. She was never allowed out of her house until she had paid him in full, and even then she was forced to remain in the house until she later married a man whom she came to love. When I met her, they had a young daughter. How I longed to see this strong-willed lady come under submission to our great God. What a Christian Asha would make!

A few years later Asha became very ill, and her mother called the witches to treat her. They mumbled their incantations over her, gave her potions, and even bit her stomach in an effort to make her well.

When Asha's husband saw her worsening condition, he ran to the Mission for help. Marilyn Van Kuiken and Zettie Finch went to the house. Immediately, Marilyn, a registered nurse, saw that Asha was very sick with hepatitis and declared that they must get her to a hospital quickly.

Asha's mother resisted that idea, and Asha's husband seemed uncertain about what to do. Finally Marilyn asked, "Are you her husband?"

"Yes," he replied.

"Do you want her in the hospital?"

"Yes," he said again.

"Then give us permission to take her!" Marilyn exclaimed, and he did.

Marilyn and Zettie rushed Asha to the hospital, but she died on the way. I am grateful, though, that Marilyn had time to lead her to a saving knowledge of Jesus before she passed into eternity.

Many times I wrote to my parents, "You must be getting your prayers through for the Lord's presence has been very real to me. I have been so happy and joyful in my work." I told of one prayer after another being answered and indicated how glad I was to have praying parents. Recalling the books my father had read to me and the talks I had with my mother, I said, "If I had my pick of parents, I would pick you two!"

In July I wrote these words of a song to them:

> So send I you to give your own with gladness,
> To let them go unhindered to the lost,
> To hide the tears, and every trace of sadness,
> So send I you to taste, with me, the cost.

One day the chiefs of Ducumbia, including the head chief, Shef Musa, asked us missionary ladies to take them to a funeral in Barentu. When we got through a place in the road where most vehicles got stuck, the chiefs clapped their hands in approval. We spent time in two mud *tukuls* in Barentu. One was full of flies but the other was very clean. In the latter we were given *tita, zigganey*, and clabbered milk to eat. "It surely was delicious," I wrote later. "The milk helped to cool the hot seasoning of the *zigganey*."

Visiting the Village of Laiday

I spent the next week with Christina Abel in village ministry in Laiday where I did much calling, playing the accordion, singing, and preaching. Christina was a Kunama believer who attended our high school in Decamere during the school year and ministered among her people at other times. While visiting Laiday during Easter vacation, Christina saw her grandmother and told her that God would take care of her. Her grandmother replied, "God doesn't love me." Christina's eyes filled with tears as she told me most of her people feel that way. Now we were back in Laiday to minister to those people.

Here we met Fatima who had been saved in the mission school in Ducumbia. Fatima was her Moslem name, but when she was baptized, she took the name of Rachel. The Moslems accused us of washing their names down the river.

Pastor Daniel and Joseph, a teacher, with children in the village of Laiday. The school building is behind them.

One day Rachel asked me to go to her home and give the gospel to her mother. We entered the *tukul* in which they lived. It was dark inside, especially after coming in from the bright African sunlight, and I had to wait a few seconds for my eyes to adjust. Rachel's mother placed a beautiful straw mat on the bed and motioned for us to sit there. After my eyes adjusted, I noticed that there were more of those beautiful woven mats hung on the wall. The *tukul* was very attractive.

There were several women seated around the room waiting to learn about God. Oh, what a joy it was to tell them how God created the Garden of Eden, man, and then woman, and gave them such wonderful fruit to eat. I told them about the tree in the midst of the garden from which they were not to eat and how sin entered the

91

world. Then God in His great love sent His only Son to die in our place that we might have eternal life. When I finished, everyone was quiet.

Finally one woman said, "This is true. This is God's Word." How did she know? The blessed Holy Spirit had witnessed the truth to her heart. Oh, what a thrill to share the gospel!

When I returned to Ducumbia, I learned that the missionaries had changed milkmen. We were thrilled to have our milk delivered right to the door. For a week, though, we noticed that the milk had a strange taste, and then we discovered that the new milkman had been putting it into a can lined with cow dung. That **did** alter the taste! He probably had lined the can to prevent the milk from leaking through small holes.

In August I spent two more nights with Christina in Laiday, and this time I took my flannelgraph. We went to another village in the area where the gospel had never been preached.

"What's wrong?" the people asked. "Why are you coming here?"

"We are coming to give you God's Word," Christina answered.

"What is God's Word?"

We started at the beginning in Genesis and tried to get through the story in one sitting. The people were very attentive. One lady who was sitting in front leaned forward to hear us better. If someone spoke, she rebuked that one by saying, "I want to hear what this foreigner has to say." They were so receptive that Christina decided to try to find a donkey to ride there when I would not be present with a vehicle. Donkeys were quite common in Laiday.

One time when Christina and I shared our personal conversion story with each other, I was so thrilled with hers that I immediately began to sing the following song:

> Once in the stillness of the late midnight hour,
> I felt the presence of the Lord's saving power.
> I fell on my knees and cried to Him there,
> "Oh, merciful Savior, hear a lost sinner's prayer."

Christina loved it and asked, "When we are back in school this fall, will you teach me that song?"

"Oh, for more like her!" I wrote in a letter home. "Such young people 'pull the teach' right out of you!"

Return to the Highlands

After spending two wonderful days in Laiday, I returned to Ducumbia. The Cromers came to visit, and after a few days they took me back to the highlands. Because of my problem with parasites the previous Christmas, my blood count was low and my blood pressure was high. I did not feel sick, but I did tire easily. I returned to my doctor, and he prescribed fifteen shots over a period of thirty days to help correct my problem with anemia.

By now I had been in Africa for nearly a year. The missionaries were supposed to take one month for vacation every year, so Pauline and I decided to go to Keren, a nice town halfway down the mountain range where the climate was ideal. The Mission had a house there that we could use. As we traveled, I enjoyed looking over the view of cornfields and flowers and a busy road, not busy with cars but with people tugging stubborn goats toward the market or children with trays of food balanced on their heads.

When we left for Keren, I was still taking shots. We found some British nurses there who could administer the shots intravenously. Later we took the nurses to a restaurant in town that was operated by Americans to serve American servicemen.

In September 1962 I resumed my teaching duties. That school year, besides teaching the missionary children, I taught *Foundations of Doctrine* by Harry E. Jessop to a class of eleventh and twelfth graders and math to ninth and tenth grades. Fred Cromer helped me with the math classes when he was there, but often he was gone on mission business since he was field director.

Ninth-grade students in math class

93

It was common to see nomads as they traveled from place to place. From my doorway I enjoyed seeing the camels that were carrying the nomads' tents. I called them Ethiopian house trailers. One day when I was shopping in Asmara, I saw some camel book-ends and was tickled to be able to purchase them.

Visiting the Village of Sorona

Easter vacation began a day earlier than planned the spring of 1963 because King Haile Selassie's son had died shortly after the death of the king's wife. On Saturday of Easter vacation, Pauline, Freddie Cromer, and I went to Sorona with Pastor Belai and his family of five for Easter services. The eight of us managed to squeeze into the Chevrolet Carryall along with our provisions. Crowds thronged us upon our arrival. Belai's house, which had two rooms, was the only one in the entire village that was whitewashed on the outside. One room was full of grain, and men were busy white-washing the other one. After a policeman's wife served us tea, Pauline and I transported the grain to the market in the Carryall, thus freeing the other room.

Tshaitu, Belai's wife, set up a charcoal burner, fried ground meat in *tesme* or butter, and proceeded to make spaghetti. Because of a lack of dishes, she set the bowl of spaghetti in the center of the table, and we all ate from it, each with our own spoon or fork.

"It's beginning to rain. You had better go and move the Carryall," Belai suggested.

Pauline hurried out to comply. I stepped out to watch and was approached by a woman speaking Tigrinya. I went back inside to ask for an interpreter, and the woman followed me. "Oh, this house is **clean!**" she exclaimed, and I thought she probably never saw a house whitewashed inside.

Belai planned to build his wife's *magogo* high enough so that she could stand while baking their bread instead of sitting on a low stool. A *magogo* is a large round oven made of clay, generally built outside and heated with wood or cow dung chips, and is used only for making their native breads. Belai wanted to show his people how to improve their way of living.

Saturday night Pauline and I tried to share a small bed in one room while Tshaitu and her children shared the other room. Freddie and the men slept on rope beds in the courtyard. "Is that a hyena outside our door?" asked wakeful Pauline in the middle of the night. She went out to inquire and found that it was "just a bull."

Leroy Adams arrived for the morning service as was his weekly custom. He played his trumpet and accordion simultaneously to call the people to the Easter service, which was held under the trees in an open area of the market. I was surprised to hear the children sing all the words to "Christ Arose" and many other songs that he played. Belai certainly was doing a good job of teaching them. He was the first one to introduce them to spiritual things.

Belai Berhe conducting an outdoor service in the village of Sorona

I was also surprised at the number of Moslem men who came to the service and stayed for the preaching. A lump came into my throat as I silently praised the Lord for the good that He was accomplishing in Sorona. After the service Belai introduced the missionaries to the chief of the Moslems. "When God wanted to save us, He sent Belai," the chief said. "I attend the services so my people will come, too."

Following that service we returned to Belai's house. While watching Tshaitu prepare sheep *zigganey* for our Easter dinner, I lost

95

my appetite. I had enjoyed chicken *zigganey* the day before and knew that I enjoyed the taste of sheep *zigganey,* but I had never watched a woman wash the sheep stomach and intestines. "Something like that is all right if you don't have to see it," I told someone.

Sunday night Leroy preached again, and the Spirit moved with conviction. Many of the men left the service to ponder the truth they had heard. They wanted to think seriously before making a life-changing decision. I had a burden of prayer for those men and for the many in the surrounding villages who had come to ask Belai to preach to them.

Arrival of New Missionaries

The following summer Ronald and Anna Smith with Douglas were to arrive on a Tuesday in mid-August, the hottest time of the year. Since the ship company often did not know for sure when their ships would arrive, Carrie, Kubra, and I went to the port city of Massawa on Saturday to be sure we were there when they arrived. We knew it would be hot and thought we could endure it, but when we got there, it was almost unbearable. It was very humid, and the temperature was about one hundred twenty degrees.

We three ladies stayed at the Swedish Mission guest house because it was inexpensive. However, we did not have a fan the first night, and we were miserable. Neither Carrie nor I could readily go to sleep, so we lay there and talked about how hard the early missionaries had it and how much better it was for us. I guess we were trying to keep up our courage. Finally we did go to sleep.

Sunday morning was worse than Saturday had been. The perspiration just stood out all over our bodies. I was about half sick, so we had prayer and asked the Lord to send some cool breezes. Praise His name, He did! Oh, how we thanked Him.

We had an ice chest with us that we had filled with ice in Asmara. I purchased extra mineral water on Saturday to hold us over Sunday. Carrie laughed a little when I bought sixteen bottles, saying, "You must plan to get thirsty!" However, by Monday morning we had only one bottle remaining and were thankful I had bought so much.

Though the Smiths were not due to arrive until Tuesday, they actually arrived Monday afternoon. They were lovely people and their baby, Douglas, was so cute. A few days later we kept him while his daddy and mommy went to Asmara to check on their ID cards.

Monday, September 2, 1963, I invited Anna Smith over for tea. Then the Mark Budensieks came and reminded us that it was Labor Day and invited all the missionaries to a picnic in their yard. I quickly put potatoes and eggs on the stove to boil and made potato salad. The Smiths made ice cream, the Adams family made cookies, and the Budensieks provided hot dogs and hamburgers. The Ray Chamberlains also were present.

The Chamberlains had come to Africa to spend a year in evangelism, giving six months to Egypt and the other six months to Eritrea, where they held revivals in Decamere, Sorona, Asmara, Agordat, Tessenie, and Ducumbia. In Decamere they stayed in the apartment building where I lived. One day it was time for revival service, and I was running late. I grabbed my Bible and hurried down the stairs of our apartment building. Just as I reached the bottom of the stairs, out of the corner of my eye, I saw what looked like a coil of rope. Then I saw it move!

Of course, I took a hop, skip, and a jump and got out of there. As soon as I got to the chapel, I told Pauline about it. She told me to notify some of the high-school boys, which I did. They went right after the snake and killed it.

When the Chamberlains, Pauline, and I went into the building after service, we stopped to chat a few minutes at the Chamberlains' door. I told them about the snake I saw right down their hallway just before service. Brother Chamberlain, in play, moved as though he were going to strangle me. "Girl," he said, "you didn't leave that thing in here, did you?" I laughed as I told him I had called some high-school boys, and they had killed it.

On September 25 I wrote, "Well, I have been in the land of His choice for two years, and they have been blessed years!" Later that fall Anna and I had a cottage prayer meeting at Teacher Amare's house on a Saturday evening. My, how we did enjoy it! The Lord came in our midst and the people appreciated it greatly. Oh, what a privilege it was to be able to work in Eritrea for Jesus!

Events During My Third Year

During my third year in Ethiopia, I did not teach the missionary children but did more teaching in the high school. The months rushed by as I taught my five classes including sixth-grade English at the orphanage. I also did secretarial work for the Mission and supervised the clinic at the high school. Elsa, a high-school student, took care of the simple, medical needs of the girls, and Benjamin, a high-school boy, did the same for the boys. My clinic duties included keeping the clinic records, buying the medicines, and signing permission slips for students to go to the government hospital.

On Saturdays I occasionally drove to town and of necessity learned how to avoid hitting people, goats, and bicycles even when going around the many curves. We were always thankful for a good horn. However, during that year the Ethiopian government decided to change from driving on the left side of the road to driving on the right side. Sometimes Eyob or Job, one of our high-school students, rode with me during that time of change. He often reminded me, "Keep right."

Because the horn on the jeep was not always working, every time we came to a curve, I would say, "Blow your horn, Eyob." He would then put his baritone out the window and blow. Later Eyob became a doctor, and the last I knew, he is still practicing in Eritrea.

Along with my school work I sometimes helped with services in other places. One time Pauline and I returned to the village of Sorona on a Saturday to be there for the Sunday services. Besides attending the services in Sorona, in the afternoon we traveled to five nearby villages for services. When we returned to Decamere on Monday morning, Pastor Belai, his wife, Tshaitu, and their children went with us. They were going to Agordat to see Tshaitu's father, who had just been promoted in the police force.

During that year I wrote to my parents and described an especially busy school day. That day I was out of bed by 6:15 and dressed, ate breakfast, and had my personal devotions. At 8:00 I taught tenth-grade English and attended chapel from 8:45 to 9:30. Then it was time to go to the orphanage and teach sixth-grade English. However, we were late getting out of chapel, and then one of the high-school girls was sick, so I had to write a permission slip for her to go to the hospital. I arrived at the orphanage at 9:50 and stayed until 12:05. Then I was off to Pauline's apartment for lunch. After lunch I went to my apartment, graded papers, had another time of prayer, rested a little, and read some of the missionary book *Jungle Pilot*.

At 2:00 Tekah, Adamses' maid, brought little Arlene Adams since I had promised to keep her while her mother went to the dentist. I also had little Dougie Smith to watch. While they were with me, I tried to study for church history class but did not get much done. Arlene's father came for her at 3:00, and soon after that Dougie went home. I studied for my class and spent a little time with Amati, my maid, studying Tigrinya before I went to teach church history class at 3:30. The next period I taught Bible to the eleventh graders.

The only phone on the compound was outside the door of my apartment, and I frequently answered it. That afternoon someone called for Mark Budensiek, and I was on my way to summon him when I saw Abraham, one of our students, on the ground with many students around him. Another student told me that Abraham had a broken leg. I asked the boys to get some wood for a splint while I went to get a car. I drove the little Volkswagen up the path to the boys' dorm. At that moment Pauline came for supper. It was already 5:30 and church service was at 6:30. After I told her what happened, she supervised preparation of a splint, and I got the car ready to take Abraham to Asmara. Mark was just walking to the chapel when I drove away from the boys' dorm, and the car stalled. He pushed it backward to get it started again. When he heard that I was taking Abraham to Asmara, he offered to take him. I was so relieved because the tires on the Volkswagen were not in good shape. In Asmara the doctor confirmed that the leg was broken and that Abraham needed to go to the government hospital.

When I returned to my apartment, Pauline had everything ready for my supper. I ate a little and we hurried to the service. The service was good, and the Lord dealt with souls. Praise His holy name! Returning to my apartment, I found Gabrielle, one of our girls, waiting for me. She asked, "Miss Hemmeter, would you pray with me?" We prayed until after 10:00, and I believe she received definite spiritual help. After she left, I remembered that I had promised one of the orphanage teachers that I would have the grades averaged for him the next day. At 11:30 I started to get ready for bed. I had a grateful time of prayer and then retired, thus ending an especially busy day.

A Year in Ducumbia

In July 1964 I was privileged to move to Ducumbia to spend a year with Zettie Finch and Marilyn Van Kuiken. Zettie was the overseer of the station. Marilyn was in charge of the clinic, and I was in charge of the school and taught all the subjects for sixth grade.

My first responsibility was to teach a summer course on Christian Culture to our pastors and teachers from the area. One day while we were in class, I looked out the window and could not keep from laughing. Marilyn was standing at a safe distance from our donkey

Missionary house in Ducumbia where I lived with Zettie Finch and Marilyn Van Kuiken during the 1964-65 school year

and leaning toward him to give him a shot of penicillin. That night a hyena killed and ate the donkey. Marilyn lamented having wasted the penicillin on a hyena.

On a Saturday evening in July, a man from the Tigre tribe came and asked Marilyn to go to his village and deliver his daughter's baby. The poor girl had been in labor for two days. I went with Marilyn and drove the Land Rover. The man said his village was by the first big well between Ducumbia and Barentu. As usual, it was farther than he indicated. While I drove, he sat behind me and pointed out the way by reaching his hand around my head.

The mother had a successful delivery, but she would not have if Marilyn had not been there. The baby girl was premature, and we felt quite sure that she could not live. As Marilyn directed, I held the baby for a while with her head lower than her feet. Her lips were blue, and she was not breathing properly. A few days later we went back to see how the mother and baby were doing and were told that the baby died the next morning. The mother had a fever, so Marilyn gave her an injection of penicillin. We also took a tape recorder with us and played a message for them in their own language. They were shocked that a machine could speak their tongue when we could not, and they listened attentively.

I was still trying to learn the difficult Tigrinya language. Kubra was helping me, and I hoped to learn all the characters of the alphabet that summer so that I could read. If I could conquer that, I could begin on the grammar and vocabulary. I had learned quite a few words by just being with the people and the other missionaries but was not making rapid progress. I also was trying to learn some of the Kunama language.

That fall we went to a village that had never been visited by a missionary. I later wrote in an article in the *Missionary Herald*:

We realized we had found another village where the name of Jesus had not been heard. The result was that instead of simply speaking to the children of the village, we spoke to all who were there. The women seated themselves on the ground before us, and the men and boys stood over at one side. I wish you could have seen the earnest expression on their faces as they listened for the first time to the story of redemption!

Where does one start when his audience knows nothing at all about the story of creation, God, or His plan of salvation? Well, we started in the only place we could—the beginning, the story of creation, the fall of man, and on to the story of redemption.

Our next problem was to find a stopping place. Where do you stop when seated in front of you is an elderly woman who is eagerly drinking in every word you say? When you are interrupted from time to time by questions? When you realize that it may be a long time before those to whom you are speaking will again be privileged to hear the words of life? ...

It was growing dark when we left them with promises that sometime we would return and tell them more. ...

Tablitz, a Kunama girl who attended our high school in Decamere, went calling with me one Sunday afternoon. I had the boys in my personal evangelism class go, too. We went up on the nearby hill to visit some Kunama people. At the first *tukul* where we stopped, we called a greeting to which they responded and invited us into the compound. There we found a young girl and her baby as well as her father, mother, and a little boy. I supposed that her husband was out in the field. With Tablitz interpreting I asked if they knew how sin came into the world. They answered that they did not. Prayerfully I told them the story of how God created the world and man and put him in a beautiful garden. I continued by telling them that God enjoyed walking in the cool of the day with Adam and Eve and how Satan tempted Eve and caused man to sin. The Lord helped me as I told how grieved God was when He knew that man had sinned. Those dear people hung onto my words as I explained how God made a plan of redemption whereby man can be saved. When I finished, I asked them if they had any questions. The young girl said, "We understand, but how can we know by just hearing the story once?" When we asked if we could come back every week, they said, "Yes!" We also invited them to attend our church services.

At the next place when we asked if there was anyone who would like to hear God's Word, they answered, "Is there anyone who doesn't?" They seemed to think the entire world would be happy to hear God's Word. Oh, if only it were so!

Seeing the Elephants

In January 1965 the families of Fred and Marilyn Cromer, Mark and Nancy Budensiek, Ronald and Anna Smith, and Meredith and Marteena Armour came to Ducumbia to be with us for the Ethiopian Christmas, which is January 7. Hearing reports of elephants in the area, the men set their alarms for 4:00 a.m. hoping they could find them. They were successful. When they returned, they told us women that they had made an arrangement with the elephants to meet us at 4:00 in the afternoon!

We all laughed, of course. In the end, though, we went with the men that afternoon. Arriving where the elephants had been, we took a villager with us to help find them. After driving through the thick underbrush until we were near them, we stopped and the villager got out of the vehicle. Soon he motioned for us to come quickly and quietly. We followed him arriving just in time to see four **big** heads with large ears moving through the brush. They must not have been more than fifty feet from us.

Marilyn Cromer and I started running toward the river to get a better look at them. I got so excited that I went hysterical and started laughing silently. Three times Marilyn turned and whispered, "What's wrong with you?" I knew I had to get control of myself. Finally I whispered back, "I guess I'm just so excited!" Seeing wild animals on foot is much more exciting than seeing them in a zoo or from a vehicle in a game reserve.

By the time Marilyn and I got to the river, my head was throbbing from laughing and running in the heat. Then someone said, "There they are!" I looked across the dry riverbed and there was the biggest elephant I had ever seen. The elephants I had seen in zoos were Indian elephants, which are smaller than the African elephants. I wanted to get closer to get better pictures, but Marilyn would not allow me to do so as one elephant was already agitated and waving his ears. She had heard stories about elephants killing natives when they became disturbed. When we got back to the rest of the group, we learned that they had seen the whole herd walking with the baby elephants holding to the tails of their mothers with their trunks.

Exposure to Hepatitis

I was alone in Ducumbia the day a Moslem man came to the house. He was a short fat man named Bedani, and I knew his shop in the marketplace. Carrie had told me that years before he had taken a twelve-year-old bride and had never allowed her to go outside their house or compound even to her mother's home since their marriage.

Carrie had scolded him for making his wife live in such a pigpen. She finally persuaded him to build a nice house of two rooms, which had a cement floor. Now here was Bedani at my door begging me to come and take care of his baby who, he said, was dying.

"I am not a nurse." I protested. "I am a teacher."

"That's OK. Just come. You **must** come!" So I went with him.

His house was right on the market square. He took me down a narrow entryway and through the backdoor of the house. When I entered the house, I saw two little girls sitting to the side. One girl was very yellow, and I thought, *I wonder where in the world that child's mother found a Chinese man!*

Bedani took me past the girls into a room where his baby was lying in a crib, struggling for his breath. I told them to boil water with something like Vicks in it and make a tent over the crib to help the baby breathe easier. Then I prayed for the baby who later recovered.

The young wife asked me to have tea with her, and I complied even though I felt I should not because of the dirty surroundings. The blankets looked as though they had never been washed, and the children had used the floor for a bathroom. I thought a dirt floor would be better for them; it would at least absorb some things.

While I was sitting on the bed, the only place to sit, the woman brought me tea and dates. I wanted to refuse the dates, but when I thought of this poor woman's years of isolation and loneliness, I accepted them. As I ate the dates, I continued to study the little **yellow** girl. I noticed that her eyes were not slanted. *That must not have been passed on to her in the genes*, I thought, *just the yellow skin.*

I walked back to my house through the marketplace, past the unsanitary place with my fragrant hankie to my nose. Moslem women liked to put perfume on guests when they entered their homes. I always gave them my hankie and asked them to put the perfume on that instead. A couple months later I was in the hospital with hepatitis. I learned during that time that the yellow girl, who was Bedani's daughter and not a visitor as I had supposed, had died of hepatitis.

Other Lowland Activities

Carrie Boyer had returned from furlough, and one day we four ladies—Carrie, Zettie, Marilyn, and I—went to visit Laiday where the Mission was building a classroom. Abraha Haile, one of our teachers, went with us and went hunting while we were in Laiday. He was successful in shooting a gazelle, a small African antelope. We had gazelle *zigganey* and more gazelle *zigganey* until I got tired of it after several days.

"Isn't there any fruit?" I asked Carrie one day. "I am so tired of meat!" Carrie also was tired of meat. Searching through our supplies she found a can of peaches and opened it for the two of us for lunch. The others were not tired of meat *zigganey* and thus did not want any peaches.

One Sunday after we returned to Ducumbia, we were all invited to Josephina's mother's house for dinner. She had such good *tita*, the bread that was made with white grain. On it she had some of the best *zigganey* I had ever tasted.

Carrie had taken her small tape recorder with her. Previously she had some of the preacher boys and Christina make tapes with music and preaching. Josephina's mother, Durena, along with other women outside, listened closely. After we finished eating, the women came inside so that they could hear better. The gospel was getting out to those who would not attend church. Durena promised she would come the follow-ing Sunday morning.

About nine o'clock one evening Marilyn and I were sitting in the living room singing by lamp-light, and Carrie was reading when we heard a knock at the door. Carrie answered and ran back to tell us that someone had brought a boy who had been bitten by a snake. I went with Marilyn to the clinic where she cut his

Holding a starving boy who was brought to our clinic in Ducumbia

leg so it would bleed and then gave him two injections of snake serum. After checking his pulse and breathing, she gave him a pain pill. When they left, Marilyn gave them instructions that if he got worse during the night, they should call. Thankfully they never called.

Language School and Hepatitis

When summer came, Zettie Finch and I went to Decamere to stay so that we could attend language school in Asmara where a six-week course in Tigrinya was being offered. On June 21, 1965, Ronald and Anna Smith, Amos and Ruth Tillis, Meredith and Marteena Armour, and Arlene Troyer along with Zettie and I drove twenty-five miles to Asmara to start language school. We commuted for the six weeks. The course was arranged for evangelical missionaries and some Peace Corps volunteers.

At first the teachers planned to divide the students into beginners' class, intermediates, and advanced class. However, everyone wanted to be in the beginners' class. So we were divided into the real beginners' class, the more experienced beginners', and the advanced beginners'. Our newer missionaries were in the real beginners' class. Zettie, Marteena, and I were in the more experienced beginners' class. Fred and Marilyn Cromer, who were living in Asmara at that time, were in the advanced beginners' class.

The teacher that I had the first period knew very little English. Besides knowing Tigrinya, he also spoke Italian and Amharic. Mr. Bird of the Presbyterian Mission, who oversaw the course, sat in our class and helped us when we got too far behind in what the teacher was saying. Sometimes I felt almost as if I were listening with my whole body. In those days we had no Tigrinya/English dictionary. All we had was a syllabus that Mr. Bird had compiled.

It was not until three years later that I passed my First Tigrinya Language Examination. I thought at that time that if I could ever take and pass the second exam, I would really know the language. However, when I took and passed it on August 1, 1970, I sadly discovered that I still did not know much of the language. At one point I told a missionary lady from the Sudan Interior Mission that maybe if I could study it until I was old and gray, I would really know it.

The weekend before the final classes I fixed a special dinner for Arlene's birthday, which is July 25. Since I had invited the other missionaries for an afternoon birthday celebration, I wanted to make two cakes. We had no mixer and had to mix by hand. My arms began to tire and ache so badly that I asked Arlene to help mix the batter for the two pineapple upside-down cakes. I was trying to make the cakes secretly so that Arlene would not catch on to what was happening.

Zettie and I had chosen a gift for Arlene from an Indian souvenir shop. When we were at the dinner table, we presented Arlene with her gift. Zettie left the room and came back singing "Happy Birthday" to me! My birthday would be August 3, and Zettie and Arlene had bought a gift for me from the same shop for they had learned what I liked. Later we felt that including my birthday in the celebration was providential because by the time my birthday came, I was in the hospital.

On a previous evening I noticed that I had a rash. I was immediately reminded of having measles as a child. I thought, *If I didn't know better, I would say I was coming down with something.*

The night of the birthday party I noticed that lights bothered my eyes, so I started wearing dark glasses. I felt nauseated and thought that I needed to have my glasses changed. On the morning of the last day of language school, I wanted only a piece of toast for breakfast. As I tried to eat it, my appetite suddenly "closed on me" as they say in Eritrea.

"I don't like your color," Zettie said.

"Oh, I am all right," I responded. "God is just helping me lose weight."

That day in class I ached all over. I just sat there resting my arms on the desk and trying to survive the class. Unfortunately the teacher called on me more than anyone else that day. Maybe he thought I was not concentrating enough, or perhaps my answers were fuzzy.

Zettie had made doughnuts for the teatime at the close of school. I loved doughnuts, but I did not want even one that time. I thought I could not even endure standing while pictures were being taken.

"I feel as though I am coming down with the flu or something," I told Marilyn Cromer. "I think I will just go and sit in the mission's Tanus." The Tanus was a small eight-passenger van made in Germany.

The following Monday morning Zettie wanted to take me to the eye doctor, but I did not feel up to it. However, Zettie insisted that we go. Zettie, Arlene, and I went by bus to Asmara and then walked to the Cromers' house. When we got there, Fred took us to the eye doctor's office, but the doctor was not there. We made an appointment to come back later. I continued to feel worse, so Zettie took me to an Italian medical doctor. He told me that my liver was swollen. "You must have amoeba in your liver," he said, and gave me Epsom salts to take.

That afternoon, though I did not feel like it, I peeled potatoes to help with the supper for American guests who were coming to Cromers' house. At mealtime I took just three tiny portions of vegetables and salad, avoiding the meat but trying to eat to be sociable. However, I was unable to retain the food I did eat.

The next morning Zettie insisted on taking me to the American military hospital. "Do you know what is wrong with you?" the doctor asked.

"No."

"You don't have any idea?"

"No."

"You have hepatitis. I want you to go home and get your things and inform those with whom you have been for the past month so they can take gamma globulin shots. Then you must enter the hospital." I was put in isolation in the American military hospital for two weeks, and then the Cromers asked if I could be released because staying there was expensive. "You may go," the doctor said, "but only if you stay in bed. That doesn't mean lying on the couch either! Be very careful, or you will end up in the hospital again."

The Cromers took me to their house where I was in bed for two weeks, and then I spent two more weeks in bed in Decamere where I lived after I had moved back from Ducumbia. Even after those six weeks I experienced days when I could not force myself even to get up. I found that eating hard candy gave me strength and took away the nausea. Eventually I was able to return to the classroom.

Difficulty in the Classroom

One day during the 1965-66 school year when I went to teach my tenth-grade English literature class, I encountered a problem. As I walked through the doorway, I saw written on the blackboard in huge letters—WE WILL NOT STUDY LITERATURE. We had prayer to open the class, and then I asked them to get their literature books and turn to a certain page. One of the students raised his hand and said, "Miss Hemmeter, I think you didn't see what was written on the blackboard."

"Yes," I said, "I did, but I will be fair with you if you will be fair with me. I have prepared our lesson for today. I would like us to study this lesson, and then I will talk to Leroy Adams after class and give him your request." They did not like the book we were studying because it used some colloquial English with which they were not familiar.

I then told the class that those who wanted to stay and study the lesson with me could do so and would get credit for the day. Those who did not want to study could leave, but they would get a zero for the day. All but two students left, and I had class with those two. By the time the bell rang, it was nearly noon. I went to my house burdened since I had to teach the same group right after lunch. I went to prayer and asked God to speak to the students and finally received the assurance that He was speaking.

When I went to class, all the students were present. We had prayer, and then Tecklesghie stood and asked for permission to speak. He said, "Mother Hemmeter, during the noon hour we got together to decide who was right, you or us. We decided that you were right, so on behalf of the class, well, maybe not quite all the class, we want to ask your forgiveness." Of course, I accepted their apology and everyone was happy. God had intervened, and we then had a normal class. I later talked to Leroy Adams, the high-school principal, about their request and he indicated that we could give them a different book. The students enjoyed the change.

Farewell

At the end of that term, the high school had a farewell for the Norton family and me in the chapel before we left for furlough. Later the high-school seniors also had a farewell for us with John Bairu being in charge of the event, which was held in one of the classrooms.

At that time John was the overseer of the garden for the school. He was allowed to raise some popcorn, which was his favorite. When I walked into the classroom that evening, I saw a washtub full of fluffy white popcorn.

Several students made speeches, but the one I remember best was John's. He told us that he was not much of one to welcome new missionaries because he did not know what they were like when they arrived. However, he was ready to tell them good-bye because now he knew what they were. We appreciated his kind words even though we did have to laugh.

The day the Nortons and I left Ethiopia in May 1966, Leroy Adams had the high-school band out to play for us. It was hard to leave all of them, and yet we were looking forward to seeing family and friends in the States whom we had not seen for nearly five years. One thing that made leaving easier was that I planned to return after a year of furlough.

Chapter 7

Events During My First Furlough
1966-1967

My Trip Home

For the first part of my trip home, I traveled with Roy and Esther Norton and their boys, John, Daniel, and Donald. We stopped in Cairo, Egypt, for a few days, and Guy Troyer, one of our missionaries there, met us at the airport. Later he took us to visit some of the highlights of the Cairo area including the place where it is thought that Joseph and Mary fled with the child Jesus, a museum where we saw mummies of ancient Pharaohs, and the pyramids. We climbed those huge stones that make up the Great Pyramid. We also climbed a sloping, inside passageway to the empty room at the peak of the pyramid, and then we had to back down because the passageway was too steep to walk down in a forward position.

While in Cairo we met Irene Maurer and Ruth Franklin who had come from Upper Egypt for the summer months to avoid the intense heat. We also visited some of the Faith Mission churches in the area.

From Egypt we flew to the Holy Land. The church and school at Milan, Illinois, where I had taught, sent me money for touring the

Roy and Esther Norton with their sons, John, Daniel, and Donald with whom I traveled to the Holy Land in 1966

Holy Land. We stayed at the American Colony hotel where we met the daughter of Horatio G. Spafford, the man who wrote the song "It Is Well with My Soul." That daughter, who was born in Jerusalem after the shipwreck, shared with us some of the details behind the writing of that song.

While Mrs. Spafford and her four daughters were sailing to England, the ship on which they traveled was involved in a shipwreck and the four daughters perished. Following the shipwreck Mr. Spafford sailed to England to join his wife. When they were near the place of the accident, the captain of the ship called Mr. Spafford to his cabin and told him that they were over the approximate place where the ship sank.

Mr. Spafford returned to his cabin and asked the Lord if it was sin in either his or his wife's life that caused them to lose their four daughters. God showed him that it was not. Then it was that God gave him the words to the song including the words,

> My sin—oh, the bliss of this glorious tho't—
> My sin—not in part, but the whole—
> Is nailed to His cross and I bear it no more.
> Praise the Lord, praise the Lord, O my soul!
> It is well with my soul. It is well, it is well with my soul.

While we were in the Holy Land, we had the privilege of visiting Bethlehem and seeing the place where Jesus was born. Sunday morning we attended a Baptist church in Jerusalem. The building was packed with people, many of whom were tourists. The pastor asked all the missionaries and preachers to stand. There was a large number of us. The congregation then sang "All Hail the Power of Jesus' Name" and almost raised the roof as we sang, knowing we were in the city where Jesus walked, died, was buried, and rose again. It was glorious! That afternoon we walked to Gordon's tomb where they said Jesus had been buried. It was beside a rocky hill that is shaped like a skull. While we were in the tomb, Roy Norton prayed the Lord's Prayer. That was a blessed experience.

From the Holy Land the Norton family flew to northern Michigan where their oldest child, Glenda Ruth, was living. I flew to Holland. There I enjoyed the windmills, tulips, and some of the villages where the people were still wearing wooden shoes. While I was in Amsterdam, Holland, my alarm clock was stolen and that caused me considerable confusion over the next few days.

Right before leaving Ethiopia I received a letter from my mother telling me that she had received a letter from my brother who was stationed in Alaska with the military. He indicated that I should not come to Alaska since he could not get any time off. However, I had prayed through on the matter, and God told me I could go.

We left Amsterdam at 5:00 p.m. and flew over the North Pole to Anchorage, Alaska, which meant that we did not have any darkness throughout that night. Because we crossed the International Date Line, we arrived at 4:00 p.m. the same day we left Amsterdam. The stewardess gave us each a card saying, "You have now joined the ranks of such men as Admiral Byrd who crossed over the North Pole!"

After arriving in Alaska and going through customs, I got a hotel room. I called my brother, John, and he asked, "Sis, where are you?" When I told him I was in Anchorage, he said, "Do you know what? My job was changed just yesterday, and I have five days off." That was just the length of time I had to spend with him.

Someone had told my father that if the Army said no, there was no use for me to go to Alaska since they do not change their minds. I said, "Yes, but God is higher, and He told me I could go." Praise His name, He worked it all out!

After talking with John I went to a restaurant. I was hungry for breakfast although it was 6:00 in the afternoon. When the waitress came, I said, "This may sound foolish, but I really would like some breakfast." She smiled, said it was all right, and brought my order.

After breakfast I returned to my hotel room and called the Greyhound bus station. The person informed me that there was a bus leaving at 10:00 a.m. to Seward where my brother was stationed. I then slept for a while, and when I awoke, it was 10:00 and it was still light outside, but was it morning or evening? Calling the man at the front desk I asked, "Could you, please, tell me what time it is?" He replied that it was 10:00. I laughed and asked, "Is it a.m. or p.m.?" He said that it was p.m. It was a relief to learn that I had not overslept and missed the bus to Seward.

When I arrived at the bus station the next morning, I was surprised to find that the Greyhound bus turned out to be a station wagon. There was only one other passenger. On the way to Seward, we passed through a place called Moose Pass, and a sign said the population was nine.

After checking into a hotel I called my brother, and he told me he would come as soon as he could. Before long, John knocked at the door and called my name. I recognized his voice and quickly opened the door. What a joyous reunion we had. However, after a hug I said, "John, this is awful, but I feel almost as if I am with a stranger." When I last saw John, he was only fifteen anxiously waiting the day when he would be old enough to get a driver's license. Now he was twenty and a mature man. We had five wonderful days together.

From Alaska I flew to Cleveland, Ohio. As I was getting off the plane, I heard my father's voice saying, "Hello, Faith." I was surprised that he was right there beside the plane and asked him how he got there. He told me he had seen another man walk out the door to the plane and decided he could do it, too. Inside the airport I met my mother, Aunt Naomi, Aunt Pearl, Aunt Gladys and Uncle Ralph, and my cousin Warren with his wife. They gave me a grand welcome. When we

With my brother, John, outside a cafe in Seward, Alaska

got to the home of my mother's family, Uncle Ralph asked me if I could say the alphabet in the Tigrinya language. As I laughed, I asked if he could stay there all night and then explained that there are approximately three hundred characters in the alphabet. I gave the family some samples of the sounds, and they were satisfied.

Mama's Tears

When I returned to the States for furlough, my parents were living in Shirley, Indiana, where my father was teaching in a Christian day school. They lived in a small mobile home but had a room prepared for me in what had previously been the girls' dorm. Mama had put all the gifts I had sent them from Ethiopia in the room so that I would not get too homesick for Africa.

Since I had been gone for five years, Mama looked forward to me being at home whenever I was not in services. Shortly before time for me to come home, she wrote to me quoting III John verses 13-14, "I had many things to write, but I will not with ink and pen write unto thee: But I trust I shall shortly see thee, and we shall speak face to face."

When I got home, a letter from EFM's director, Victor Glenn, was waiting for me. It said that Wayne States had written to him asking if I could teach in their school in Phoenix, Arizona, during my furlough. Victor Glenn said he would let me make that decision. When Mama knew what the letter said, she cried as if her heart would break. "Oh, honey," she said, "you aren't going to do that, are you?"

When I saw how her heart was broken, I said, "No, Mama, I will not do that unless Jesus tells me to do so." Accordingly, I stayed with my parents whenever I was not in deputation work. I was home only a short time when Daddy took the pastorate of the Wesleyan Holiness Church in Huntingburg, Indiana.

Sharon Schwanz, who was going to Guatemala as a missionary with Evangelistic Faith Missions, and I traveled together for deputation services. On one of our tours, we traveled to churches in the southern part of our country. Several of those churches gave us money to buy towels. The Canon Towel Company had outlet stores in that area, and since I had the money and the towels were so beautiful, I bought quite a few sets. At that time I wondered why I was buying so many but did not feel checked.

Later when I returned to Ethiopia, our missionaries in Egypt were evacuated because of the war between Israel and Egypt in 1967 and were unable to take much with them. When they arrived in Ethiopia, it was my privilege to give to the Ronald Robbins family, Irene Maurer, and Ruth Franklin each a set of towels. Our Heavenly Father

With Sharon Schwanz in Greensboro, North Carolina, during deputation

was looking out for them even though I did not understand when I purchased the towel sets.

My Wish List

Before I came home for furlough, one of my fellow missionaries advised me, "Faith, you ought to start a list of things you want to bring back for your second term." That list included personal clothing, greeting cards such as birthday or get-well cards, baby clothes to be given to new mothers, good holiness books for myself and for my high-school students, and an ironing board.

After I arrived home, I got a Montgomery Ward catalog and started figuring how much those things would cost. My heart sank lower and lower as I saw that I could not purchase much on my salary. The Holy Spirit spoke to me and said, "Faith, do you remember the song you sang before you went to the mission field the first time?

> I never shall doubt that my needs will be met,
> The ways and the means my dear Father controls,
> Who watches the sparrow will never forget
> The one who must labor for perishing souls."

I fell on my knees and cried, "Oh, Jesus, forgive me. I know you can do it, and maybe you see I don't need everything on that list. I am just going to leave it in Your hands. If there is anything on my list that You do not want me to have, then I do not want it either. You just give me what You see is best."

Shortly after that I was at a neighbor's house when she opened her closet door, and an ironing board fell out. "This silly thing is always falling out," she complained. Turning to me she asked, "Could you use an ironing board?"

"Oh, yes," I replied. That was one thing I could mark off my list.

Later while in deputation services I went to a church in Kansas where Victor and LaVena Gibson were pastoring. While I was in their home, LaVena said she had a question for me. "Faith, could you use some baby clothes?"

"Yes," I replied. "I have been praying for some to take for the babies in Ethiopia."

LaVena then told me about a woman in her church whose baby had died, and she had a lot of baby clothes she wanted to give to me if I could use them. Immediately she called the woman so that she would have time to gather them and bring them to church that evening. That was another item off my list.

Later when I visited the school at Milan, Illinois, R.C. Boynton took me to their bookroom, gave me a large box, and told me to fill it with books. There were Brengle's books on holiness, Mrs. Charles E. Cowman's devotional books *Streams in the Desert* and *Springs in the Valley*, and other books I had been wanting.

One day while visiting in Cleveland, I called my cousin Judy Mitchell, and she asked, "Faith, could you use some greeting cards?"

"Why, yes, Judy, but how much do they cost?"

"Oh, they don't cost anything. I sell greeting cards, and at the end of each year, I give the cards I have left to some missionary." Later she gave me a bag full of boxes of greeting cards.

God had given me everything on my list, far exceeding my expectations. When I returned to Ethiopia for my second term, I had four barrels and one wooden box of supplies.

Deputation Services

The Mission also sent Sharon and me to Hiawatha, Kansas, where Keith and Neoma Gibson were pastoring the Wesleyan Holiness Church. Sharon was driving when a deer suddenly ran across the road. It hit the front of the car damaging the radiator, then hit the door on the driver's side, and finally ran off into the woods.

We stopped beside a field where a farmer was plowing. Sharon could not get her door open and had to get out on the passenger's side. We called to the farmer and asked if he could call a tow truck for us, and he did. From the garage in town, we called Keith Gibson and asked him to come and get us. The mechanic said he would do only the necessary repairs, and we could get the car the next day. After the service that evening, I called Victor Glenn to tell him what happened. Sharon wanted to talk to him, too, since she felt responsible because she was driving at that time. When she told him about the deer hitting us, he jokingly said, "And you didn't even get his license number?"

When we got to the garage the next afternoon, we were disappointed that the car was not ready. We were scheduled to speak that evening at the Wesleyan Holiness Church in Wichita, Kansas. I called Victor Glenn again and told him I was afraid we would not be able to get to our service. His response was something like this: "Oh, please, Sister Hemmeter, if you ever went anywhere, be sure to go to that service. They are the only ones who called the Mission three times asking for you to come. Call the pastor, Kenneth Johansen, and tell him what your situation is, and then take the Kansas Turnpike and go the speed limit."

Well, we did just what Victor Glenn told us to do. We called the pastor who said he would keep the congregation singing until we got there. I wondered later if Victor Glenn realized the speed limit on the turnpike was 80 miles per hour. As we traveled, both Sharon and I felt that something was going to happen. Neither of us spoke about it, but we were praying silently. Suddenly the tread flew off one of our tires. Thank God, Sharon was able to keep the car on the road, and we finally got stopped.

My father had given me a flashlight with a red flare on it, so I got out and waved it at the next car that came along. I was frightened since I did not know who might stop. Just before the car stopped, the driver turned on the flashing lights on the top of his car. What a relief to realize that it was a highway patrolman. As he walked toward us, I said, "Praise the Lord!"

"I don't know why I came this way tonight," he said. "It is not really my route." Of course we understood that God, our ever-watchful heavenly Father, had sent him.

The patrolman got to work immediately. Sharon had been buying supplies to take to Guatemala, and I had been buying supplies to take to Ethiopia; consequently, the trunk was full. We had to take everything out so that we could get to the spare tire.

Just then another highway patrolman came down the other side of the turnpike. That patrolman also stopped and came over to help. When he saw everything at the side of the road, he said, "You'll never get all that into that trunk."

"Oh, yes, we will," replied the first patrolman. "It all came out of there!"

We finally made it to the church in Wichita, and after the message the church insisted that they wanted to give us a personal offering. I spoke up and told them that we were scheduled to go to Tacoma, Washington, and requested that they permit us to use the money to buy new snow tires for the mission car. It was November, and we knew that we were not prepared for bad weather. They agreed to buy them, and the next day they took us to a store that was having a sale on snow tires. The church also paid to have an alignment done. What a blessing that was! Sure enough, when we got to Idaho, we drove into a snowstorm. Had we not had those snow tires, we might not have made it through the storm.

One of the last places the Mission sent me was back to Shirley, Indiana, where the Shirley Gospel Mission had asked me to hold a revival. While driving there it dawned upon me that it was nearing my time to return to Ethiopia, and I was away from my parents. I knew that after that revival, EFM was going to send me to St. Louis, Michigan, for a missionary convention with Dennis and Emma Reiff, missionaries to Guatemala.

While traveling to Shirley I was asking Jesus to please, if it would be His sweet will, to allow Mama to go with me to Michigan. My parents had planned to come to Shirley to attend revival services that weekend. When they arrived on Friday evening, the first thing my father said to me was, "Faith, Mama is going to Michigan with you." Oh, how happy I was. Then I suddenly realized that Daddy would be left alone, and I did not like that idea. However, when I expressed my concern to him, he said, "No, Faith, that is all right. I will be OK. Mama is going with you." So it was settled, and Mama and I rode to Michigan with the Dennis Reiffs. God gave us a wonderful convention.

With Mama in 1967

During my furlough Mama asked me if during the millennium I would take her to Africa and show her the places where I had worked. On another occasion she said to me, "Oh, Faithie, I haven't said or done anything that would keep you from going back to the mission field, have I? I don't want to do anything to keep you from doing God's will." I assured her that she had not.

While I was with my parents in Huntingburg, the Wayne Sanders family came to visit me several times. They were living in the Shoals, Indiana, area not far from Huntingburg and were under appointment to Ethiopia. The Sanders told me that they let their questions accumulate until they could stand it no longer, and then they would come to see me.

Mama told me that she was praying that Victor Glenn would not send the Sanders to the field until I was ready to go. I said, "Oh, Mama, don't pray that way. Brother Glenn will not keep them from going just so I could go with them." Mama continued to pray that way. Guess what! God answered her prayer, and it was my privilege to sail in June 1967 with Wayne and Eileen Sanders and their four children: Iona, 8; Victor, 7; Darlene, 4; and Connie, 2.

Chapter 8

Women's Ministry in Ethiopia
1967-1971

Returning to Ethiopia

Wayne and Eileen Sanders with their four children and I boarded the *Concordia Fawn* in May 1967. Their daughter, Iona, who today is married to Timothy White, a minister, was my cabin mate.

As we crossed the Atlantic Ocean, I prayed, "Lord, would You give me one soul on this journey as a token of what You are going to do through me in Ethiopia?" There were only five passengers besides our little group, and I did not feel particularly drawn to witness to any of them. When we stopped at Genoa, Italy, though, a beautiful young woman named Luisa boarded the ship. Her mother was an Eritrean and her father was an Italian.

Luisa's mother was her father's African concubine, and he had brought Luisa to Italy to meet his wife. Now she was returning to

The Wayne Sanders family with whom I sailed to Eritrea in 1967

her home in the Ethiopian province of Eritrea. I immediately felt that Luisa was the one God wanted me to win to Him on that voyage. I was not sure how to go about it and asked the Lord to show me the way, and He did.

"Luisa," I asked, "do you read your mother's language?"

"Yes, I do," she readily replied.

"I have my Tigrinya Bible with me. I wonder if you could give me some reading lessons."

"Sure."

"I'll read in Tigrinya, and you correct my pronunciation."

"I'll be happy to do that."

I purposefully chose to read from the Gospel of John. It was not long before Luisa began to ask questions about what I was reading, just as I had hoped she would. After several days of such lessons, one afternoon I suddenly felt a strong desire to pray for Luisa. I went to my cabin to be alone. "Lord," I prayed as I walked back and forth across the cabin, "would You please show Luisa her heart and her need of You?" There seemed to be no barriers to praying. "Lord, it's so easy to pray! I feel that someone else is helping me pray for Luisa." When I looked at my watch, I saw that it was about 2:00 p.m.

The ship's crew had told us that the way to avoid seasickness was to keep your stomach full, so I decided to go up and have tea, and it would give me another chance to be with Luisa. When I got to the dining hall, I looked at Luisa and wondered if she also had been weeping. Nothing was said, however, so we took our tea without either of us learning what the other had been doing.

After supper that same evening I said, "Luisa, would you like to go to the lounge to visit?'

"Yes, I would like that."

God had arranged that no one else was in the lounge. I began telling Luisa how God had saved and sanctified me. Suddenly I had an intense desire to see her saved and started to cry. "Oh, Luisa, wouldn't you like to give your heart to Jesus right now?"

"Yes," she said, "I would."

"Do you want to pray here or go down to your cabin?"

"Let's pray right here."

I began by rebuking the devil. "Old devil, this has been your territory until now." Then I turned quickly to Jesus, "Lord, tonight it belongs to You!" Luisa prayed until she prayed clear through and then looked up with a beaming face.

"Did Jesus forgive your sins?" I asked.

"Yes." Then she said, "Do you know what happened right after dinner today?"

"No. What happened?" I asked. I had a sneaking suspicion that Luisa had been praying, too.

"I had such a desire to know Jesus that I went down to my cabin and prayed, 'Lord, would You please help Faith to pray for me?'" No wonder it had been so easy for me to pray. We had a complete triangle with God at the apex!

The next day Luisa asked, "Faith, did you feel something when we prayed last night?"

"Yes, I did."

"Well, what was that?"

"That was God," I replied.

Luisa was pleased to understand that it was God whom she had sensed the previous evening.

The Sanders family and I had been having devotions together each evening and Luisa began to join us. However, when we reached the Ethiopian seaport of Massawa, Luisa said, "Faith, I don't think I will come for devotions tonight because I need to get ready to disembark." When we were about halfway through with devotions, we heard a knock at the door.

"I couldn't stay away," Luisa said.

Thus God gave me a soul for Him on the freighter as a token of what He was going to do through me in Ethiopia. After we arrived in Ethiopia, I visited with Luisa a few times, but then she married, moved away, and I lost contact with her.

War was looming in the Middle East as I returned to Ethiopia. Our ship was one of the last to pass through the Suez Canal before the start of the Arab-Israeli conflict in June 1967. It was soon after our arrival in Ethiopia that our missionaries in Egypt were evacuated because of those hostilities.

Beginning an Outreach to Women

During my second term I again lived in the highland town of Decamere where I had lived most of my first term. My primary duties at that time were teaching in the high school and the Bible school.

High-school faculty and students. Missionary teachers from left: Leroy Adams, Ronald and Anna Smith, Faith Hemmeter, Irene Maurer, and Arlene Troyer

One day I was in the marketplace, and seeing all the women I asked myself, *What are we doing to reach the women?* One reason we had not been reaching the women was that many of our pastors were young, unmarried men, and they dealt mostly with the men. The women, seeing many men in the services, did not feel comfortable attending our churches. God began to burden my heart about ministering to the women in our town. About that time I wrote an article for the *Missionary Herald*:

> Look out my window with me some evening and you are likely to see women plodding their way home with a large load of wood on their backs. Stop and consider with me the prospects that await them upon their arrival at home. In all probability they will prepare a scanty meal for a hungry family by the flickering light of a small oil lamp made from a tin can with a piece of rag for a wick. Added to this is the heavy burden of sin with no hope of eternal life. I am describing the poorer ones, but even those who are better off materially are often heavy-hearted and burdened with sin and uncertain about life beyond the grave.

A number of us missionaries lived in Decamere where we had an orphanage, a high school, a Bible school, and a print shop. We began our women's outreach by pairing a missionary lady with a national lady and going into the community two by two doing visitation. Sunday afternoons we met for prayer at 2:00 and then went visiting, except for the last Sunday of each month when we shared our experiences and spent time in prayer for special needs.

Maraf Tedla, a teacher's wife and the sister of Mesgun Tedla, and I often visited the women in the police compound. I felt strongly the following words of this poem:

Have you ever read the sorrow in a heathen woman's face,
As you met her eye to eye amid a throng?
She who is by sex your sister, though of different race,
Have you ever wondered why she has no song?

It will take no occult power to fathom all her secrets deep,
And it needs no cruel probing just to know;
If you're filled with Christ's compassion and can weep
    with those who weep,
All her inmost soul will then to you outflow.

—Mrs. W. M. Turnbull

The Story of Rashan

One day after Maraf and I started visiting the police compound, I received a call from one of our teachers whose father was a policeman. "Would you come to the police compound to visit a policeman's wife? Her name is Rashan, and her baby daughter has just died."

"I will be glad to go," I replied.

Taking Maraf with me, we went to the one-room house where many were gathered to comfort the family in their loss. The people were sitting on chairs placed around the sides of the room. Maraf and I joined them and were served hot, strong, sweet coffee. We visited with the guests as we drank our coffee.

"May I read a passage of Scripture to you and pray?" I asked.

"No," Rashan replied. I was surprised with her answer. In all my years of ministering in Ethiopia, that was the only time I was denied the privilege of reading and praying with a hostess when I visited in her home.

As we were leaving, a Catholic priest arrived. I supposed that it was out of fear of him that Rashan did not want me to read or pray although she had given other reasons. "Let's not be discouraged, Maraf," I said as we walked home. "Let's return next week with some sugar or coffee as a gift according to your custom. Maybe then she will let us read the Bible and pray with her."

The next week we took a gift of sugar to show our concern that the family had lost a loved one, and again Rashan refused permission for me to read and pray with her. We left feeling that there was no point in returning. In my mind I wrote off Rashan.

A number of months later when Maraf and I were visiting in a Moslem lady's home, the woman asked me, "Would you go to visit Rashan? Her twelve-year-old daughter, Zewdi, is sick." *How strange*, I thought, *that others want us to read and pray with Rashan, but she herself does not want it.*

"Would you go with us?" I responded.

"Yes. My daughter and I will accompany you."

While we were visiting, the little girl who came with us sat on my lap. I was delighted, thinking that it would help Rashan to see that even a little Moslem girl was not afraid of me. Then I said to Rashan, "Jesus can heal sick people."

"I believe that," she responded.

"Would you like me to pray for your daughter?"

"No!" Her answer was definite and emphatic.

I was quite discouraged. Bowing my head I prayed silently and wondered why I had not remembered to do that sooner. "Lord, I do not know how to reach this woman. Please show me what to do."

"Ask her if there is something else you can do for her," the Lord prompted.

Quickly I asked, "Is there anything I can do for you, Rashan?"

"Oh," she said, "Zewdi's head aches so badly. She is so weak and cannot eat. Her head has been aching for such a long time."

"Do you have any aspirin?"

"No, we don't."

"I will send you some this evening."

Rashan followed me to the door and said, "You have been here three times, but I have not allowed you to read the Bible and pray. If you will come back next Sunday, I will."

Anna Smith had just returned from furlough, and I told her about Rashan and invited her to go with me on Sunday. I indicated that Rashan was friendly on our last visit, but I did not know what would happen this time. When we arrived, we found that Zewdi was still ill, but true to her word Rashan allowed us to read the Word and pray. I asked God to touch Zewdi so that her parents might see that He alone is all powerful. In a few days we heard that God had answered our prayer and healed Zewdi. The Holy Spirit used a few aspirin to open the door of that home to the gospel. Praise God for His faithful leadership! After that incident I visited them frequently.

Another time when we visited Rashan, her husband, *Abo* or Father Tesfamichael, was there. As we discussed God's Word together, I asked Tesfamichael, "Do you have a Bible?"

When he said he did not, I asked, "Would you read one if I gave it to you?"

"Yes!" he replied, so I took him a New Testament.

After Rashan had finally accepted me, she asked, "Tell me something. Did you like to come here when I hated you?"

From left, Rashan, Zewdi holding her daughter, and *Abo* Tesfamichael

"No, I did not," I admitted.

"Then why did you keep coming?"

"It was God who kept leading me back," I explained.

One evening I prayed that God would put a desire in the hearts of Rashan's older children, Zewdi and Teweldemedhin, to read God's Word. The next morning they knocked on my door and asked, "Would you give us Bibles?" What a quick answer to my prayer. My heart rejoiced again for that family.

On a later visit a neighbor woman was present, and *Abo* Tesfamichael commanded her to leave. When she did not go, he repeated his command. Finally he said very emphatically, "I told you to get out. Now go!" I was shocked but wondered why he had never commanded me to leave.

Some days later Tesfamichael enlightened me. He was sitting in a chair that had arms, and he made this application. "Let us say that the arm of this chair represents this life, and at the end of the arm is hell. Our people are walking up and falling off, walking up and falling off. You know what? Our priests are walking up and falling off, too. You are the first person who has ever come here and told us the truth."

The next Sunday Maraf, her sister-in-law Zewdi, and I shared the Word with Rashan and some of her relatives in a nearby courtyard. Afterward, Rashan asked us to come to her house and drink some Ethiopian coffee with her. I was inclined not to go because I felt she had heard the Word that day, and we needed to get the Word to someone else. However, when I learned that she had prepared the coffee just for us, I agreed to go.

While we were drinking coffee, Rashan's husband, who was a lot older than she, came. Zewdi asked me if he was interested in the Bible. I told her that last Sunday after hearing the Word he said, "What you have told us is the truth." Today the Holy Spirit directed us to read Ezekiel 33:13-18. Oh, how Jesus did speak! Tesfamichael was so quiet, and one could see he was thinking. We then had prayer before leaving.

One day *Abo* Tesfamichael told me that he could sometimes hear us praying at the Mission at night. He said, "It is your prayers that are protecting this town." Once when I urged him to give his heart to Jesus, he responded, "I would, but I fear what my neighbors would say." As far as I know he never yielded to the drawings of the Spirit.

Rashan's youngest girl who was about six years of age began attending Sunday school at our high-school chapel. She loved it and wanted to attend every Sunday. Once when her mother took her away on a Sunday, and she could not come, she missed it so much that she said to her mama, "Mother, will there **ever** be another Sunday?"

Then came the fateful Sunday when Rashan took her little girl with her to a village over the mountain road from Decamere. On the way they had an accident, and the taxi in which they were traveling went over the side of the mountain. The child was killed when she was thrown out, and the vehicle rolled over her. Rashan picked up her little daughter and covered her with her apron. Rashan and the others that had been in the taxi were rushed to the government hospital in the capital city of Asmara.

Rashan's daughter, Zewdi, came to me crying and told me what had happened. She was afraid her mother was going to lose her mind. When Rashan was released from the hospital, I visited her and did my best to comfort her. I felt that since her daughter had little light and loved coming to Sunday school that she was covered by the blood of Jesus and was in heaven.

(Note: This story about Rashan took place over a period of approximately two and one-half years.)

Working with Moslem Women

One Sunday following our Ethiopian Christmas vacation in January 1968, Maraf and I were again visiting in the police compound where we had become well-known. I greeted two Moslem women seated on small rope stools outside their one-room house. To my surprise they asked, "Why don't you ever come and read the Bible to us?"

"Do you want us to?" I asked.

"Why, yes!"

"If you want us to, we will come now." We did and frequently went thereafter.

"You know, we are taught that women have no soul," one of the women said. "We don't have anyone to tell us about God." Maraf and I took that challenge.

The elderly grandmother of the home always sat on the floor, and I sat on the floor beside her. Younger women hurried to get pillows to make me more comfortable. At teatime I was served tea in the grandmother's special large cup given to her by her policeman son. I hesitated to use it.

"Do it," her daughter-in-law said. "It is the will of the grandmother!"

With the grandmother's teenaged grandson interpreting, I explained the way of salvation to her over and over. "The only way to God is through His Son, Jesus," I instructed.

The grandson often told me, "Now, I don't believe that, but I will tell her what you said." Grandmother said she understood.

"Do you want to pray and ask Jesus to forgive your sins?"

"Yes," she said, "I do."

We prayed and she confessed her sins and asked Jesus to come into her heart. A short time later God awakened me in the early hours of the morning and impressed me to pray for the little grandmother. That morning when the phone rang at the high school, someone was calling to tell me that the grandmother had died. I was not in class, so I went immediately to her home. "Did she say anything as she was dying?" I wanted to know.

"Yes, she did," one of the family replied. "We were crying, and she asked us why we were weeping. We said, 'Because you are dying.' 'I'm not dying,' she said." I felt that she did not believe she was dying because she was going to be with Jesus.

God was fulfilling a promise He had given to me previously. While I was walking down the stairs from my apartment to go calling that day, the Holy Spirit spoke to me. "Faith, if you remain faithful, I am going to give you some of those people from the police compound."

"Praise the Lord! I hope to see them in heaven!" I responded.

Visiting Rosa in Massawa

Rosa was brought up in the Faith Mission orphanage in Decamere. When Pauline Keith and I lived in adjoining apartments, Rosa was in high school, and part of her work assignment was to help Pauline and me in our homes. We would often pray for her.

When Arlene Troyer came to Ethiopia, we shared an apartment. She suggested that we pray for revival each evening at 7:00. During those prayer sessions the Lord again laid Rosa on my heart.

During the Ethiopian Christmas vacation in January 1969, we single missionary ladies visited Massawa. Since Rosa had married a naval officer, we went to the navy base to search for her. When we arrived at her house, we were greeted by Rosa who was now a beautiful, young wife and mother. She invited us into her lovely home, and while we were visiting, we encouraged her to come to our chapel that evening there in Massawa. She accepted our invitation.

It was my privilege to give the message that evening, and I must admit that I was fishing especially for Rosa. During the altar call I went to her. "Rosa, would you like to pray?" In answer to my question, she just fell on her knees and began to cry and pray. Later she looked up with a beaming face.

"'Rosa, did Jesus save you?" I asked

"Yes," she replied.

"I've been praying a long time for you, Rosa."

"I knew you were praying for me," she said. "Every time I was alone, God was speaking to me." He is faithful to work as we pray.

Students of Special Remembrance

Ghermai Yohannes

At the age of seven, Ghermai Yohannes became totally blind when he contracted measles, and his parents did not know how to take care of him during his illness. He attended a school for the blind in Addis Ababa, Ethiopia, where he learned to read and write in braille. Ghermai graduated from twelfth grade from that school.

One day Ghermai attended the Faith Mission church in Asmara where he responded to the wooing of the Holy Spirit, and God transformed his life. When he applied to attend our Bible school, the committee accepted him with grave misgivings.

Summer Bible school students with teachers Ronald Smith and me. Solomon Tesfamichael is fifth from left, and Fernando Fradiani seventh from left.

131

I was privileged to teach Ghermai and found that he could learn quicker than our seeing students. He used a braillewriter to take notes in class. I would put his tests on a cassette, and he would type the answers on an English typewriter. He certainly was not a problem student. That young man was always cheerful and brought sunshine wherever he went. What a joy it was to have him in my classes.

Ghermai was a good singer, and he could sing the glory down. Once he said to me, "When you sing in front of people, you can see their responses, but when we blind people sing, we cannot see and thus sing only for God's glory."

Solomon Tesfamichael

Solomon Tesfamichael was from a poor home in Tessenie where he lived with his mother. In 1961 he entered our school in Decamere as a seventh grader and was one of my first students in Eritrea. He proved to be one of the three top students of the class. From the beginning Solomon purposed in his heart to serve the Lord, and during that year he organized a prayer band among the boys. After he was sanctified, he sang the words of the song "My Soul Is Filled with Glory" and changed the last part of the chorus to read "sanctifies me holy" for each verse.

Solomon was able to attend our Bible school in the late 1960s. He began his first pastorate while still in Bible school by going to Massawa on weekends. His ministry among the young men stationed there in the navy was fruitful. Upon completing Bible school Solomon moved to Massawa as pastor.

When Solomon gave his report at conference one year, he said, "God is always with me even in Massawa!" He said that because some people who visited Massawa thought it was the end of the world. Following his pastorate in Massawa, he pastored several other churches in the Mission. Eventually Solomon served as national chairman of EFM's work in Ethiopia. He was killed in a vehicle accident while on mission business on March 3, 2003, after working for the Mission for 36 years.

Fernando Fradiani

Fernando Fradiani lived in our mission orphanage as a child. There he learned to love Jesus. While attending our high school, he was called to preach. After he received his call, he pastored a market church in Decamere and then one in Asmara. Eventually he was able to attend the mission Bible school. During his years in Bible school, he was known as a man of prayer. Finally he became co-pastor of our high-school church in Decamere.

Being very good in the English language, Fernando taught English in our elementary schools and also classes in our Bible school for a number of years. At this writing Fernando is the pastor of our high-school church in Decamere. His wife, Lemlem, and their son Peter are also teaching for the Mission. Fernando has given nearly forty years of service to the Lord through EFM.

Physical Problems and Furlough

During the summer of 1968, I held a VBS for the missionary children and several other children of Americans living in the area. The 1968-69 school year had been such a joy for me. Four of us single ladies—Irene Maurer, Arlene Troyer, Ruth Franklin, and I—lived and worked together. Arlene and Ruth were scheduled to go home for furlough at the end of that school year. I thought Irene would still

VBS in 1968. My helpers from left were Myrtle Adams, Margaret Robbins, Nancy Budensiek, and Ruth Franklin.

From left, Ruth Franklin, Irene Maurer, Arlene Troyer, and I who lived
together during the 1968-1969 school year

The building on the high-school compound where we lived in the
upstairs apartments

be with me, but Victor Glenn, our mission director, called and asked
that she return to the States to help in deputation work. That left me
as the only single missionary in Decamere.

Since I am a people person, it is very hard for me to live alone.
That summer I taught summer school and kept myself occupied with
other activities to keep from being too lonely.

During the following two school years, I was kept busy teaching
in both the high school and the Bible school and doing evangelism.
However, they were still difficult years for me.

One highlight for me during those two years was a wonderful baptismal service held on a Sunday afternoon at the high school. There were about fourteen converts from our Asmara church who were baptized, including Mengastub, a young man whose father was a Coptic priest. Mengastub's father and older brother had beaten him unmercifully, and his father had put him out of the home. Mesgun Tedla, the pastor of our church in Asmara, had asked us to take him into the high school. The day before the baptismal service Mengastub's father and brother were at the high school trying again to get him to go with them. When he told them he did not want to go, they tried to force him, but Mark Budensiek called the police, and they intervened for him. Mengastub testified at the time of his baptism, "I don't care what happens to my body. I am going to serve Jesus."

Among the candidates for baptism was the first girl to be baptized from the Asmara church. There was also a hunchbacked young man who testified that, before he was saved, his parents did not seem to care what he did, but since his conversion they watched his every move. He said he was born with two crooked natures. "Now my spiritual nature has been straightened," he exclaimed!

The last young man to be baptized testified with tears rolling down his cheeks. First in Tigrinya and then in English, he told how much he appreciated the missionaries leaving their homes and coming to tell him the story of salvation.

By the time the 1971-1972 school year was to begin, I was sensing the need for a change. I told Carrie Boyer, who had come up from the lowlands for a visit, that if I did not get away for a while, I would not be able to make it. She kindly took me to Massawa for a few days of rest beside the Red Sea. Carrie urged me to stay longer, but I felt I had to get back to prepare for classes.

Soon I began to develop nervous problems that affected my stomach. When I developed diarrhea, I purchased an over-the-counter medication called Enterovioform. I began to have dizzy spells, so the missionary committee decided I should go to the Red Sea Rest Home in Asmara for a time of recuperation.

The first Saturday I was there, I tried to walk from the rest home to our church to see if I could do it the next morning. I did not want to use public transportation to get to church on Sunday. After walking

EFM missionaries with Victor Glenn in 1969.
Adults from left: Ronald and Margaret Robbins, Meredith Armour, Zettie Finch, Marteena Armour, Ruth Hobart, Victor Glenn, Maurice Hobart, Arlene Troyer, Faith Hemmeter, Mark and Nancy Budensiek, Eileen and Wayne Sanders, Ruth Franklin, Irene Maurer, Leroy and Myrtle Adams.
Children from left: Dennis Robbins, Timothy Robbins, Lowell Adams

only a few blocks, I had another dizzy spell and ended up calling the rest home and asking for someone to come and get me. They kindly did so and indicated that they thought I should spend Sunday in bed. Sunday morning as I lay in bed, God gave me a three-point sermon: 1) Rest, 2) Be still, 3) Trust. That is what I endeavored to do.

Finally I returned to my classes and later met with the missionary committee who told me they believed that I needed to return to the States. I asked them if I could return to the field later. "Yes," they said, "if you are well enough." I told them that if the Lord had not spoken to me through His Word that very morning, it would have been hard for me to accept their decision. However, that morning God had given me the verse "In the multitude of counselors there is safety" (Proverbs 11:14b). I accepted the committee's decision as God's will for me and returned to the States during the Christmas season of 1971.

Chapter 9

God's Marvelous Touch
1971-1973

Struggling with My Illness

My parents met me at the airport in Chicago and took me to their home in the countryside near Canton, Illinois, where my father was pastoring an independent holiness church. We enjoyed Christmas together and then shortly after Christmas, I entered the hospital in

With my family in the farm house near Canton, Illinois, in 1972

East Moline, Illinois. I felt God placed me there to help someone. My roommate was a young married woman named Judy. She told me that her mother was a Catholic and her father an atheist and that she did not know whether or not to believe in God.

My doctor scheduled various tests but could not find the cause of my dizzy spells. One morning while I was lying in bed, the devil tried to discourage me by saying that the doctors were not going to find anything wrong with me and that this would be the end of my missionary career. Realizing that I could not fight the devil in my own strength, I told Judy that I wanted to close the curtain between our beds because I needed to talk with God. She indicated that it was all right to do that. I prayed silently and told the Lord that I was going to open my Bible where I had been reading in my devotions and that I needed Him to speak to me and let me know if I would ever return to Ethiopia.

At that time I was reading in Isaiah, so I turned to chapter 40 and read the entire chapter. It was good, but there was nothing especially for me. I continued reading in chapter 41 when suddenly the last part of verse 9 and all of verse 10 almost jumped off the page at me: "Thou art my servant; I have chosen thee, and not cast thee away. Fear thou not; for I am with thee: be not dismayed; for I am thy God: I will strengthen thee; yea, I will help thee; yea, I will uphold thee with the right hand of my righteousness." Later when I told Judy what God had said to me through His Word, she thought that was wonderful.

That same morning the doctor came and said that he had a question for me. "Have you ever taken Enterovioform?"

"Why, yes," I admitted, "that is exactly what I have been taking."

The doctor snapped his fingers and replied, "I just read an article in a medical journal last night about Enterovioform. It can cause the very symptoms you are having." Then he told me that I should never take any of those pills again. He indicated that he was going to photocopy the article for me to take to my mission board, and he emphasized that they should warn all their missionaries against taking Enterovioform. That medication was sold over the counter in Ethiopia for dysentery. Incidentally, the doctor did not charge me anything for taking care of me for a week while I was in the hospital. May God bless him.

When the doctor left, Judy exclaimed to me, "Why, Faith, just think of all the doctors there are in America and that God would lead you to the one who read that magazine article. That just proves there is a God!" Then she added, "Just listen to me telling you!"

All the doctor could prescribe for me was to get plenty of rest, eat good food, and take some good vitamins. He indicated that he had no idea how long it would take to get the Enterovioform out of my system, but if I followed his instructions, eventually I would get well. After I was released from the hospital, I returned to my parents' home.

I was amazed at how much rest I needed. It seemed that I slept day and night for a while. Finally I began to feel more like myself. During those days of recovery, I meditated on the wonderful verses God had given to this unworthy servant of His. Glory to His name!

I was scheduled to go to Bedford, Indiana, right after Easter to work in the EFM office. Shortly before it was time to go, I decided to help my mother do some housecleaning. I worked one day and felt fine. The next day I did not feel well, but I thought to myself, *Why should I not work just because I do not feel well?* So I worked anyway. However, that really set me back physically. Mama wanted me to call the Mission and tell them I was not ready to come yet, but I did not want to do that. In a few days I went to Bedford and began working in the office. I continued to tire quickly, though, and was told to come to work only when I felt up to it. Even then I found I could work only half days.

I had been praying that I would be able to go to Cleveland, Ohio, to visit my Aunt Pearl who had helped pay my way through college. She had suffered several strokes and was then in the hospital.

One day Mark Budensiek, who worked at the U.S. headquarters of EFM in Bedford, called me into his office and said, "Faith, if you want to stay in the States the rest of your life, just keep working here. But if you want to return to Ethiopia, you should take another six weeks to rest." Then he asked an amazing question. "Don't you have relatives in Cleveland?"

"Why, yes," I replied.

"Why don't you go and visit them?"

"Oh, Brother Budensiek," I exclaimed, "I have just been praying about going to see them if it was God's will." Being assured it was His will, I was soon on my way to Cleveland. While there I stayed with Uncle Fred and Aunt Naomi. I also visited Aunt Pearl. I really enjoyed being with my relatives.

At the end of the six weeks, the Mission arranged for me to go to the Cleveland Clinic for an evaluation. The doctor there told me that he thought I could return to Ethiopia. "Just don't let yourself get into a corner," he said.

After returning to Bedford I lived with Ruth Franklin, and we both worked in the home office. A few weeks later Mark Budensiek called me and told me to prepare to return to Ethiopia. I was thrilled, but one morning God spoke through His Word, revealing His plan for my future. He said, "In quietness and in confidence shall be your strength" (Isaiah 30:15). That very morning Mark Budensiek called me on the phone. He told me that Victor Glenn, the president of EFM, had contacted him and said that he thought I should stay in the States for another year. Everyone thought I would be devastated, but God had prepared me.

Other Furlough Events

While traveling for the Mission in deputation services, I became very hungry. I told the Lord I really would like to find a Pancake House if it would be all right with Him. I expressed, though, that I wanted to find one near the highway because I did not want to spend mission money looking for one.

I drove and drove, but no Pancake House appeared. Finally I saw a picture of a large black skillet on a billboard that was advertising a restaurant. I said, "Well, Jesus, maybe you don't want me to have pancakes this morning. That's OK with me. I'll just eat at that restaurant."

Following the directions on the sign, I took the next exit and crossed over the Interstate. The restaurant where I had planned to eat was on the left, but on the right I saw a Pancake House. "Thank you, Jesus," I said, as I drove into the parking lot of the Pancake House. That experience has been such a blessing to me through the years.

Some time later the Mission sent me to Texas to speak at the Wesleyan Holiness Church in Dumas where John and Mary Copeland pastored. On my way there about noon, I suddenly got hungry for fish and chips and prayed, "Oh, Jesus, if you could help me find a restaurant that has fish and chips and a gas station nearby with a telephone, I would really appreciate it."

Just then I looked up and saw a sign advertising fish and chips. I turned off the highway and went directly to the restaurant. Nearby was a gas station that had a phone. I bought gas, called to make reservations at a motel, and then went and enjoyed fish and chips. As I left, I got blessed and said, "Oh, Jesus, You take such good care of me!"

My brother, John, married Margey Zimmerman on August 4, 1973. I was privileged to attend the wedding and sang the song "Each for the Other and Both for the Lord." Mama played the piano, and Daddy performed the ceremony. Later that month I had the joy of getting on a plane and returning to Ethiopia. God keeps His promises. Praise His dear name!

Chapter 10

Political Problems and a New Work in Jinka
1973-1977

Returning to Ethiopia

On my flight from New York to Paris in September 1973 for my third term in Ethiopia, I was seated beside a young man who was accompanied by his mother. During our conversation he asked me with what mission I was associated. After telling him about Evangelistic Faith Missions, I shared with him how God saved me and later sanctified me. His repeated exclamation of "That's wonderful!" indicated that he had a hungry heart. Then he revealed to me that he was a Jew. That led to quite a discussion. What a joy it was to witness to him. Once again God had arranged my travels so that I could meet and speak with a hungry soul.

During that term the women's ministry continued to be a priority for me even though most of my time was taken up in class preparation and teaching in the classroom. The women's prayer meetings in Decamere on Sunday afternoons were followed by visitation in the neighborhoods.

Adai Tshaitu

I was thrilled to hear how *Adai* Tshaitu, a godly woman in our Asmara church, was faithfully laboring with the women and girls of that congregation. Largely through her efforts, thirty-five young women began attending the services along with nine young married couples who had been saved and were establishing Christian homes. God was blessing the work among the women.

First Bible and a Wedding Cake

Irene Maurer and I lived together on the high-school compound in Decamere. Each month a man would come to collect payment for our electric bill. During the Christmas season when the bill collector arrived, I invited him to come inside and see our Christmas decorations. While I went to get the money, Irene offered him a Christmas card that had a picture of two angels on the front.

"Do you believe in angels?" he asked me.

"Why certainly!" I answered. "There are many of them in heaven even now."

"Yes, but do you believe they can save?"

I got my Tigrinya Bible and read I Timothy 2:5 to him: "For there is one God, and one mediator between God and men, the man Christ Jesus;" The man was quite surprised. He was able to read, so he took the Bible and read the verse several times to himself.

"Do you have a Bible of your own?" I asked.

"No, I do not."

"Continue collecting the money for the bills," I said, "and then return and I will give you one."

After the man had gone, I exclaimed, "Thank the Lord for our print shop!"

I immediately sent someone with a note to the print shop indicating that I wanted to buy a Tygrinia Bible. By the time the bill collector returned, I had marked several verses for him including John 3:16 and I Timothy 2:5. He was delighted. Opening his briefcase he laid his new Bible reverently inside. "I will read all of it," he said. "I promise you!" I rejoiced at the opportunity to share God's Word with another hungry soul.

It was such a blessing that God had made it possible for Evangelistic Faith Missions to operate its own print shop. Our national workers, under the leadership of Wayne Sanders, produced Sunday school literature, other teaching materials, and tracts in the Tigrinya, Kunama, and Amharic languages. In addition to printing material, they operated a bookstore where they sold Bibles in the different languages. They also sold holiness classics and study books in English.

Another interesting event that took place in the early part of that term was making a cake for a wedding. The orphanage children considered the missionaries as their parents and would sometimes ask us to make their wedding cakes. One of the girls who had been in our orphanage was marrying a believer who was in the Ethiopian navy, and I was asked to make the wedding cake. Carrie Boyer suggested that it look like a ship and drew the design. Irene baked

Cake I made for the wedding for one of our orphanage girls

the cake, and I assembled and decorated it. When the newlyweds and their attendants entered the room and saw the wedding cake, they were really amazed. Praise God, He helped us do something special for them.

The Deteriorating Situation

The ongoing military struggle between the Eritrean freedom fighters and the Ethiopian army was growing in intensity. The Eritreans were increasing their efforts to gain their independence from Ethiopia. Tensions further increased in the country as word spread that two missionary nurses from the *Mihireta Yesus* or Compassion of Jesus Hospital at Ghinda had been kidnapped on May 27, 1974. The report indicated that Anna Strikwerda, a nurse from Holland, had been killed while the other nurse, Debbie Dortzbach, an American, was being held captive. It also was rumored that the kidnappers hoped to seize several more Americans. Eventually Debbie was released unharmed after being held hostage for twenty-six days. Praise God for His mercy to Debbie in response to the prayers of Christians around the world!

In July the mission church leaders, pastors, church delegates, and other church members met in Decamere for their fourteenth annual church conference. As they gathered for three days of services and business sessions, they did not realize that it would be their last conference for several years. Some months later the Ethiopian government, a monarchy under Haile Selassie, was overthrown by communist members of the Ethiopian army.

Our hearts were blessed during conference when Aforkie, who had just completed eleventh grade in our high school, testified. "Thank God," he said, "He has called me to preach the gospel of holiness." During his high-school years he had been a leader of a prayer band in the boys' dorm, and now God had called him to preach.

One Sunday afternoon following conference Aforkie knocked on our door. "I have come," he said, "because I was thinking that you missionaries have no one to be a pastor to you. I want to read some words of encouragement from God's Word."

That caring young man had once been a member of the Coptic Church of Ethiopia. He, along with other young men, began seeking God at our Faith Mission Church in Massawa. Aforkie was saved, and when he returned home with a glorious testimony, his father was enraged. As a leader in the Coptic Church, his father declared that no son of his could claim such an experience and remain in his house. Though his mother pleaded for him, Aforkie, then a teenager, was put out of his home with no place to go.

Aforkie went to the pastor of our mission church in Massawa and found refuge. Eventually he came to our high school in Decamere. Shortly after he finished eleventh grade, our high school was forced to close. Later he attended the Faith Mission Bible College from which he graduated and became one of our pastors. At the time of this writing, he is still preaching in Eritrea.

Fighting in Asmara

In January 1975 the Mission asked Irene, who had served in Egypt for many years, to visit Egypt and preach during their annual convention. In those days our works in Egypt and Ethiopia sometimes exchanged speakers for their conventions. However, because of the communist takeover in Ethiopia, a number of new rulings had been passed, one of which prevented Eritreans from leaving the country.

On January 31 Tesfai Debas, our national chairman, and Ronald Robbins, our missionary chairman, took Irene to the airport in Asmara. No other women accompanied them because of the tense political situation. That night the smoldering conflict between the Eritrean freedom fighters and the Ethiopian army broke out in full force.

Irene and the two men had to spend the night in the airport, and she did not fly to Egypt until the next day. Although Tesfai and Ronald had to remain in Asmara, they were unable to contact their families in Decamere. Reports from the British Broadcasting Corporation (BBC) told about the outbreak of fighting. They also indicated that there was neither water nor electricity in Asmara. I commented to Tekie Mebrahtu that perhaps Tesfai and Ronald would have to leave the country. Tekie answered rather prophetically, "Why, Miss Hemmeter, God put them there to get you folks out."

The Adams and Robbins families lived at the far end of our high-school compound. Carrie and I knew that Margaret Robbins was feeling rather apprehensive, so we invited her to come with her two little boys, Timothy and Dennis, and baby Rachel and stay with us at the front of the compound.

The missionaries made preparations for whatever situation might develop. We stored water in case it might be cut off and made sure we had candles and matches in the event there was no electricity. We purchased canned peaches, Coke, crackers, cheese, and other items in case we had to leave. Each of us packed two suitcases. Irene had experienced an evacuation from Egypt in 1967 and told me that you usually were allowed only one suitcase when you were removed from an area, but that it was good to have a second one packed in case they would allow you to take it.

Knowing that the Ethiopian army had closed the road between Asmara and Decamere, we prayed that God would reopen the road for us to leave if He saw that was best. I thought that the words "Ready to go, ready to stay," were just as true on the mission field as they were at home.

Ethiopian Soldiers Visiting Our High School

In the meanwhile I was teaching my tenth-grade English class one morning when I looked out the window toward the road outside our compound and saw an army truck that was loaded with young Ethiopian soldiers. When it stopped, the soldiers began jumping off the back and running into the compound. Startled by what was happening, my students gathered their books and started to jump up. I was afraid that if the students ran, the soldiers would open fire on them, so I said, "Don't you move. Don't you dare move." The situation was tense.

We had no idea what had just happened with Tekie Mebrahtu, our high-school director, and Manna Hagos, the director of our orphanage. They had gone to the market and bought potatoes for the schools. In returning they had to pass a barrel that had been set up in the middle of the road at that end of Decamere. No one was allowed to pass that barrel without special permission. Normally we just went around the barrel and came to our compounds, which were just a short distance beyond the barrel. We had done that several times without any problem because the soldiers stationed in Decamere knew us. However, new soldiers had been sent from Addis Ababa and knew nothing about our Mission. So when Tekie and Manna passed the barrel, the soldiers stopped and questioned them about what was inside the compound. Our directors told them it was a high school, but the soldiers did not believe them.

Prior to that time Tekie had erected an antenna from the chimney of his apartment building to our water tower in order to get better radio reception. When the soldiers who stopped them saw the antenna, they thought our compound was a base for the Eritrean freedom fighters. Our men could not convince them that it was a school, so a truckload of soldiers was sent to investigate.

The soldiers surrounded the buildings inside the compound. When we looked out the classroom door and windows, we saw soldiers everywhere. In the meantime I kept trying to teach. In just a moment or two, Tekie came running and told us that when the bell rings, he wanted all the students to go to the ball field. After what seemed an eternity, the bell rang. The students hurried to the ball field, and I went to my apartment where I found a soldier talking to Carrie with his gun pointed at her. She was trying to convince him that her radio was not a two-way radio. The soldier thought it was since it was also connected to the outside antenna.

The Ethiopian soldiers finally became convinced that it was a school when they saw the students, teachers, and blackboards. One of the girls said to me afterward, "Miss Hemmeter, we were all scared to death, but you just stood there like a rock."

"I might have stood like a rock, but my heart was beating like this," I said and demonstrated by hitting my right fist into my opened left hand.

After the soldiers left our compound, we tried to return to our normal routine. However, political tensions in the country continued to build.

Flight to Addis Ababa

It was an exciting time as Tesfai and Ronald drove up to our compound gate blowing the car horn. They had been unable to leave Asmara for almost a week because of the fighting. I stood on the porch of our second-floor apartment and cried for joy as I saw them being reunited with their families.

Soon all the missionaries were summoned to a meeting with our national field committee. They told us that Tesfai and Ronald had gone to the American Consulate in Asmara to ask what we should do. The consul had arranged with the Ethiopian army to reopen the road between Asmara and Decamere long enough for Tesfai and Ronald to come to Decamere, make arrangements for the ongoing of the work, and take us back to Asmara. Thankfully we already had turned the mission work over to our capable national brethren a couple years previously, so that was not a problem.

It was not long until Tesfai and we missionaries were on our way to Asmara. I wish you could have seen the people we passed along the way who were fleeing the city where war had begun. Their faces were marked with terror but also with looks of incredulity as they saw us going toward the city. They appeared to be wondering why anyone would go to the place from which they were fleeing, but that was our only way out of the country.

First we stopped at the American Consulate and were given a list of hotels where we could stay. We were instructed to stay away from the windows, and when fighting broke out, we were to get on the floor. They also told us that there was no water or electricity in the city. Someone would come and get us as soon as possible, but no one knew how soon that would be.

That night Leroy and Myrtle Adams with their children: Marie, 15; Melvin, 14; Arlene, 12; Edith, 10; and Lowell, 7; Ronald and Margaret Robbins with Timothy, 11; Dennis, 10; and Rachel, 2 months, met in the room where Carrie and I were staying. I served supper, playfully asking each person whether he wanted hamburgers or steak, but such fancy foods quickly became a couple of crackers with cheese and a half glass of Coke. We rationed our food because we did not know how long we might need to stay in the hotel. After having devotions the two families went to their rooms.

During the night I was awakened by the whistling sounds of flares as they lit up the sky and the noise of bombs exploding. I awakened Carrie and exclaimed, "They're at it. They have started!"

"Hit the floor!" Carrie declared. We began crawling to the safest place, which was a small hallway between our bedroom and the bathroom. We waited there for some time but became so tired that we crept back into the bedroom. Pulling the mattress onto the floor, we spent the rest of the night trying to sleep there. Every now and then, although the windows had wooden slat shutters over them, we could see the sky light up as the fighting continued.

Unknown to us at the time, there was an all-night prayer meeting taking place in Addis Ababa, the capital of Ethiopia. Meredith Armour, who was working for the Mission in the home office, had arrived in Addis Ababa. He knew about the war in the province of Eritrea and called the men of our church to prayer.

Sometime during the early morning hours, God gave Meredith the assurance that we would be coming to Addis Ababa. In fact, God let him know that we would be arriving later that day. So certain was he that he talked to the people in charge of the Baptist rest home and reserved an apartment for one of the families and then went to a hotel and got several rooms for the rest of us.

By daylight the fighting in Asmara had stopped. Relieved, we gathered in our room again for a breakfast of crackers, cheese, and Coke. It was not long before a knock came on our door. A young man from the hotel was there to tell us that the U.S. Marines had come to get us. We hurriedly grabbed our suitcases and went downstairs. The Marines had brought a truck and a couple of jeeps. They wrote our last names on our suitcases and threw them into the back of the truck while we got into the jeeps. There were American flags on the vehicles to let everyone know that we were neutral. It was February 7, and amid the chaos I remembered it was my brother's birthday.

When we arrived at the consulate, an American government official explained that the U.S. government would give us tickets to depart on an Italian plane that had come to evacuate their own people, but we would need to sign a paper promising that our Mission would repay the U.S. government within a certain length of time or we would lose our passports. We gladly signed, knowing that EFM would pay.

Again with the American flags flying, the Marines took us by bus to the airport. It was a tense ride because we realized that fighting could break out again at any time. However, God took us safely to the airport.

Inside the airport we found a long line of Italians waiting to board a plane. Two men were actually fighting for a place in line. As we joined the group, the American consul approached the Italian consul and spoke to him. Our names were called, and we moved toward the front of the line. I felt a little guilty about getting in line ahead of those who had been waiting for a long time.

Dr. Mafadonia, an Italian medical doctor who had been a personal physician for some of our missionaries, said, "Mothers and babies go first." With the consul's permission Margaret Robbins with Rachel moved to the head of the line. Margaret then asked if her husband, boys, Carrie, and I could go with her, and the request was granted.

When we disembarked in Addis Ababa, Meredith and some Ethiopian believers met us. Having prayed through on our getting out of Eritrea safely, in faith they came to meet us. Since the Adams family was coming on a later flight, we waited in the airport until they arrived.

Some days later after the fighting subsided in Asmara, I received a call from our Eritrean national field committee asking me to return to Decamere and teach in the Bible school for the remainder of the school year. They also suggested that I could go through my belongings in Decamere in preparation for sending them to Addis Ababa. The offer was inviting; however, Carrie Boyer, who was listening, suggested that I pray about the matter, so I told them that I would pray and let them know. As I prayed, I distinctly felt that God was telling me not to go. After I had declined their invitation, Carrie said to me, "Now I am free to tell you. I had a dream in which you went back to Decamere and were killed." Eventually my belongings were packed by our maid and shipped to Addis Ababa.

A few weeks later Leroy Adams and Ronald Robbins returned to Decamere. Ronald packed their belongings since they were soon due for furlough, and both men returned to Addis Ababa. The Adams family then returned to Decamere to finish the school year. Following the first battle after their return, some of the Adams family went to the apartment where I would have been living. They found a number of broken windows and a bullet embedded in the wall directly above my pillow. God knew the danger I would have faced if I had returned to Decamere.

A New Work in Jinka

Some years before the communist trouble, a young sailor, Fessehaye Asgodom, gave his heart to the Lord as he stood outside our church in Asmara and listened to Irene Maurer preach in 1973. When he returned to his ship, he began holding services.

Danye, another young sailor, was wonderfully saved in one of those services. When I visited our church in Massawa, I heard Danye testify and say, "Won't you please pray that someone will take the gospel to my people in Jinka? It is a beautiful place, but there is no one there to tell them of Jesus."

After I heard Danye testify, a desire was born in my heart to take the gospel to the unreached people of southern Ethiopia where Jinka is located near the border of Kenya. Carrie and I began to pray that

Mesfin and Roma with their children, Sadal, Daniel, and Samuel

God would open the way for us to go there. We even asked our executive committee in Eritrea for permission to start such a work, but they told us that we were needed where we were. We continued to fulfill our duties but also continued praying for God to open the door to Jinka.

On February 7, 1975, the day we arrived in Addis Ababa, Danye came to Carrie and me and asked, "Now will you go to Jinka?" We told him that such was our desire.

In March Leroy Adams, Ronald Robbins, and Mesfin Yohannes made an exploratory trip to Jinka. While there they made arrangements with the Ethiopian army major who was in charge of that area for EFM to open a work in Jinka. They also rented a house for Mesfin's family. In a few weeks Mesfin and his wife, Roma, moved to Jinka with their three children. Carrie and I then made preparations to join Mesfin and his family. As we prepared, Carrie said to me, "Faith, we are going into a primitive area. There will be no tools there, so we must buy all that we will need." Among the items we purchased were a saw, a hammer, pliers, nails, a meat grinder, and a coffee grinder.

Leterberhan, one of the ladies in our Addis Ababa church, went with Carrie and me by plane to Jinka. When we descended the steps of the DC-10, we found that the airstrip was just a grassy field, and the terminal was a tin building. There was also a small bamboo building with a cone-shaped grass roof that served as the waiting room. The Ethiopian Airlines was the primary means in and out of that beautiful mountain valley. The overland route was only a trail and required several days of arduous travel.

Mesfin was at the landing strip to greet us and led us to the place where we would be living—a house made of sticks and plastered with mud. Roma and the children were there to greet us. As we walked into our house, I noticed that the floor was dirt. How happy I was, though, for I realized that, at last, I was in a place where we could do pioneer missionary work. In 1962 I had asked the Lord that if it was His will, He would allow me to help Carrie open a new work some day. Now that prayer was being answered.

Carrie and I ready to leave Addis Ababa to fly to Jinka

151

The house where Carrie and I were going to live was divided so that Mesfin's family had the large room for their living area. We had a bedroom and a small room that had served as a chicken coop. We cleaned out the small room and made it our kitchen. The Mission purchased a small gas stove with an oven, and that stove became a bright spot for me. When my parents were in home-mission work and did not have much, Mama always found something positive that she would call her "bright spot."

In the kitchen we had a rough wooden table and two folding chairs. Later Carrie made a cupboard using tree branches, cardboard, and some blue plastic we had brought with us from Addis Ababa. In the market we bought some blue material with which I made a curtain for the cupboard.

Jinka was located in a lovely part of southern Ethiopia where everything was lush, green, and beautiful with lots of flowers and trees. It was a large village with approximately 500 people who lived in mud houses similar to our house. There was an open market area in the center of town. Nearby villagers came to Jinka on Saturdays and sold their wares in the market and made needed purchases. There were only two stores in Jinka. In them you could purchase such things as sewing materials, shoes, sweaters, lanterns, kerosene, matches, margarine, canned peaches, writing paper, pens, and bottled gas.

The wife of the army major who governed Jinka had been educated in a Sudan Interior Mission school, so he was favorable to missionary work. The first week we were there, Carrie said to me, "Faith, I am going to give you the privilege of preaching the first message to these people." When Sunday morning came, we went to the public school building where Mesfin had secured permission for us to hold services. We gathered in one of the classrooms that had desks with benches attached in which each unit was made for two students. A large Moslem man dressed in his billowing *galabiyah*, a long flowing garment, had difficulty squeezing into one of the seats. No women attended that first service.

God had given me a message from the story about Lazarus and the rich man. At the close of the message, I wanted to give an invitation but realized there was no place for me to invite them to come and pray since the room was full. I asked them to raise their hands if they wanted to ask God for forgiveness, thinking maybe three or four would raise their hands. To my surprise **everyone** did. I then instructed them how to pray. Subsequent developments indicated that many of these had not fully understood at that time or had not completely settled the issue of living for God.

On my way home that day I was thrilled and told God how happy I was to be in Jinka and to have the privilege of giving the gospel to those who had never heard. I told Him that I would not care if all I owned were two sticks if I could just have the joy of serving Him. Glory to His name!

One day we purchased some grass mats in the market and put them on the dirt floor of the entrance hallway at the back of our house. That hallway led to Mesfin and Roma's part of the house and also to our kitchen and bedroom areas. The grass mats made it easier to keep our house clean. We would step into the hallway from outdoors, remove our shoes, and put on our house slippers. In that hallway we placed a little stand on which we put a basin of water and a bar of soap and hung a towel on a nail.

We had no running water. Tesfai and Loboco, two of our guards, brought us water from the nearby river, transporting it in a canvas bag that hung over a donkey's back. We used that water for washing,

Our guard bringing water on a donkey to our house from the nearby river. This water was used for household purposes. Roma and I are in the background straining the water.

but our drinking water came from Gezehane's well. For light we used kerosene lamps and candles. Our "bathroom," which was outside, was enclosed with grass mats that overlapped in the front to serve as a door. It had a lovely ceiling that was black at night with twinkling stars. When it rained, though, we had quite a task to hold an umbrella overhead. Since our living quarters had limited space, Carrie cleared away some of the brush behind the house, and that area became our place of prayer.

When we arrived in Jinka, I asked if there were termites there. "In Jinka? No, there are no termites in Jinka," people assured me. The first day we were there, Carrie put nails in the walls by our beds so we could hang some clothes, and Leterberhan hung a nice spring coat on one of the nails. The next morning I noticed a little tunnel of mud leading from the floor up to her coat. When we investigated, we found that termites had built the tunnel and used it to reach her coat. They had a special treat during the night, eating the entire lining from the garment. But, you understand, there were no termites in Jinka.

Later I asked someone why they had told me there were no termites. The reply was that in comparison with the town of Afelagemway, there were none. They said that in Afelagemway at certain times of the year, if you stand still too long, the termites would eat the soles out of your shoes.

I also asked if there were lions in Jinka. "No, no lions in Jinka," was the reply. We learned differently on that score, too. One day we waded through the shallow river on our way to see where the men were breaking rock for the foundation for our house and the building for the church and school. While we were there, a sudden storm came up, and a kind man invited us into a shelter he had built of bamboo. He served us strong coffee with salt instead of sugar along with roasted peanuts and cooked sweet potatoes. We learned to take a handful of peanuts and then a sip of coffee, and in that way we salted our peanuts. We did the same with the sweet potatoes.

As we sat there visiting, the man told us that a lion had come into his yard the night before and killed two of his cows. That was within easy walking distance of the mission compound. I guess when they said there were no lions in Jinka, they meant the village of Jinka and not the surrounding countryside. They also told us there were no snakes in Jinka, but we soon learned that it was the same story.

Progress in Jinka

While we were living with Mesfin's family in the rented house, Carrie and Mesfin were busy supervising some of the men from the village as they were building a duplex for the Mission. They were also constructing a building for a church and a school. Things went well until the Coptics became upset because of the large number of people who attended our services. Inspired by the Coptic priests the village men demanded a huge price for their work. Mesfin then located a Tigrinya man in Arbaminch who was a builder. We made an agreement with him to complete the work on our buildings.

Mission duplex on left and church/school building on right in the village of Jinka. Local airport runway, marked by white stones, is in the foreground.

We moved into the duplex when it was almost finished. However, during the daytime the door was left open because the builders were going in and out doing their work. One day as I was working in our kitchen, I sensed that someone had entered the room. When I turned to look, I saw an Arai man with his mud cap made of red, black, and white mud and a white ostrich feather in it. He had only a loincloth for clothing. In one hand he held a spear and in the other hand a transistor radio.

I said *"Abo,"* which was the only word I knew in his language. Since it means peace, I thought it was quite appropriate! I then called to Mesfin who was on his side of the duplex and on the other side of our kitchen wall. I told him one of those men was in our kitchen, and I did not know what to do.

"OK, Miss Hemmeter, I will be right there," Mesfin answered. Soon he appeared and began talking with the man in his Shankala language and asked him what he wanted.

"Well, we live under communism. Everything belongs to everyone, so I want this house," the man responded.

"You are right, and I want your radio," Mesfin replied.

"Oh, no," responded the man. "I just bought it."

Mesfin answered, "Well, just as that radio belongs to you, so this house belongs to us."

"Oh," he said and walked out the door.

After we moved into our house, L.W. Barbee, who preached for the Mission on many of our fields, made it possible for us to have a refrigerator. It was a real blessing for our food situation. That model could be powered in three different ways—kerosene, bottled gas, or electricity. There was no electricity, and of the other two power sources, the bottled gas worked better.

The inhabitants of the area were known as the Shankala people. They were represented by two tribes, the Arie and the Bana. The Arie tribe believed that people who had white arms and legs could communicate with God, so some of their men painted themselves accordingly. That belief helped them to accept what we were

A group of Arie people

156

preaching. They also dressed in bark skirts. The Bana tribe, on the other hand, wore animal skins.

Carrie and I watched the procession of tribesmen pass our new house in Jinka as they went to market. Frequently we prayed, "God, help us to reach them for You. Help us reach both the Arie and the Bana tribes."

Our mail came by air, and the plane was scheduled to arrive three times a week. When it came, the pilot swooped low over the landing strip to scare animals from the field so that he could land. However, the same plane was used to carry wounded soldiers from the area of fighting in Eritrea, and there were times when the mail did not come for three weeks. I remember admitting to Carrie, "When the plane doesn't come for three weeks, it bothers me."

Carrie encouraged me with her answer. "Don't kid yourself. I'm human, too."

Leroy Adams and his family made a trip to Jinka in August 1976 bringing a Land Rover for us to use. They traveled with several trucks in a convoy so that there was always someone to pull an unfortunate vehicle out of a hole. They covered 500 kilometers or 310 miles, the first day. After that the going was so difficult that it took them an additional five days to drive the other 500 kilometers. The convoy passed through "villages" where there were no huts or houses, but the people slept on the ground or in trees.

Because of the communist influence in our area, I was concerned that we would not have many students when school began. Pastor Mesfin suggested that we send a letter to the people in nearby villages and inform them of the new school in Jinka and invite them to send their children. We also sent a second letter as the opening day drew near.

To our surprise forty-five Arie children and teenagers came to enroll. Our joy knew no bounds when we discovered among them one lad who could speak both Amharic and the Arie language. Chanyalo was about sixteen, and he immediately became our interpreter.

Our kindergarten class, held in the morning, was made up of teenagers. They all came with the hope of learning to read and write, but first they had to learn the Amharic alphabet, which has 231 characters. What a daunting task!

It was interesting to see the students' reaction as they heard the story of Adam and Eve and how they made clothes of leaves after they sinned because the Arie tribe wore skirts made of strips of bark. Then when they heard how God made Adam and Eve clothes of animal skins, quite a murmur went up since the Bana tribe wore skirts made of animal skins.

Our students with their teachers—Gherima on left and Bekele on right

We had two fine teachers, Gherima and Bekele. Both of them loved the Lord and wanted to bring their students to know Him. Gherima constantly drilled the children in the truths of God's Word as he taught them scripture verses, gospel songs, and choruses. "Sing these songs as you walk the village paths so you won't forget them," he admonished.

One day as I was sitting at my desk, I heard some children singing outside, "He's coming back! He's coming back! Jesus is coming back!" Thinking it was our school children, I looked up to see which ones. Imagine my surprise to see that they were not our students but others who had learned the song from our students. The Word of Truth was being spread along the road and paths throughout the surrounding area. Praise the Lord!

Our afternoon classes were made up mostly of tiny tots from the town, all of whom spoke Amharic. Most of them were four to seven years of age. They were so sweet and soon were used by Jesus in their homes as some of them persuaded their families to pray before eating.

158

At the time of our second Christmas in Jinka, December 1976, Carrie and I planned to go to Addis Ababa to be with the Adams family. For three weeks we were prepared to go, but the plane did not arrive. When it finally came, there was such a backlog of passengers that there was no room for us, and there was no way we could contact the Adamses.

Mesfin and Roma invited us to their home for Christmas dinner, and instead of turkey and dressing we had chicken *zigganey*. The next day we held our Sunday services, and Danye's brother was saved. Remaining in Jinka for Christmas was worthwhile.

A Sunday morning congregation

At our only baptismal service in Jinka, held in early 1977, Carrie exclaimed, "God gave us the perfect number to be baptized. There are exactly seven!" The first one was a tall young Arie student named Bekele. The previous summer he had come to the Mission wearing a loincloth, shirt, and mud cap. His mud cap was done up in three colors with a fine ostrich feather sticking out the top; he wanted his picture taken. Since that day Bekele had given his heart to Jesus. Eventually he learned to read and was given a New Testament in his language.

After Bekele's conversion he asked if it was wrong to grow tobacco. I told him it was, and he said, "I kind of thought so. I have a whole tobacco field back home with which I am going to have to do something."

159

Mokonen was another Arie school boy of fourteen who had been saved during a chapel service. He testified that his parents had seen a change in him. Whereas he used to be disobedient, now he was quick to obey.

Abaash was a tall fourteen-year-old Arie student who also had given her heart to Jesus during chapel. Several times she testified that Jesus had brought her out of darkness into light.

Admasu was a young man of twenty-four who came to school to learn to read so that he could read God's Word. "Even if they take my head off, I am still going to serve Jesus," he testified.

Abinish was a young mother of three little boys. She was faithful in attending services, usually carrying her youngest to church. Her husband was a policeman stationed in a remote area and attended with her when he was home. That little mother had taken off her gold, and in many other ways had taken her stand for Jesus. The last two candidates were a young man who taught in the Jinka government school and Shumeta, who was one of the three mission guards.

Baptismal service in Jinka

Difficulties

Sometime in the spring of 1977, I was out at the clothesline when God spoke to me, saying, "Faith, you're not coming back to Ethiopia anymore. Remember your call to Bolivia?" That was all He said, but I knew what He meant.

Worsening political circumstances led Carrie and me to leave Jinka on a Missionary Aviation Fellowship plane flying to Addis Ababa in April. Shortly after our arrival there, we heard that the government had forced all missionaries out of Gema Gofa province, which included the Jinka area. That news meant that we would not be returning to our beautiful valley. Later we heard that, just a few days after we left Jinka, the communist authorities came in to kill all the missionaries. Thank the Lord He already had taken us out of the area.

Sometime before we left Jinka, the Lord impressed me to sign the report cards for the students. Even though we had been evacuated, the students received their report cards at the end of the school year. The local authorities allowed the school and church to remain open for a short time after we left.

We called the home office of Evangelistic Faith Missions in Bedford, Indiana, and told them about those events and asked what we should do. Since it was almost time for my furlough, they told me to return to the States and for Carrie to go to Egypt to help Irene Maurer. Carrie and I traveled together to Egypt where I visited with Irene and the Guy Troyer family for a few days. I then visited Zurich, Switzerland, as well as London and Newcastle-upon-Tyme in England, arriving back in the States on June 9, 1977.

Part III

My Years in Bolivia
The Country of God's Second Calling

Chapter 11

Spanish Language Study and Mama's Sickness 1977-1980

God Keeping Me with EFM

Just before I left Addis Ababa, Ethiopia, in May 1977 to return to the United States, Leroy Adams, the field director, said to me, "I want to advance your June salary so that you have enough money in Europe. I will let the home office know."

After arriving home I called the office in Bedford to let them know about my arrival. I talked with Meredith Armour for a while, and then he said, "By the way, Miss Hemmeter, I put your June salary in your checking account."

"Didn't you get Brother Adams' letter?" I asked. "He gave me my June salary before I left Addis Ababa."

"Oh, that can be for July then," Meredith said.

Later when I was in the home office talking with Leonard Sankey, he said to Jennie Glenn, "You want to get that for her?"

"What's that?" I asked.

"Your June salary and travel expense money."

"I've already been paid for June and July."

"OK, then it can be for August," he replied.

When I arrived back home, I told my father that the Mission had paid me for three months in advance.

"Faith, I think the Lord is trying to tell you something," he suggested.

"Yes, I will have to stay with EFM at least through August."

Since I knew that Evangelistic Faith Missions did not have mission work in Bolivia, South America, my mind was filled with many thoughts and possibilities. Because my parents were getting older, I wondered about staying with them for a while. I thought of going to nursing school since I had wanted to be a nurse or maybe going back to college to update my teacher's certificate. Everything I pondered seemed bleak. While praying about it, the Lord said, "Just wait!"

A short time later I received a letter from Irene Maurer in Egypt. "How about coming to work with me in Egypt?" she wrote.

I answered, "Irene, I do not know anyone I would rather work with, but God has called me to Bolivia."

Then I received a letter from Abrahet, an Eritrean lady whom I had trained in child evangelism. "How about coming to help me with the women's work in Sudan?" she asked.

"I would enjoy working with you, Abrahet, but God has called me to Bolivia," I wrote.

Then in July 1977, I went to the Tri-State Holiness Association Camp in Clinton, Pennsylvania, and heard Victor Glenn tell about his being laid up with a blood clot in his leg. During that time the Lord spoke to him about three things:

• Starting prayer bands in America

• Starting a work among the American Indians

• Starting a work in Bolivia

My heart jumped! I was so excited! I wanted to talk with him about my call to Bolivia after the service, but no opportunity arose, so I thought to myself, *I'll be in other services with him. I can talk with him then.*

I went with Steven and Kathy Hight to another camp in Pennsylvania where Victor Glenn again told his account of God's leadings. After the service I said to him, "Brother Glenn, do you know that God called me to Bolivia before I ever went to Africa?" His eyes got big and his mouth fell open. He did not say anything, and I did not know what to think.

When I met the Board in March 1978, they asked me to tell my story about God calling me to Bolivia. After they heard me, they did not say anything about me going to Egypt or Sudan. They simply asked one question regarding my yearning to go to Bolivia. "How soon do you want to go?" I indicated that I wanted to go as soon as possible.

After deliberating, the Board replied, "You will need money for language school plus going to the field. You probably won't be able to raise enough money before language school starts in Costa Rica this fall, so plan to go in December."

The previous December the Mission had sent Doris Warren to Bolivia to try to secure permission for Evangelistic Faith Missions to enter that country. Doris had spent more than twenty years in Bolivia with another mission organization, and when they nationalized the work, she was no longer needed. She then applied to EFM and was placed under appointment to Honduras. Later the Board decided that it was God's time to launch out into Bolivia.

My first deputation tour after meeting with the Board took me to southern Ohio where the Mission had arranged seven services for me. The first service was at Fairview Holiness Church near Burr Oak State Park. They gave a good offering but specified it for general mission expenses. *I am sure the Mission needs that money,* I thought, *but I wonder how I will ever get to the field if the other churches do the same.*

The next five services were cancelled because of sickness in those churches. I was discouraged since I had only one service left on the schedule. I did not want to drive back to Bedford, Indiana, and then back to southern Ohio several days later for that one service. Since I was staying with Ralph and Bonnie Cantor, I asked Bonnie about camp meetings that I might visit in the interim.

"Faith, why do you want to go to a camp meeting?" I explained the situation and indicated that I wanted to have an inexpensive place to stay and at the same time get into some good services.

"You're staying right here," Bonnie said.

The next Wednesday I went with the Cantors back to Fairview Holiness Church, and after the service Pastor Arnold Van Horn asked me, "Are you going to be here on Sunday? How about speaking to the children in the morning?" I agreed to do so, and they gave me an offering of $100.00.

That afternoon I figured out exactly how much money I needed to go to Costa Rica and to Bolivia. I subtracted the amount I already had and wrote that balance on a piece of paper. I had been asked to sing a special in the evening service, and when I finished, Edgar Parsons stood up and said, "Folks, I think it is time we get back to sacrificial giving." He then told the story of Mary Christman, his sister-in-law, washing clothes by hand to earn money for a washing machine. When she had saved enough, she heard Victor Glenn tell about people who had never heard the gospel. *How can I spend money for a washing machine when there are people who never heard the gospel*, she thought to herself and gave that money to EFM. "I think we need to get back to that kind of sacrificial giving," Edgar repeated.

Myra Sue Van Horn, the pastor's wife, said, "I don't know how the rest of you feel, but I think God would have us pay the rest of Faith's way to language school." After a few others spoke in agreement, the pastor turned to me.

"It seems to be unanimous. How much do you lack?" he asked. I was afraid to state the amount I had calculated that afternoon because it seemed so much. However, I did so. "Write a check for her for that amount," Pastor Van Horn told the church treasurer.

Praise God! He had supplied in full. Now I realized why God kept me at that church. After going to the last service on that tour, I returned to Bedford. I spent the summer months representing the Mission at camp meetings and preparing to go to Costa Rica in September for one year of language school.

With the Van Horns in front of the Fairview Holiness Church in Ohio

Language School in Costa Rica

I arrived in San José, Costa Rica, on September 27, 1978, and began a year of studying Spanish. I roomed with Lois Beatty, who was going to serve in Guatemala under EFM. We lived in the home of a *tico* or Costa Rican family that was composed of a mother with her son, Gabriel, and her daughter, "Cookie." The father had died previously. Gabriel was a teacher at the Costa Rican University and taught Contemporary Latin American History. "Cookie" had been married to the Costa Rican ambassador to Mexico. Their house had hardwood floors and was well kept. There were even orchids hanging in the showers.

Shortly after Lois and I arrived, we had a conversation with Gabriel in order to avoid misunderstandings. I shared with him how we felt about such things as watching television and drinking alco-

168

holic beverages. At the end of our conversation, he commented, "I'd hate to think that I have a couple of nuns living in my home."

Gabriel's family had a pet parrot named Rosita that lived outside and was perched on a large ring near the laundry room. She learned to say my name, *Fe*, and said it from time to time. When she started saying *Fe*, she repeated it until I answered. Rosita also learned to laugh like Lois.

One day there was a fire on the property next to where we were living. Our "mama" was afraid that it would burn the fence around the back patio, so we got the hose to wet the fence, but there was not enough pressure. Lois and I found some buckets and began running back and forth dousing the fence with water. One time Rosita attacked Lois as she was going into the house to fill her bucket. Lois called for help, and I told her to throw water at the parrot. At that Rosita began to cackle in her "Lois laugh" as if to say, *Ha, ha, I fooled you!*

Learning Spanish was frustrating. It was easier than learning Tigrinya, but all the classes were taught in Spanish. We could not ask intelligent questions in a language we did not know, and when we did manage to ask a question, we could not understand the answer. Comprehension developed more quickly than speaking skills, though, so that when we did begin to understand what was being said, we found it hard to respond.

Partial view of the language school campus in Costa Rica

Frank and Leah Klassen, EFM missionaries, were in language school at the same time. We would often go on the city bus together trying to find our way around San José, the capital city. I would ask directions, not understand, and get us lost. Frank was fond of saying, "We're traveling by Faith."

In early December I asked God for money to buy children's materials in Spanish for our work in Bolivia. To my delight the Union Gospel Tabernacle in Zanesville, Ohio, who had supported me since I first went to Eritrea in 1961, sent me a sizable check for Christmas.

After I got the check, I went to the Child Evangelism Fellowship store in San José. I found a wealth of materials including illustrated songs and story books with big pictures. They had everything I needed to begin children's work in Bolivia.

I collected a large supply of materials, and when I took them to the counter to pay for them, the woman in charge of the store bubbled over with joy. She told me that just that morning she told her workers she did not have money to pay them. They prayed together and asked God to meet their need. She now said that the money I was paying would make it possible for her to pay her workers. Our hearts rejoiced together at the realization that our heavenly Father, who knows all and does all things well, had providentially arranged everything for them and for me. Our heavenly Father works in **wonderful ways!**

At Christmas time Gabriel offered Lois and me glasses of wine. When we declined, he exclaimed, "You can't do anything!"

"But I don't want to do those kinds of things because I have something so much better," I replied, and then testified to him about God's saving grace.

When I finished, Gabriel said, "That was wonderful. We will have to talk about that again sometime."

Some months later Gabriel knocked on our door wanting spiritual help. After talking with him for some time and answering his questions, we prayed and he asked Jesus to forgive him and take charge of his life.

I was forty-two years old and trying to keep up with Lois, who was an energetic young lady, besides trying to adapt to a new culture and learn a new language. I was also concerned about my mother, who was ill. It all took its toll on me. As we neared the end of our Spanish study, I developed a nerve problem and began to have bouts of anxiety and physical weakness.

The Mission advised me to drop out of school and not take the final exams. I did not need the credit hours for any academic program. My only interest was to acquire the language. Thus I dropped out of classes.

About that time Gabriel told the Klassens and me some disturbing news. "You are going to stop in Panama on your way to Bolivia," he said. "They charge high customs there, so you better have extra money." We contacted the home office, and they wired us a check for a thousand dollars. Frank cashed the check and carried the cash in a money belt when we traveled to Bolivia.

Caring for Mama

Before leaving for Bolivia I received a phone call from Guy Troyer in the home office. He told me that my father had called and told him that according to one of the nurses who was helping to care for Mama, she only had a few months to live. He indicated that if I wanted to return home instead of going to Bolivia, I could.

I knew the mission policy stipulated that I would have to pay my own way home since it would be a personal trip. Although I did not have the money to pay for such travel, I did not want to tell Guy Troyer that, so I said I would go on to Bolivia. "Well," he replied, "after you get there, if you decide that you want to come home, you may."

I sort of laughed and said, "Well, I won't have any more money then than I do now." Nothing more was said about it, and on August 11, 1979, the Klassen family and I left Costa Rica. We spent that night in the airport in Panama City and flew to Bolivia the next day.

Doris Warren met us at the airport. After we cleared customs, we drove through part of the city of La Paz and through a mountain pass on a dirt road to a suburb of La Paz called Bosque de Bolognia where the mission's rented houses were located.

A day or two after arriving in Bolivia, Frank said to me, "I want you to call your father and see how your mother is. If you don't have money for the phone call, I will pay for it."

With Doris Warren, the missionary God used to open EFM's work in Bolivia

When I made the connection and heard Daddy's voice, I could tell that he had hit bottom. Being concerned for him, I asked if I should come home. "I don't know, Faith," he answered. "Pray about it."

Several days before I called, Daddy came home after shopping and found Mama on the floor. He did not know how long she had been there. He felt so bad about it that he vowed never to leave her unattended again. The only time he went for groceries was during the time a nurse came to care for her.

After praying about going home, I felt strongly that I should go. My heavenly Father provided the finances for that trip in an unusual way. In Panama we did not have to pay even one penny for customs, so we had the extra thousand dollars on hand. I asked Doris to wire the home office and ask if I could use that money to buy my ticket and if I could have two years to repay it. They answered in the affirmative.

Only nine days after arriving in Bolivia, I departed for home on August 21. Daddy was so happy to have me home. He and Mama were living in a rented mobile home in Shirley, Indiana. Whenever I returned home from some errand, he would come out onto the little porch and pretend to play a trumpet to joyfully announce my arrival. Once after I had returned he asked, "Faith, do you think we could invite Charles Riggs and his family over for a meal?" I replied that we certainly could. My father had not been able to fellowship with others while he faithfully cared for Mama, so their visit was a special treat for him.

On Sunday mornings I stayed with Mama and got her ready for the day and prepared our Sunday dinner while Daddy went to church. Then I attended the evening services while Daddy stayed with Mama. The youth leader asked me to give a study on the Pentateuch to the young people in their Sunday evening services, which I greatly enjoyed.

Two or three times during those months, I offered to take a leave of absence from the Mission. Their response always was, "You have been with us for so long—just stay with us," so I did. I prepared the monthly prayer letter for EFM and had a few deputation services.

One Saturday while I was cleaning my parents' bedroom, Daddy was reading a book to us. We always enjoyed his reading aloud. When I turned to look at Mama, I saw that she was unconscious. Immediately I elevated her feet so that her head would be at a lower level, and then I called for an ambulance. I rode with Mama to the hospital in Greenfield, Indiana, and Daddy followed in the car. She looked at me with such gratitude in her eyes. Although she could not speak, she kept smiling at the ambulance attendant who remarked about it and said that Mama must be a wonderful lady.

Mama was kept in the hospital, and while there she suffered a major stroke. She could not eat or talk and just kept rolling her tongue around in her mouth. One of the doctors told me that she would never be anything but a vegetable. He suggested that we place Mama in a nursing home, but I could not accept that.

I went to church the next morning and told the people about Mama's condition and requested prayer for her. One of the young married men in the congregation, Dale Miller, offered to be anointed for her. When we went to see her that afternoon, she could both talk and eat. Praise God, He answered prayer.

On Monday morning someone called from the hospital and told me that they could not keep my mother any longer. We would need to take her home the next day. I went to prayer and told the Lord that we needed a hospital bed by Tuesday morning. It was an SOS to heaven.

After praying I decided to call my Spanish-speaking friend who lived in Shirley. She was a Costa Rican lady who had married an American. I visited her frequently to study the Bible with her in Spanish. I had a double reason for my visits—to help her spiritually and to remember the Spanish that I had learned in Costa Rica.

That morning when I called, I did so only with the intention of maintaining my contact with her and to practice a little Spanish.

While we talked, she asked about my mother, and I told her the situation. To my surprise she said, "Why, Faith, don't you know that there is a women's group right here in town that has hospital beds for those who need them?" That was unexpected because Shirley was just a little town in the middle of a farming area. Daddy used to say that Shirley was a crossroads in the middle of a cow pasture.

Excitedly, I asked how I could contact the women's group. She told me of a woman who worked in the Bible bookstore who knew about it and that I could call her there. Daddy and I went to see her, and providentially, her mother was the president of the group. Most of the beds were operated manually, but there was one that was operated electrically, which we were able to secure. When I asked about the cost involved, she said, "Oh, nothing. It is for anyone who needs it." Praise God!

My father and I then went to see our pastor since he had a pickup truck and asked him to haul the bed for us. He agreed to do so, but he wondered if it would fit in our mobile home. With confidence I responded, "Do you think God would give us a bed that would not fit in our mobile home? It will fit but may take a little work. It might have to be taken apart to get it through the door, but it will fit." He brought it to our place and it fit. I knew that my heavenly Father knew the size of our mobile home.

That organization also gave us bedsheets and some gowns for my mother. Daddy and I purchased two white gowns with pink roses on them for her in addition to the gowns that had been provided.

Anticipating My Return to Bolivia

In early spring I began to feel that the time was approaching for me to return to Bolivia. I prayed for God to speak to some good holiness woman about helping my father to care for my mother. I asked God to make His will so definite that it would be almost like a missionary call.

Then I wrote to Gertrude Campbell, who was a widow living in Michigan, and asked her to help me pray for God to send a godly woman to help Daddy take care of Mama so that I could return to Bolivia. She later told me that when she read that part of my letter, she thought to herself, *Why, certainly, I will pray.* Near the end of the letter I asked, "And if God should call you, would you be willing to come?" When she read that part of the letter, she thought, *Now why did she have to say that?*

Gertrude then wrote and explained all the reasons why she could not come. One was that she had a rash on her hands that was quite bothersome. However, in spite of all that she was saying in the letter, the joy bells began to ring in my soul as the blessed Holy Spirit said to me, "She's coming. She's coming. She's coming."

One Sunday night when I came home from church, my father said, "Faith, Sister Campbell called from Michigan. Why don't you return her call?"

I did, and she was so excited as she said, "Oh, Faith, God has called me to take care of your mother, and it is so definite that it is almost like a missionary call!" God had spoken to her in exactly the manner that I had asked Him. Praise His name! Several weeks later Gertrude came to Shirley, Indiana, and I made plans to return to Bolivia.

Chapter 12

Adventure and Evangelism
1980-1982

Arriving Back in Bolivia

After being in the States for nine months to help care for my mother, I returned to Bolivia on May 9, 1980. Doris Warren and I had planned to work together in Bolivia; however, that was not to be. One month before I returned, she left Bolivia because of a blood clot in her leg. The altitude of the suburb of La Paz where she lived was 11,000 feet. Since the high altitude causes the blood to thicken, and EFM had no mission work at a lower altitude at that time, it was not advisable for her to stay.

While Doris was in Bolivia, she was able to get the Mission registered with the government and obtained permission for us to work in the country. She also did personal evangelism with older women and started our children's work.

Building on the foundation Doris had laid, Leah Klassen and I held our first DVBS in Bolivia. That was the first of many Daily Vacation Bible Schools I would conduct in an effort to reach the children of Bolivia for Jesus.

Conducting a DVBS in Bosque de Bolognia with Leah Klassen

I lived in the house where Doris and I had planned to live. It was a cute little pink house on *Calle Uno* meaning Street One. Doris had planted a vegetable garden in front of the house, and on one side of the house she had grass and beautiful flowers. At the edge of the patio was a wall, and beyond that another patio and a house where *Doña* Yali lived. She owned that house and the one in which I lived.

After I was in Bolivia for a while, Gertrude Campbell wrote some interesting news from home. She had to use bleach water to make sure Mama's things were sanitized, and through that God worked a miracle. He used the bleach to cure the rash on Gertrude's hands—the same rash that she said would keep her from caring for Mama. We both rejoiced in God's goodness.

Gertrude cared for my mother for four months in Shirley, Indiana. Then it was decided that she would move back to Gladwin, Michigan, and Daddy and Mama would also move there. They would live in Gertrude's mobile home instead of paying rent where they were living in Shirley. They had learned that the state of Michigan would pay Gertrude to care for my mother in her home.

Gertrude's mobile home had only two small bedrooms, so there would not be room for my father. However, several years earlier her son Bob had built a large garage onto the side of it. She questioned why he had erected such a large building, but he assured her that she would use it. In preparation for their moving, Bob partitioned off a bedroom in the garage for my father and made an opening directly into the hallway of the mobile home.

Two other details show how God had prepared the mobile home so that Gertrude could care for my mother. One was the foundation. When Gertrude and Clair, her husband, moved the mobile home onto their property, they decided they did not want steps leading up to the door, so they set it on a permanent foundation that was low enough to eliminate steps. Thus, there would be no problem going in and out of the mobile home with Mama in her wheelchair.

The other detail involved an opening between rooms. Gertrude had asked Bob to make an opening in the wall of the smaller bedroom, which she used as her sewing room. She wanted to be able to see into the living room so that she would not feel so closed in while she sewed. When Mama stayed in that room, she was able to look into the living room and see Daddy and anyone else who was there. Isn't God good? We all rejoiced over God's planning of every detail.

Lost on a Mountain in Bolivia

On the night of September 14, 1980, I accidentally took the wrong bus and got lost in a mountainous suburb of La Paz. That day is the anniversary of the Obrajes *barrio* or neighborhood. All around me were drunken Indians who were celebrating. The men were wearing masks, and the women were dressed in their colorful billowing skirts as they danced and chanted in the street. Frankly, I was afraid.

Earlier in the day I left home with Julia Fulton, a missionary with the Central Friends Mission who taught their missionary children. She had been visiting me, and I went with her to Obrajes to make sure she got on the right bus. After I saw her leave, I waited for a bus to take me back to Bosque de Bolognia.

I was not only enveloped in the darkness of the night and surrounded by the strange music and the dancing of the celebrants, but also my mind was troubled about my mother. Gertrude Campbell had called me a few days earlier to explain that she and my parents would be moving from Shirley, Indiana, to Gladwin, Michigan. They would have less expense that way since Gertrude had her own mobile home there.

Mama would go to Michigan on a medical flight. It all sounded good on the phone. Later I foolishly began to worry because my mother had never been on an airplane. I thought she would be so frightened that she might have another stroke.

I stood watching for a bus and wondering if any vehicle could get through the streets that were crowded with revelers. Finally, a bus came inching its way through the crowd with the dancers moving to one side. A sudden surge of people who wanted to board the bus swept me along, and I found myself at the doorway wondering if any other buses might come. Almost forced to enter the bus by the pressing crowd, I asked the driver if he was going to Bosque meaning Bosque de Bolognia. He said he was, so I paid my fare and found a seat near the back.

Looking around I soon realized that we were in an area I had never seen. As I was searching for a familiar landmark, the bus came to a stop, and everyone got off. The driver said in Spanish, "This is the end of the line, and everyone must get off."

"But sir," I answered, "I don't know where I am. When I got on this bus, I asked if you were going to Bosque, and you said that you were." I did not know the local people called it Bolognia and not Bosque.

The driver did not deny it. He simply repeated, "This is the end of the line, and you must get off the bus."

I did not move. It was dark outside, and I did not know where I was. I did not feel that I could leave the bus since my heart was filled with so much fear that I felt chilled. "*Cuando tengo temor, confiaré en el Señor*" meaning "What time I am afraid, I will trust in thee." I repeated those words from Psalms 56:3 over and over to myself. I liked saying that verse in Spanish because it rhymes.

God then moved on the driver's heart, and he turned the bus around and drove back to an intersection with a road that went to Bolognia. I got off the bus hoping another one would come that was going to Bolognia, but I was still disoriented.

Now what should I do? The logical thing was to look for a telephone, which I did, but there was no phone. Well, I did not need a phone to call my heavenly Father since I had a direct line to Him. The God who had called me to Africa and kept me there for sixteen years was the same God who had called me to Bolivia. He knew exactly where I was in the land of my second calling!

"Father, You know I am lost on a mountain here in Bolivia. Around me are drunken men and there is no telephone. Please, let the Klassens know I am lost and send them to find me. Thank you, Jesus," I prayed.

As I stood there waiting for the Klassens, a bus finally came. I did not know then that the Klassens arrived just in time to see me board the bus. I got off the bus at their street in Bolognia intending to let them know that I had arrived. Then I clearly heard Leah Klassen's voice calling, "Faith, we are right here." She sounded like an angel, and I ran joyously to the mission vehicle.

As the Klassens took me home, I told them how I had used my direct line to Jesus. With excitement Leah responded, "Now let me tell you our side of the story. My husband had just said, 'I think it is

Frank and Leah Klassen with Carla, Rhonda, and Kelly

about time for us to go to bed.' 'No,' I said, 'I feel Faith is lost and we must go and find her.'"

How it thrilled me to hear that God worked on both ends just as I had believed He would. As I walked into my house, He spoke to me. "Now, Faith, if I could take care of you when you were lost on the mountain with drunken men all around you and no telephone, don't you think I can take care of your mother as she flies to Michigan?"

I fell on my knees and cried, "Yes, Lord, I know You can do it. Forgive me for doubting." Because I knew I had hold of His hand, I said, "Lord, I am going to ask you for only two more things. First, please let Daddy go with Mama on the plane; second, please don't let her know she is on a plane."

Gertrude drove her car to Michigan a day before Daddy and Mama flew. She was at the airport to meet them when they arrived. Seeing them she said, "Well, Mama, how did you like your trip?"

"Well, I got a little sick on the bus," Mama answered. The God who took care of me when I was lost on a mountain in Bolivia also answered my prayers regarding my mother.

New Neighbors

After *Doña* Yali moved out of her house, which was behind my patio, Jorge and Nancy, a young couple with a baby and two little girls, rented it. One day after Nancy had washed the diapers, she laid them on the wall between our patios to dry. Later the wind blew them onto my patio. That gave me a wonderful opportunity to meet my new neighbors. I took the diapers and knocked on her gate, and soon the young mother came. I explained what had happened and told her my name was Faith, and that I wanted to be her friend.

She told me her name was Nancy, gave me a big smile, and replied, "I want to be your friend, too. Come in." Once we were inside she asked, "Would you like to see my baby?"

"Yes, I would enjoy that," I replied. Little Luis, only a few months old, was sound asleep in his bed.

We sat and talked for a while, and then I asked, "Nancy, would you like to study the Bible with me?" She agreed and we set Tuesday and Thursday afternoons for Bible studies, one day at my house and the next time at hers. We had tea together at the end of our Bible studies.

Nancy's in-laws, Ignacio and Marcela, thought it was a sin to read the Bible. They believed that only priests were worthy to read it. Several times during the first few months of those studies, Nancy had a bad report to give me.

"Faith, do you know what my mother-in-law says?"

"No, what does she say?"

"She says so-and-so lost his job because you and I are reading the Bible together." Another time it was, "So-and-so is sick because we are reading the Bible together." When I met the mother-in-law on the street, she would turn her head and not even acknowledge me.

Frank Klassen had been holding Bible studies in various homes in the community. Then he decided we should invite the people to his home on Tuesday evenings for a Bible study together. I invited Nancy to join us in those studies. One night at the close of the study, she gave her heart to Jesus.

During a later Bible study in my home, Nancy asked me to attend a birthday party for Luis' first birthday. I was not sure what might transpire at such a party, so I hesitated. Soon I felt God's assurance that it was the right thing to do and consented to attend. She then asked me if I would make their son a birthday cake like a football field.

"How many people will be there?" I asked.

A group of ladies who attended Bible studies in Klassens' house
in Bosque de Bolognia

"About thirty or forty," she replied.

I thought that would take a rather big cake, but considering it prayerfully, I again felt the Lord's assurance.

At the party Nancy asked me to cut and serve the cake. During the time I was present, nothing questionable transpired. Among those present were Ignacio and Marcela. The heart of a grandmother is the same around the world. When Marcela saw the cake I made and served, her heart was touched.

"Do you know what my mother-in-law said?" Nancy asked the week after the party.

"No, what did she say?"

"She said, 'I would like to study the Bible with *Hermana Fe*, but I don't know if she would let me after the way I have treated her.'"

"Nancy, you tell her that, of course, I would like her to study the Bible with us!"

Two days later I saw one of the happiest sights of my life. Coming up my walk were Ignacio, who used a walker because of some strokes he had had, Marcela, and Nancy to study the Bible with "the hated Evangelical." I welcomed them to our Bible study.

I knew the doctor had told Ignacio that he could die at any time. I explained to him the plan of salvation and then asked, "Ignacio, do you have the assurance that your sins are forgiven?"

"Not yet."

"Why?" I questioned.

"There are too many obstacles. I cannot go directly to Him for forgiveness."

Turning in my Bible to the book of Hebrews, I read, "Seeing then that we have a great high priest, that is passed into the heavens, Jesus the Son of God, let us hold fast our profession. For we have not an high priest which cannot be touched with the feeling of our infirmities; but was in all points tempted like as we are, yet without sin. Let us therefore come boldly unto the throne of grace, that we may obtain mercy, and find grace to help in time of need" (Hebrews 4:14-16). That afternoon he sought God but did not find forgiveness then.

At the next Bible study I presented a chart showing the high priesthood of Christ, hoping that it would help Ignacio in his search for God. As we studied together, a flicker of hope passed over his face. A month later Marcela gave her heart and life to Jesus. "Has Jesus forgiven you?" I asked.

"Yes!" Marcela exclaimed with a shining face.

Some months later after Ignacio had more strokes, there were times when his mind was lucid and times when it was not. One day God told me that it was time to visit him. I went to their home and asked his wife how he was.

"Why, he is fairly well today. Come in and see him," Marcela replied.

I read to him from Revelation 3:20, "Behold, I stand at the door, and knock; if any man hear my voice, and open the door, I will come in to him, and will sup with him, and he with me."

"Ignacio, Jesus is here. Won't you ask Him to come into your heart?" I asked.

"Why not?" the sick man responded. I led Ignacio in praying the sinner's prayer and inviting Jesus into his heart. What a glorious experience! Just a few weeks later he went to heaven.

Nancy later suffered with cancer for more than five years before passing away. While in the hospital she assured me that she was ready to meet God.

Spiritual Victories

Another family with whom we had contact lived in Chacoma. They were Nicolas and Christina with their two little girls, María and Lucía. Christina repeatedly refused to attend the services of a cult with her husband. "Come with me," he begged.

"No," Christina responded. "If I go to church anywhere, it will be to the Evangelicals." She proceeded to tell Nicolas of evangelical relatives of hers and how she was impressed by their lives.

The Mission had held only a few services in the village of Chacoma when Nicolas began attending, bringing with him three-year-old María. He pondered the words he heard.

"My wife is sick," Nicolas told the Christians one day, and he asked that they pray for her. After Christina improved, Nicolas brought her and little Lucía along to the services. Later a son was born three weeks prematurely with a serious physical problem. Nicolas and Christina gave me the joy of naming their little boy, and I called him Daniel. Christina and baby Daniel lived with me in Bosque de Bolognia for a while so that Daniel might receive the needed surgery at the children's hospital in La Paz. The operation was successful, and they returned to their home in Chacoma.

During the next camp meeting I was speaking from Matthew 7:13-14 and ended by asking, "Which road will you take?" Out of the congregation came Nicolas' voice, "I'm going to take the strait and narrow road!" He and Christina traveled it together.

Shortly after the above events I received a definite answer to prayer. It concerned our work in Collana. I had specifically asked God one Wednesday to send three sisters in the Lord—Dalia, Margarita, and Raquel—to service that night and sanctify them.

After praying I loaded my accordion, songbooks, and Bibles into the Toyota Land Cruiser and headed for the mountain pass that separates Bosque de Bolognia from the rest of La Paz. There I met Manuel Paco, and we traveled up the *autopista* or modern highway to the high plateau and the two-lane highway to Collana. In our new adobe brick chapel I began playing my accordion to help gather the crowd. Dalia and her parents were among the first to enter, and they were soon followed by Margarita and Raquel. The girls were shepherds, and often one of them could not attend church because she was herding the sheep. On that Wednesday all three were able to attend. Following a message on holiness, Dalia and her mother were among the first seekers, and the other two girls soon followed. They all sought holiness, and some of them found victory.

Nano and Marisol

Marisol had been attending Frank Klassen's Bible studies on Tuesday evenings with her grandmother Antonia for two years. However, on Sundays she, along with Nano, a young man, attended the Catholic Church. "Marisol will never come to our services on Sunday morning," the grandmother had explained to the Klassens, "because she plays the guitar and helps with the singing in the Catholic Church." However, an interesting incident took place during the Easter service at the Catholic Church in 1982.

Often the priests emphasized only Jesus' death, but when the priest spoke of the resurrection of Jesus, Nano could not hold his peace. He responded by saying, "Praise God, my Jesus is alive!" That response and the "Amens" of Nano and Marisol so startled the priest that he lost his place in his reading. He rebuked them and told them to leave the church. When they left, several others walked out with them. That night Nano, Marisol, her brother José Luis, and several others came to the service in the Klassens' living room, which resulted in a full room.

The following week Marisol's mother, Christina, came to beg Frank to tell Marisol to return to the Catholic Church. The priest had come by and apologized for demanding their departure. "You are the mother," Frank told her. "That is your job." Then he added, "I am zealous for your children. I would like to see them attend here. In fact, I would like to see José Luis become a preacher."

"José Luis?" Christina replied. "It's more like Marisol. She's the one who preaches to us all the time."

Later I asked Christina, "Have you seen any change in Marisol since she gave her heart to the Lord?"

"Yes!"

"What change have you seen?"

"She's more fearful."

"What do you mean?"

"She's afraid her father and I are going to go to hell."

People in the community soon began telling the missionaries that Marisol was witnessing and saying, "The Bible nowhere teaches the worship of Mary."

When the Klassens were preparing to leave Bolivia, I approached Marisol about teaching the children's Sunday school class. She was thrilled about the prospect of serving her Lord in that way.

Marisol told me she was trying to obey the Lord in every way in spite of opposition at home. When she refused to attend the movies, drink alcoholic beverages, and participate in fiestas, her father, who was a dentist for the Bolivian army, accused her of being unsociable. She shared her burden for her parents' salvation. Eventually Marisol married Nano, who was the youth leader in our church in La Paz, and today they have three daughters and a son.

Chapter 13

Filling the Leadership Role
1982-1984

Leadership Transition

Furlough time was drawing near for the Klassens in the spring of 1982, and I was feeling overwhelmed with the idea of leading the work in Bolivia. "If I didn't have a definite call to Bolivia," I said to Frank, "I would be packing my bags and heading to the States." But I did have a call and knew the Lord would help me. My first concern was trying to direct a work in a land where masculine leadership is so strong. I knew our only hope was the sanctified national believers who were working with us. I also had the anticipation of Irene Maurer, who had worked with me in Ethiopia, arriving in May to help me with the work.

Before Irene arrived, the Klassen family and I all succumbed to typhoid. God undertook so that the diagnoses were made and medicines purchased before a strike occurred by the doctors and pharmacists in the area. Wasn't God good?

The lease for my house was up a short time before the Klassens were scheduled to leave. Since the house the Mission rented for them had more space for our services, it was decided that I should move in with them.

Irene arrived in Bolivia on schedule in spite of having been in a car accident the day before departure. By then I had recovered enough from typhoid that I was able to accompany her to Cochabamba in the lower altitude where the doctors wanted her to stay for two weeks to aid in acclimatization. La Paz is 12,000 feet above sea level while Cochabamba is only 8,000 feet. I was delighted to see how quickly Irene adjusted to the altitude.

Shortly after Irene and I returned to Bolognia, the Klassens left for the States at the end of May. Though saying farewell was difficult and sad, Irene and I felt God's sustaining and empowering presence.

We were thankful for the wonderful groundwork that the Klassens had laid regarding both salvation and sanctification. God helped Walter Pope, a man active in the congregation in Bolognia, to announce publicly that he was seeking holiness and to ask his brethren to join him. "I know we all have to be sanctified if we want to see God," Walter said.

"Let us pray right now," I urged, "God wants to sanctify you, and His presence is so real. He is ready and waiting to do the work." We knelt there in our home on that Sunday evening, and the men sought God for heart holiness.

God graciously sanctified Walter. The next day, as he sat around the dinner table with his family, God blessed him so greatly he did not know what to do. Tuesday evening he testified that God had burned something out of his heart. Walter continued to lead his fellow workers by saying, "God has placed *Hermana Fe* and her American sister over us and under Himself to guide our people in the strait and narrow way.

During the following November, Carlos Flores of the Central Friends Mission held a revival for us in our Bosque de Bolognia church. He was a white man of Spanish descent and of the same culture as our Bolognia people. His preaching was excellent, and God met with us.

At that time there was a young woman named Bridgett Belmonte who attended our services. She was dating a young man who was learning to fly. One evening after the revival service Irene and I invited them to join Carlos, his wife, and us for a snack. While Irene prepared the snack, Bridgett and her boyfriend stayed in the chapel, and Carlos spoke with them doing his best to lead the young man to the Lord. However, he would not yield.

A few nights after the revival ended, we were ready to retire when the phone rang. I answered. Bridgett was calling, and she was crying so hard that it was difficult to distinguish her words. "Bridgett, do you want us to come to your home?" I asked.

"Yes," she replied.

Irene and I got ready quickly and went to the Belmonte home. When the tragic story came out, we learned that she had been invited by her boyfriend to go on a date that evening. The hour arrived, but he did not come. Finally, his family informed her that he and three other young men, including the son of the Venezuelan ambassador, had decided to fly a small plane to the Yungas, which is a lush, green area of Bolivia. Evidently there was a strong downdraft over the mountains that caused their plane to crash. It caught fire, and two burned to death at the site of the crash while the other two died later in a hospital in La Paz. Our hearts were saddened by the fact that Bridgett's boyfriend did not seek the Lord while he had an opportunity.

Taking a Brief Vacation

In November, soon after the revival with Carlos Flores, Irene and I became aware that we needed a rest and decided to take a brief midweek vacation in the quiet little town of Sorata. It is nestled in the mountains at 9,000 feet and backed by a towering snowcapped peak. The final descent was on a narrow ledge with part of the way having only one lane for two-way traffic. "It's fraught with perils!" Irene exclaimed.

At the first checkpoint on the way to Sorata, the policeman accidentally kept the mission car registration paper. Irene and I did not discover the loss until the next checkpoint where we needed to show only the pass received at the previous checkpoint. I prayed that we would be able to regain our registration paper.

At the Sorata checkpoint I was able to get our pass stamped the day after arrival and told the officer about our loss of the registration paper. He told us that when we returned, we should ask for it at the checkpoint where it had been kept. Then he asked if he might ride with us back to La Paz, and we consented.

Our arrival in Sorata coincided with a night of festivity which was part of the All Saints' Day. The unsaved Aymara Indians believe that the souls of their deceased loved ones return for a day or two to visit them during that feast. They buy sugarcane stalks to serve as canes for those souls. They make horses and llamas of bread dough for the souls on which to ride and ladders of bread to help them get back to heaven. They prepare food and carry it to the graves where they eat it, drink native beer, sing, dance, and play music. They put bottles of *chicha,* a strong drink made from fermented corn, on the graves with the stalks of onions that have gone to seed for the souls to use as straws to drink. If even a fly lands on the food, someone is likely to say, "Oh, that is the soul of some departed loved one just arriving."

When Irene and I took a walk to explore a little stream and waterfall, an Aymara woman said to us, "Why don't you go to the cemetery and pray for the souls? The people are dancing there, and you can dance, too!" When I told her about Jesus and how we need to confess our sins directly to Him, she was surprised.

After a few days of rest and relaxation in Sorata, it was time for us to return to our duties. The officer who wanted to go to La Paz accompanied us, and that turned out to be God's providential care for us. We were not able to get gas for the vehicle in Sorata because gas was scarce at the time, so with only a quarter of a tank of gas, we started up those treacherous, narrow roads with their numerous curves and multiple switchbacks. Along the way the officer told us of places to check for gas, but there was none available. We prayed earnestly that God would stretch our gas and help us get to La Paz.

A typical gas station in the outlying areas of Bolivia. Gasoline is stored in fifty-gallon drums.

Steadily we climbed over the ranges until we reached the high plains. Eventually Irene started to drive, and that gave me time to rest and an opportunity to do personal work with the officer. Earlier he accepted Spanish tracts that Irene offered him and told us he had an evangelical background.

While Irene was driving slowly to save gas, suddenly there was a rumpled, bumpy sensation. She knew it was a flat tire and pulled to the side of the road. Thankfully, the officer changed the tire, which would have been difficult for us to do.

When we reached the final checkpoint, the officer there recognized us and returned our vehicle's registration paper. How relieved we were! As we entered the city of La Paz, we were grateful to our heavenly Father for stretching the gas. We both felt our brief vacation was restful and profitable as we returned to our responsibilities.

Mama's Final Days

Vividly, I recall the first day of March 1983. It was Tuesday and started as an ordinary day. I shampooed my hair, did my laundry, prepared for my evening Bible study from Hebrews 9, and then knelt

Daddy and Mama celebrating their fiftieth wedding anniversary in 1982

to pray. As I prayed, I was burdened for the salvation of my cousin Ida Mae Jackett. She had a stroke, and I wanted to see her saved. While praying I said, "Lord, you are even able to make it possible for me to go and see Ida Mae." Surprised by my own prayer I thought, *What am I saying? She is in Florida in the States and I am here in Bolivia, South America.* Then the phone rang.

"*Buenos tardes*," I answered but got no response.

"Good evening?"

"Faith?"

"Yes?"

"Faith, your mother isn't expected to live much longer." Gertrude Campbell was calling from Michigan. When I finished speaking with Gertrude, I told Irene the news.

"You'll need to go."

"Yes, I want to go. I have prayed that I could be with Mama when it is her time to leave this world. But now, with Klassens on furlough. ...."

"I can oversee the work in your place for a while," Irene replied.

"Are you sure?"

"Yes, you need to be with your mother."

I then telephoned Juddie Peyton and received permission to return to the States.

That evening I led the people in a study of the tabernacle and God's perfect plan for its construction. God met with us and assured me that He also had a perfect plan for my mother, for my father, for me, and even for Gertrude. After the Bible study I shared with the Bolivians the news of my mother's approaching death and my desire to be with her and told them that Irene would lead in my absence.

With the help of Bruce Johnson, a Central Friends missionary, I was able to go to the Association of National Evangelicals in Bolivia (ANDEB) office the next morning and get clearance from the government, secure an exit and reentry visa, and buy a ticket to the States for that very day.

Bruce asked Umberto, the headman of ANDEB in La Paz, "Do you think we can get her out of the country today?"

"We have to!" Umberto replied.

After going to Immigration, Umberto said to me, "You'll have to fill out a form saying you do not owe money to anyone. Wait in that line for the form."

I waited in line for some time and finally got to the window and asked for the needed form. "We ran out of forms," the man announced. "We will have more at 3:00."

Bruce stepped around the corner and approached another man. "I don't know what to do," he explained. "I have to get Faith

Hemmeter out of the country today, but your people have run out of forms."

Bruce had picked a true gentleman, for though he was a complete stranger, he immediately replied, "I have a form in my office, and I have no urgent need for it. If you will take me there, I will give it to you." Bruce took the gentleman and me to his office where we discovered the form already had the government stamp on it.

I pondered those things in my heart. God had helped Bruce to speak to a man who had a form that was already stamped, enabling me to leave the country that day. It was a miracle. What a great God I serve!

Back in Immigration I filled out more forms and answered more questions. Anxiously, I looked at my watch. Bruce and I should have left for the airport at 6:30 p.m., and here it was almost 7:00. Umberto was diligently trying to get the last signatures on all the papers. We watched as he walked to a desk and asked the man for a signature. He shook his head no, pointed to his watch, and said, "It's quitting time." We prayed quietly asking God to cause the man to sign, and in a moment he did!

My flight was to leave at 8:00. Bruce and I rushed to the Central Friends headquarters at Pura Pura where my suitcases were delivered earlier in the day because it was closer to the airport than our headquarters. We arrived at the airport just in time for me to check in, hurry out to the tarmac, and board the plane. By divine providence I was seated beside Mark Frink of the Bolivian Holiness Mission.

When I disembarked in Miami, Florida, at 5:00 the next morning, Mark Frink helped me put my suitcases in a locker. He handed me a key and directed me to Delta Airlines to buy a ticket to Saginaw, Michigan. I ran down the corridor to Delta, purchased the ticket for a plane leaving in ten minutes, and rushed back to the locker.

In haste I tried the key but could not open the locker. Then I realized the number on the key did not agree with the number on the locker. No other locker bore the number of the key either, so I went to Mark Frink and told him my problem. He went to the locker and tried the key and it opened! I hurried back to Delta only to discover that I had missed my plane.

"There are no more flights to Saginaw today," the young woman at the counter said. "Let me see if I can find any connecting flights. Ah! Here is one to Chicago that connects to Saginaw. Look! It will cost you $31.00 less than the other one."

"Oh, God, that is all part of Your plan! Thank you, Father, You wanted to save me $31.00!" I sang in my heart, "Praise God, from Whom All Blessings Flow." I arrived in Saginaw at 1:20 p.m. on Thursday.

I wanted to be with my mother at her promotion to glory because she had sacrificed so much in allowing her only daughter to go to the mission field. Now God was working out every detail to grant me that privilege. As her death approached on Sunday night, I spent some time alone with my mother and read to her John 14:1-3: "Let not your heart be troubled: Ye believe in God, believe also in me. In my father's house are many mansions: If it were not so, I would have told you. I go to prepare a place for you. And if I go and prepare a place for you, I will come again, and receive you unto myself; that where I am, there ye may be also."

Mama cocked her head a little as if to tell me she could not hear clearly. I leaned down by her ear and repeated the verses. "Mama, Jesus has gone to prepare a place for you, and I think He is coming to get you soon."

"Uh-huh," my mother responded in spite of the fact that she had not spoken for days.

My heart rejoiced as I thought, *She's looking for Him to come!* Lillian Hemmeter, who had served God faithfully nearly all her life, went to be with her Lord on March 6, 1983, at the age of 77.

My only opportunity to visit Ida Mae was on my way back to Bolivia. I made arrangements with her father, my Uncle Ralph Jackett, to meet me at the airport. Together we went to the nursing home where she was a resident. I rejoiced when I learned that Uncle Virgil Hemmeter had already led her to Jesus. After a short visit Uncle Ralph took me to his mobile home. As we sat in the living room, I realized that he might be hungry for Jesus. I asked, "Uncle Ralph, have you ever given your heart to Jesus?" He responded by falling on his knees there at the davenport and saying, "Oh, Faith, pray for me." Praise God he prayed through. About two months after

I returned to Bolivia, I received the news that he had a heart attack, and Jesus took him to heaven.

After spending three weeks in the States, I returned to Bolivia to rejoin Irene. We continued our shepherding of pastors, holding Daily Vacation Bible Schools, planting new churches, and overseeing the work. One of my primary responsibilities was pastoring the church in Bosque de Bolognia. Both of us were privileged to help dedicate the new church in Chacoma on July 3, 1983.

Problems with My Pancreas

During the fall of 1983, I began to develop a physical problem and finally went for x-rays of my pancreas on December 20. The next day I took the x-rays to my doctor in La Paz. "You must return to the United States immediately," the doctor said when he examined the x-rays. "You have no choice in the matter." Quickly I made arrangements to leave Bolivia and arrived in the States on December 24.

Carrie Boyer accompanied me to the Caylor-Nickel Medical Center in Bluffton, Indiana, the following Monday. That night we stayed in a room reserved for patients needing to spend the night. The next morning as Carrie and I were having our private devotions, I prayed, "Lord, if you want Carrie to anoint me, have her ask me if I want to be anointed."

Almost immediately Carrie came to me and asked, "Faith, have you been anointed for this condition?" I responded by telling her what I had just prayed. "I will anoint you and pray for you," Carrie replied. "I am going to ask God to have the doctors take new x-rays because if they accept the ones from Bolivia, they will operate on you."

The next day we rejoiced when the new x-rays showed no growths on the pancreas. One doctor exclaimed, "If you had pancreatitis, you no longer have it." A few days later I went to the Bedford Regional Medical Center in Bedford, Indiana, and there I was told that in order to avoid having the problem again, I must not overeat. So it was that God healed me. Praise His dear name!

Since it was time for my furlough, I stayed home for a year and traveled for deputation services. My father was then living with my brother and his family, but he was very lonely because he missed

Mama so much. I decided to take him with me on some of my travels. That fall he moved to Point Pleasant, West Virginia, and in December 1984 he married Margaret Smith. The wedding was performed by Juddie Peyton in the mission house in Bedford, Indiana.

Daddy's marriage to Margaret Smith
in December 1984

Chapter 14

New Ministries
1985-1989

Returning to Bolivia

Shortly after my father's wedding I returned to Bolivia singing "Sweet Will of God." My heart filled with praise as I flew over the snowcapped Andes and landed on the high, barren, windswept plains above the picturesque city of La Paz. I looked for familiar faces as I left the plane and entered the airport. With delight I recognized my friends who had come to meet me. My pounding heart quickly reminded me that I was at a high altitude and needed to be careful, so I walked slowly from the airport. I was back in the land of my second calling.

Celia Ormachea of our congregation in Bosque de Bolognia greeted me with the words, "Oh, before we do anything else, let us get on our knees and thank God for your return." We knelt and thanked God together.

It was wonderful to be with my Aymara Indian friends whose eyes sparkled with the joy of their Savior. How they loved to sing the songs of Zion! They usually sang for an hour before the preaching in their services. It was a thrill to share God's Word with them again.

Our work was expanding, but we did not have men trained to serve as pastors. In February 1985, Manuel Paco helped me to start the Bible Institute at Jocopampa. Manuel had received his training in another holiness Bible school in Bolivia and thus was able to help me with the teaching. We started classes with twelve Aymara Indian men.

Easter Sunrise Service and DVBS

Fathers, mothers, the elderly, youth, missionaries, and one little girl met before daylight to begin our walk along the winding trail that leads to a high bluff above the river in Bosque de Bolognia for the Easter sunrise service that year. Like believers around the world, we wanted to commemorate our Savior's resurrection. With enthusiasm

197

we sang, *"Cristo la tumba vencio; y con gran poder resuscito"* meaning "Christ was victor over the tomb; and with great power He arose!"

Twenty-six people attended that first sunrise service. Irene played her trumpet, and Marisol joined in with her guitar as we sang of Christ's sufferings, death, and glorious resurrection. Our songs rang out for some distance across the clear morning air. After we sang, many of the group voiced their testimonies telling how they had been bound by Satan but were now set free by the risen Savior! Damian Abán read the account of the resurrection from the Gospel of Mark.

Carlos, a quiet gentleman, had joined us for the first time. When he was a baby, his parents had escaped from the Nazis in Austria during World War II. As a young man he married a lovely Spanish lady by the name of Teresa, and she and two of their teenage children had accompanied him to that sunrise service. He was visibly touched by the Holy Spirit.

Julia, a lady from the neighborhood, attended with her little daughter Eslávitza whose father was from Yugoslavia. Thus, five different nationalities were represented in that group of twenty-six who were worshiping our risen Lord—Austrian, Spanish, Yugoslavian, Aymara and Quechua Indians from Bolivia, and North American.

Following the sunrise service everyone was invited to the home of Carlos and Teresa. We were served *api*, a red-corn drink, and *empanadas,* a cheese pastry, made by Julia.

The following month I held a DVBS in Bolognia with fifty-six children in attendance. The theme was "Christian Soldiers." Many of the children came from homes of military men, so it was easy for them to identify with that concept. They loved singing "I May Never March in the Infantry" and "All the Armor." They quickly caught on to the catchy tune of the latter chorus and learned it well. Marisol helped by teaching the Bible stories.

On Sunday the chapel was filled to capacity, and some people had to stand outside while the children presented a program showing what they had learned. I remembered when Marisol was younger and came to services without her parents. Doubtless among those children there were more "Marisols."

Collana

The name Collana makes any Bolivian think of the white cheese made near that town. However, to the missionaries it brings to mind the little Faith Mission church and community of believers. In August 1985 Irene, the Manuel Paco family, and I held revival services in Collana.

Going to Collana meant another steep climb in our vehicle to the rim of the bowl in which the city of La Paz lies. Soon our party of six gazed at the breathtaking view of the city below surrounded by the rugged snow-covered Andes against a bright blue sky. We passed the food vendors sitting under their white umbrella-like sunshades, and not long afterward we stopped at the checkpoint, showed our papers, and paid the toll. We were now on the main road where we soon caught sight of Mount Illimani.

As we traveled, we noticed the stone cross at the side of the road and sadly saw someone offering a sacrifice, mixing paganism and dead Christianity. After passing through village after village, at last we reached the little Faith Mission whitewashed adobe chapel by the side of the blacktopped road in Collana.

We unloaded our musical instruments and began playing gospel songs. Soon we glimpsed people making their way across the plains. Women came wearing their brightly-colored full skirts and traditional derby hats perched on top of their heads. Their babies were tied snugly to their backs with colorful, hand-woven, wool blankets. Men arrived in their bright wool caps with the earflaps pulled down to protect them from the Andean winds. Children, dressed as miniature adults, accompanied their parents.

I preached in Spanish and Manuel translated into Aymara. That revival marked the time of David Mamani's sanctification along with that of others. He testified of victory and asked the congregation to forgive him for the times he had manifested the carnal nature. David was the young adult son of Pastor Manuel Mamani. In later years David became the pastor at Collana, and today he has a wife and three lovely children.

Youth Revival

One day in January 1986 Nano Orihuela suggested, "I think it would be good to have a revival especially for our youth."

"I am in complete agreement," I eagerly responded.

We began having Friday noon prayer-and-fast services and also scheduled a chain of prayer for that Saturday night. I exhorted the church to mind God and pray. The youth made lovely posters that were displayed in various places in the community. Missionaries and youth went out two by two and gave personal invitations to each home. We played gospel music, read Scripture, and announced the services over our loudspeakers.

The Spirit anointed the services from the beginning. I had been urging our American friends and prayer partners to pray for Marisol's father, Dr. Teófano. He came to the youth services faithfully. The last Sunday evening during the service he announced, "I have some good news." He went on to tell how he had prayed in his home and found the Lord as his Savior.

Later when I visited Dr. Teófano's home, I said, "Our purpose of being in your country is to help people find God."

Dr. Teófano replied, "The church we were attending did not tell us how to come to know God."

"It was our children who pulled us toward your church," his wife exclaimed. "When they came home from services, they showed their

Dr. Teófano Bohorquez and his family

200

father where the truths they learned were written in the Bible. Marisol often cried and did her best to convince us of the way of the Cross."

Again and again Marisol's father replied, "That is not the way we have been taught." However, Marisol continued to pray and witness to her parents, and she was the one God used to bring them to Him.

Another young Christian named Susie begged me before she left for the University of Sucre, "Don't let my mama stop coming to services." Susie's mother also came to the altar during that youth revival.

"What do you want God to do for you?" I asked.

"I want to be born again like you were saying," she answered. Praise God she found Jesus as her Savior! Then she brought her two teenaged sons, Peter and Carlos, to the services, and one night Peter sought God.

"How are things?" I asked afterwards.

"Jesus is so wonderful!" Peter responded with a big smile.

Monica, a friend of Susie, came to the services. Saturday night as I preached about being a good soldier for Jesus, I saw tears in Monica's eyes. We rejoiced when she gave her heart to Jesus that night.

Susie's sister came from Cochabamba to visit, and on the last Sunday morning of the special services, she also gave her heart to Jesus. Together, Nano, Irene, and I praised God for those lost sheep who had been found by the Good Shepherd.

Bible Institute and Sunday School Convention

The Bible Institute resumed classes in February 1986 with four new students: Cirilo Flores, Barnabe (Barnabus) Miranda, Juan (John) Mamani, and Pedro (Peter) Guarachi. With three having biblical names, we sometimes felt like we were teaching in the early church.

I rejoiced that whereas we had two teachers and two subjects the first year, now we were offering four subjects by four different teachers. The Bible Institute classes were taught only on Saturdays because the students were married men who had families. It was necessary for them to work to earn a living. We met in the Jocopampa church building, and all day the men sat on boards for benches with no backs. Manuel Paco taught Gospels for two hours, I taught Pentateuch for two hours, Sinforoso Lamachi taught Acts for two hours, and Irene taught music for an hour.

Our first Sunday school convention in Bolivia was held on the high plains in Jocopampa in the spring of 1986. The first morning of the two-day convention, Manuel gave instructions about how to teach an adult Sunday school class. In one afternoon session Irene instructed them how to teach a children's class. When Irene spoke, I interpreted into Spanish, and Manuel interpreted into Aymara. During the afternoon classes some of the pastors stood in order to stay awake.

One evening I spoke about "How to Win a Soul to Jesus." I explained and illustrated how to use the Wordless Book with children. A church in West Virginia had given me construction paper, and I made a Wordless Book for each of the five churches to use. I also made visual aids to go with songs in both Spanish and Aymara.

In August of that year, Jerry and Jacqueline Kwasigroh with their children, Jessica and Jonathan, arrived in Bolivia. We welcomed them by having a service in our home in Bosque de Bolognia where services were then held. Cake was served following the service.

Bible Institute Building

Dionicio with mud bricks he was making to build the Bible Institute building in Jocopampa.

In early 1987 Dionicio, a student of the Bible Institute in Jocopampa, began making bricks to construct a building for the Bible Institute. It rained before the bricks hardened, and many of them were ruined. They looked as if they were partly melted. "Poor boy!" exclaimed Manuel Paco, thinking of all the hard work Dionicio had put into them.

During the next month Dionicio made 3,000 bricks, and they hardened in the sun without getting "melted" by the rain. "I only have 1,000 more to make to have enough for the building," Dionicio rejoiced. Christians and missionaries prayed that God would continue to give us good weather.

Before Dionicio completed making the bricks, other men gathered to begin construction. Men from the Jocopampa church and the Bible Institute laid the foundation and then began laying the adobe bricks. The men worked fast, and in just two weeks they were ready for the roof. The rainy season had arrived, and if the roof were not in place before much rain fell, the adobe bricks would be ruined.

Rain fell in La Paz and in many other surrounding towns and villages on the *altiplano*, but the institute building was spared from damaging rain. We praised the Lord for helping the men to complete the roof before the rains came to that area. How much easier it was for the teachers to have an adequate facility in which to teach their classes. What a milestone!

Transformed Lives

I was traveling with some of our young people in La Paz when we passed a group of Hare Krishnas, members of a religious group who worship the Hindu god Krishna. "I almost went into the Hare Krishnas," Susie said. "My parents had told us we were free to choose the religion we wanted. God saved me from that. You came just in time." I praised God when I heard her testimony.

On another occasion Marisol said, "The Klassens and you came just in time to save me from becoming a nun. I was the only young girl in my class at the Catholic school where I attended who was interested in becoming a nun."

I rejoiced as I listened to Marisol teach a children's Sunday school class and lead the youth group. One time she prepared a study for the young people entitled "Advice for Young People Given in the Word of God."

"God has transformed our lives and we don't want to dress like the world any longer," Marisol and her sister Saundra told me. "When our friends ask, 'Why are you dressing like that?' we answer, because the Bible says that is what is pleasing to God!"

Damian who opened his home for services told me how he used to drink and carouse. "But since Jesus has transformed my life, I don't drink *chicha* anymore."

Teresa was involved in a cult before she came to Faith Missions. She longed for her whole family to come to the Lord. On my fifty-first birthday I had the privilege of dedicating her grandson Timmy to the Lord. I rejoiced with her when her husband and daughter stood with her to dedicate that little one to Jesus.

Chacoma's Fourth Anniversary

Our church in Chacoma made plans to celebrate its fourth anniversary in July 1987. Irene and I were asked to hold special services for them. It meant days of preparing camping equipment, DVBS supplies, and food, and of ending different projects on the home base. Our national leader, Manuel Paco, and Pastor Sinforoso traveled with us, and at Jocopampa we got more supplies. Late that afternoon we arrived in Chacoma and found the little two-room parsonage vacated and freshly swept. While Irene and I set up simple housekeeping in the parsonage, the men prepared the loud speakers and a gas lamp in the church.

In Bolivia the seasons are opposite from those in the States, so it got very cold in July. We dressed warmly like the Aymara women who wear multiple skirts, sweaters, and something on their heads. We were thankful for fleece-lined, ankle-high shoes. The men slept on the church benches in the unheated church.

On Friday we made house-to-house calls and were graciously welcomed. The people felt honored to have us come to their homes, and they expressed their appreciation. On Saturday we returned to Jocopampa for Bible Institute classes from 9:00 a.m. to 5:00 p.m. and then made our way back to Chacoma for the evening service.

Irene and I took turns preaching. People from other churches came on Sunday, and we had a wonderful time of fellowship. People sought God in each service. Lucia, a believer, and her husband, Luciano, attended, and Luciano sought the Lord for spiritual help.

A few months later I welcomed Zettie (Finch) Cotton to Bolivia. Zettie, who was now a widow, had worked for a number of years in Eritrea before marrying Jesse Cotton. She came to help me because Irene had returned to the States to care for her ailing sister. Irene later returned to Bolivia in 1988.

With Bible Institute students in Jocopampa in 1989

Prison Ministry and a Birthday Party

In early 1988 I began weekly services in a women's prison. Marisol played her guitar while twenty-five to thirty women lifted their voices in song. Their daily existence was dark and dreary, and singing helped to bring them out of the depths of despair. Some were as young as seventeen while the oldest one was eighty-five. After several months of services, the inmates testified to a change in the atmosphere of the prison. God made a difference!

Later that year Irene and I had the privilege of attending a birthday party for Lourdes, one of the believers from our Bosque de Bolognia church. The celebration began with a service dedicated to Lourdes in the home of Sebastian, her husband's brother. It was opened by singing "I Will Praise Him." Choruses and gospel songs were sung first to honor the Lord and secondly to honor Lourdes. Different ones in the congregation dedicated songs or scripture passages to her. I gave a short message from John 3:16 about the greatest Gift and our freedom to accept or reject salvation. We closed the service by having a time of prayer for the unsaved among us.

Then we went next door to the home of Damian and Lourdes where we were served fried chicken, potato salad, tomatoes, lettuce, and soft drinks. Everyone, including their five children, gathered around the dining-room table that held the birthday cake. We sang "Happy Birthday" in English and then in Spanish. I never attended a birthday party where Jesus was truly honored like He was in this one.

Another Triumphant Crossing

Antonia, an older lady in our Bolognia congregation, and I had gone to visit Nimia in 1985 on the first Sunday after my return from furlough. We found her very receptive to the gospel, and we were soon holding prayer meetings in her home with her husband, Juan, two daughters, and one little granddaughter. However, at that time they were actively part of the Jehovah's Witnesses.

The married daughter, Teresa, was the first one in the family to get saved. Nimia was saved shortly thereafter and, like all new converts, she became concerned about the salvation of the rest of her family. She prayed faithfully and rejoiced when some of them chose to serve Jesus.

Just two days before Nimia died, I asked her if all was well between her and her Lord. She assured me once again that all was well. "I am not afraid to die," she said. "I am ready to go."

Nimia had wanted to live until her son, Juan, arrived from the States, but he was not able to get there until after the funeral. Just before she died, a doctor who looked much like Juan entered Nimia's room and stood by her bed. "Little Juan!" Nimia exclaimed, and she died within a few minutes.

Teresa and I dressed the body for burial. The funeral was to be held in the home, so the undertakers placed the body in the coffin in the living room. They placed a lovely blue rug on the floor under the casket and large candleholders with tall white candles at either end of the casket.

Irene set up the mission's electronic keyboard, and Fernando had his guitar. I was ready to give the message when the people began to pressure Juan to call for a priest.

"Where is the priest? We must have a priest to conduct this funeral service," someone said.

Another said, "Nimia was born a Catholic and she must die a Catholic. We must have a priest to bless her body."

Juan replied, "I am fulfilling the request of my wife. This religion is a very holy one. This *señorita* has come morning and evening to visit my wife. I cannot change now."

The funeral proceeded, and for the first time in that Catholic community songs full of hope rang forth at a funeral. We sang "The Home over There," which translated from Spanish says, "Meditate in that there is a home on the margin of the river of light where the believers in Jesus Christ are going to forever be joyful. ..." Then we sang "In the New Jerusalem."

During my message I spoke about the beautiful words of John 14, "Let not your heart be troubled." After the service the undertakers placed the casket in the hearse and drove slowly down the street while everyone else walked behind it for several blocks to show their respect. Some of the group found transportation to the cemetery for the burial. I mourned the death of Nimia but thanked God for one more precious soul in heaven.

Recovering a Lost Transformer

When I was preaching in revival services for another mission in Sucre in 1988, we needed to take a transformer with us to the services. They had an electronic keyboard that operated on 110 current, but the current in Sucre was 220. In order to play the keyboard from a 220 outlet, we had to use a transformer, and I borrowed one from Allen and Eunice McVey.

We usually walked to service, but one evening since we were a little late, Gumersenda or Gumy and I took a taxi to church. She carried the transformer while I carried my Bible and other materials. After we arrived at the church, I began to speak to an older woman seated nearby hoping to encourage her to come to the service. Gumy struck up a conversation with a young man. Finally Gumy unlocked the church door, and we both stepped inside. It was then that I noticed we did not have the transformer. "Gumy, where is the transformer?" I asked with concern.

"Oh!" she replied in despair, "I left it in the taxi." My first thought was, *Well, it's gone. I'll just have to buy the McVeys another one.*

Then God spoke to me, "Don't just stand there. Do something!" So I said, "Gumy, search for it."

"But it's gone! The taxi is gone and I don't know where it is," Gumy said in a small, sad voice.

"Search for it! Search for it," I replied.

We both started running down the street. Suddenly, I saw a parked taxi. Running up to the driver, I asked, "Would you help me search for another taxi?"

The man looked at me rather strangely but replied, "All right."

I jumped in, he started the motor, and off we went. Soon we came alongside Gumy. The poor girl was running, and I saw her face was wet with tears.

"**Stop, Stop!**" I called to the taxi driver. When he did, I jumped out, handed Gumy some money, and said, "Take this and go search for the taxi while I go back to the church to pray."

Back in the church I began to remind God of all the wonderful things He had done for me through the years. Then I said, "Oh, God, You are the only One who has eyes of fire. You are the only One who knows where in this city of Sucre the taxi is that has our transformer. Would You please help Gumy find it." I prayed in Jesus' name, and as I prayed, my faith rose. Finally, I prayed through and **knew** that Gumy had found the transformer. I got up from my knees just in time to see the door open and Gumy walk in. She was smiling from ear to ear.

"Gumy, you found it, didn't you!" In answer she held it up for me to see.

"How did you find it?" I quizzed.

"Well, sometimes the taxi driver wanted to go right, and I just felt we should go left, so that is what we did. Sometimes he wanted to go left, and I told him we better go straight ahead. All of a sudden I recognized the shirt of the man who was driving the taxi in front of us. I asked my taxi driver to please stop. I paid him and got out. I ran up to that taxi and motioned for him to stop. He said, 'Lady, I can't stop here. I have to pull up a little.' I ran along till he stopped. I ran up to him and said, 'Sir, you have our transformer.' Of course, he did not know what I was talking about since it was on the floor of the back seat. I looked and sure enough it was still there! I then asked him to bring me back to the church." Another miracle was the fact that no one had stolen it while he had been picking up and letting off passengers.

Furlough and Return

During the middle of December 1988, I returned to the States for furlough and stayed home only until the middle of March of the following year. That furlough marked a new pattern for me as regarding my labors in Bolivia. From that time I had a three-month furlough every three years.

Chapter 15

More New Developments
1989-1992

Our First TLC Team

George Vernon contacted us in 1989 about a Touching Lives for Christ (TLC) team coming to Bolivia. TLC is an outreach ministry of the Hobe Sound Bible Church in Hobe Sound, Florida. We welcomed the idea and planned to use the team to help us with some Daily Vacation Bible Schools and revival meetings and also to paint the outside of our house.

TLC team for 1989. Front row from left: Christine French, John French, Ann French, Ann Marie French, Virginia Niemic, Elva Lutz, Melissa Meldau, Daryl Bozone. Back row from left: G.R. French, Charlene Olson, Irene Maurer, Duane Reiff, Matt Crocker

Immediately, I began asking the Lord to send a good preacher for our revival meetings. I thought perhaps there would be a young person on the team who could preach with God's anointing. However, **God abundantly answered my prayers** by sending G.R. and Ann French as the team sponsors. G.R. French is a very capable Bible teacher and evangelist who taught at Hobe Sound Bible College for many years.

Due to the need to adjust to the high altitude, we planned for the team to have a few days of rest and recreation after they arrived. Irene and I decided that since La Paz is in the semiarid plains of the Andes Mountains, we would take them to the Yungas, which is the lush, green area of Bolivia between La Paz and Carnavi. The two-lane road to our destination is considered the most treacherous road in Bolivia because it is carved out of the side of the mountain and has no guardrails in spite of the many curves and deep drop offs at the side of the road. I asked God if it was all right for us to take the team to the Yungas. He assured me that it was, and we had a wonderful time.

The treacherous road to the Yungas

After we returned from the Yungas, we took the entire group to Collana for the first Sunday. During the services I had the privilege of interpreting for G.R. French. On Thursday I took part of the team—Virginia Niemic, Elva Lutz, Melissa Meldau, and Daryl Bozone—along with Damian Abán to Sixilla Baja. We had a DVBS on Friday and Saturday mornings and afternoons and had the program on Sunday morning. We also conducted revival services in the evenings and Sunday afternoon. The rest of the team stayed in Bolognia with Irene. They painted the outside of our house during the day and helped with revival services in the evening in our Bolognia church.

During their last week with us, we went to our church in Jocopampa. Part of the group conducted a DVBS on Friday and

Saturday mornings and had revival services in the afternoons in Collana, and the other members held a DVBS in Jocopampa. In the evenings we all joined in the revival services at Jocopampa. That church is located on the high plains of Bolivia, and it was very cold at that time of the year. Some of the team members took blankets with them to church in an effort to stay warm. G.R. French served as an excellent preacher for the revival meetings, and many received spiritual help.

G.R. French preaching with me interpreting into Spanish and Víctor Copia into Aymara

A Growing Bible Institute

For the school year that began in February 1990, we moved our Bible Institute classes to the Villa Jesus de Gran Poder church in El Alto and used the Sunday school rooms. We had taught the classes in rural Jocopampa the previous five years; however, new churches had been started in El Alto, and it was more convenient for our students to attend classes in the city. After six years we moved the classes to the Villa Tunari church because most of the students were from that area.

As the students increased, we divided them into two groups. Irene taught those whose Spanish was not adequate for accelerated study, while I taught the accelerated group. The accelerated students completed the thirty-six subjects in three years while the other students took six years. Upon successfully completing the course of study, the students had a general knowledge of each book of the Bible as well as a clear understanding of the major doctrines of the Christian faith and the beliefs of Evangelistic Faith Missions.

Daily Vacation Bible Schools in Belén and Sixilla Baja

Daily Vacation Bible Schools were an important part of our ministry, and we made plans to have one in the village of Belén.

DVBS in Belén

From Bolognia Irene and I drove to Jocopampa where we met Lucas, a son of Pastor Víctor, and Pedro, a Bible Institute student. Those two along with Pastor Raymundo, who came by bus, were to be our helpers for DVBS during the day and revival services in the evenings. Village authorities had granted us the use of a large classroom in the public school. When we arrived for the first service, to our dismay we found many broken windowpanes in the classroom. The cold night air blowing through the broken windows was bad for our colds, and by the end of the week, Irene had lost her voice.

About thirty-five children regularly attended the DVBS. Several opened their hearts to Jesus, including the son of the caretaker of the

213

village school. Each day after DVBS we returned to Jocopampa, a few miles away, where we were staying.

In the evening the men in our group loaded the generator, public-address system, gas tanks, gas lamps, an accordion, and a trumpet into the Toyota. After the three men, Irene, and I got in, other available space was occupied by people from Jocopampa who were accompanying us to the services. One young believer even rode on the luggage carrier on the roof. Although it was **very** cold up there, he really wanted to go. After services everything had to be reloaded and taken back to Jocopampa.

Raymundo preached in the evening services. When he could not be there, I preached in his absence. Sixty to seventy people attended every evening and many responded to the altar calls. One of the new converts named Frans immediately enrolled in the Bible Institute.

A few days later we took seven windowpanes to Belén as a gift for the use of the classroom. We knew they needed seventy panes, but the Mission could not afford to purchase that many. The officials were in a meeting when we came with the panes. During that meeting they decided to allow EFM to use a classroom regularly for services and indicated that they preferred building supplies rather than money as payment for rent.

Irene and I promised the officials that the Mission would donate ten bags of cement to repair their school. On an appointed day when we delivered the cement, they said, "Could you come inside so we can show you our love?" We went to the school office where they gave us soft drinks. After visiting awhile they brought in a live sheep and presented it to us. That was quite a surprise! We tied it on top of the Toyota when we went to Jocopampa to teach our Bible Institute classes. While we were teaching, the sheep was tied to the Toyota with a long rope so it could eat grass. The local pastor agreed to care for the sheep by putting it with his flock. For several years we used the lambs from that sheep to provide meat for our Easter conventions.

Another TLC team from Hobe Sound came in 1990. That team included Michael and Ruth Williams as team leaders, Daniel Edwards, Sarah Bowell, Valerie Holdiman, Heidi Weingard, and two Taiwanese girls named Lena and Helen.

The following week I took the group to Sixilla Baja where we had a DVBS and revival services. One little girl came bringing all her handicrafts and papers from the previous year. How she had treasured them! Not only had she treasured the tangible mementos, but she had hidden some of God's Word in her heart and wanted to hear more!

That year the prize for Bible memorization was a small Spanish booklet entitled *Ruthie's Four Hearts* by Ruth Hoien. The book gives a good explanation of the two works of grace in a way that the children can understand. A good number of children earned the prize.

Huarcamarca

"I wish you could start a work in my mother's village," said Florentino, a young married student in the Bible Institute. He was referring to the mountain village of Huarcamarca near the Peruvian border. That started the ball rolling. Irene and I made arrangements to meet Florentino and one of his brothers-in-law in Upper La Paz early one morning to start on the seven-hour journey. While we traveled, we came to where Bolivia's breath-taking, blue gem Lake Titicaca came into view. How beautiful!

I was getting hungry and asked Irene, "Did you pack our lunch?"

"I made it but didn't put it in the car. Did you?"

"No." However, after reaching Vilacala, Florentino spread out cooked steak, fried bananas, and boiled potatoes that his wife had prepared early that morning, so in spite of our forgetfulness, we had a satisfying lunch.

After we ate, we drove to the trailhead and walked down a twisting mountain trail that crossed two mountain ridges and into the high valley where Florentino's mother lived. I played the accordion for the service we held in her yard. Irene brought the message in Spanish, and Florentino interpreted into Aymara. As a result of that service, a village official invited us to begin a work in Huarcamarca. Florentino, Irene, and I then discussed plans with the village leaders. Florentino wanted to personally evangelize that area, but his work and transportation difficulties did not allow him to do so at that time. One man in the village could read, so we left literature with him to share with the people.

Irene preaching during the first service conducted in Huarcamarca in the yard of
Florentino Paco's mother

Following the service we retraced our steps up the mountainous trail to the Toyota. That night we parked the car at the home of Florentino's brother-in-law. Florentino slept in the house with his brother-in-law's family while Irene and I slept in the back of the Toyota. In the morning the ground was white with frost, and ice had

The village leaders of Huarcamarca who invited us to start a church in their village

formed on the metal window frames of our vehicle, but we believed God's work was worth the inconveniences.

By May 1990 the men of the church had begun digging the foundation for the church at Huarcamarca. However, when the rainy season began, the work was postponed until the dry season.

In September our group arrived again in Vilacala as beautiful snowflakes were falling. We spent the night sleeping in the Toyota. It was very cold, but Irene and I had brought our hot water bottles, which we filled and put at the bottom of our sleeping bags. We were more comfortable than on the previous occasion when we had forgotten our hot water bottles.

Sunday morning we drove from Vilacala a few miles to where we parked the Toyota and began the thirty-minute walk down the mountain footpath to the new church site. We found the church ready for the doors, windows, and roof. The people had even laid a foundation for a three-room house for missionaries, evangelists, and pastors who would come to visit. The men had carried the materials down that twisting mountain footpath to the building site on their backs. What dedication to the Lord! That Sunday morning we had a service as usual in the yard of Florentino's mother. At the close of the service, a number of people came forward and knelt on the ground to pray.

Teaching a Sunday school class in Huarcamarca

By that time Florentino was able to go every other weekend to pastor the church. It was only 143 miles from La Paz, but the washboard roads, called *calamina*, meaning corrugated as in tin-roofing material, made the trip difficult. Florentino usually rode on top of a loaded truck, and it sometimes took twelve hours because of mechanical problems and flat tires. Such a trip was exceedingly cold, rough, and tiring.

On July 28, 1991, Irene and I again descended the mountain on the footpath along with Florentino, his wife, Benancia, and their three-year-old adopted daughter, Marlene. As we lifted our eyes, we saw ridge after ridge of mountains displaying various shades of green, blue, and purple. I was intrigued with the exquisite wild flowers at our feet. Just before we reached the end of the path, I said, "Oh, let's just stop a minute and look."

The Florentino Paco family. Florentino was the key to starting a church in Huarcamarca.

Our purpose in going that time was to inspect the new church building. What a fine little church it was. It was built of mud bricks plastered with white stucco and had a tin roof. The ceiling was cloth, the floor was dirt, and the altar and platform were hardened earth. A lovely wooden pulpit stood on the platform. Written in Spanish on a valance across the platform was "Follow peace with all men, and holiness, without which no man shall see the Lord" (Hebrews 12:14).

As we entered the church, I saw some of the congregation kneeling at the altar. I also knelt, and my heart filled with praise to our Redeemer for the privilege of worshiping in our little holiness church in the mountains of Bolivia.

During the service Irene played a small organ as we sang mostly Aymara songs in a minor key, but they sang them joyfully. For the message I spoke from Psalm 118:27, "God is the Lord, which hath shewed us light: bind the sacrifice with cords, even unto the horns of the altar." I explained that it was not nails that held Jesus to the cross but the cords of love and of delighting to do the Father's will. Before the message was completed, people began coming to the altar where they prayed with tears running down their faces.

Quillcoma

Quillcoma, a few miles from our Collana church, is a village made up of four zones covering a large area. A number of people in the Santiago II church in El Alto were from Quillcoma. When some farmland was made into a residential area in 1991, a plot was reserved for a Protestant church. The Santiago II folk asked the missionaries to seize that opportunity and open a church in Quillcoma.

In early September Irene and I visited Quillcoma for the purpose of holding a service and initiating a church. We loaded the Toyota with twelve planks for seats, some poles, two tarpaulins, and rope. The local people carried stones from the river to set at each corner of our plot for identification of property lines. It was snowing when we held our first service.

Later the newly elected secretary of justice of the village wanted to give EFM a better plot of land since the first plot was in a wet area near a stream. He met with the town leaders, school authorities, and missionaries. The village officials agreed to sell EFM a small plot of land on a higher elevation for $47.00 (U.S.).

Many individuals welcomed EFM into the village, and Gregorio Gomez became the pastor for that new work. We rejoiced about one more opening for spreading the gospel and prayed that God would raise up more workers for new areas.

First Bible Institute Graduate

Pedro Guarachi was our first Bible Institute graduate. He had spent six years in the classroom on Saturdays to complete the course of study. James McBryant, a missionary with the Central Friends Mission, gave the commencement address at that first graduation on November 30, 1991. Pedro was forty-six years old, married, and the father of seven children, six still at home. For the last year and a half of his studies, he pastored the church at Jocopampa.

Pedro Guarachi, our first Bible Institute graduate, in 1991

The story of Pedro's conversion began in early 1985. María, Pedro's wife, was very sick, so sick she thought she was going to die. In desperation she went to the witch doctor, and he asked Pedro to give him a lamb to die in María's place. The blood of the lamb was shed, but María did not improve. Next the witch doctor asked for a chicken, coca leaves, alcohol, and cigarettes. He also told María to sleep beside a rabbit. They tried several things. The witch doctor even talked to the devil, but María was still very ill. During her illness María begged Pedro to care for the children and not separate them if she died. In December of that year, María's brother Carmelo, who was the pastor of a neighboring holiness church, witnessed to them.

"You must go to church," he said. "That is where you will find help. Seek God." Instead, Pedro went out and got drunk, and with other drunkards he elected a politician.

"How can you elect an official for our community when you are drunk?" María asked. Later she decided to go to church, and then she really thought she would die. She went to our church in Jocopampa and came home with great joy, whereas Pedro went to the Catholic Church and came home sick at heart.

"Don't go to different churches. Go together to the same church," Carmelo advised.

Pedro decided to visit our church in Jocopampa on Saturday, December 24, 1985. He and María planned to go together at 7:00 p.m., but he discovered his bicycle had been stolen and went to search for it. When they arrived at the church, it was 7:30. Great fear came over Pedro, and he was afraid to go inside. When he heard them singing "Christ Is Searching for Workers," he entered. Trembling, he went to the altar, found pardon, and was overcome with joy. In February

1986 Pedro, with the moral support of his wife, started taking classes at the Bible Institute in Jocopampa, and in the spring of that year, God saw fit to restore María to physical health.

Celebrating Christmas

The Catholic custom at Christmas is for each family to set up the manger scene in their home, sometimes devoting a whole room to that purpose. Those nativity scenes are usually decorated with Christmas lights.

During that time poor children, dressed as shepherds, walk the streets playing homemade instruments. Their favorite instrument is the *chulluchullu,* which is made from bottle caps that were placed on train tracks for flattening and then nailed to a piece of wood. The children go from house to house shaking their *chulluchullus* and singing and dancing in front of the nativity scenes. It is believed that those children bring blessings upon the home, and the owners give them fruit, cookies, and candy.

On Christmas Eve most Bolivians go to the Catholic Church at midnight to celebrate the "mass of the rooster." It is believed that when Jesus was born, a rooster crowed, and all the animals except the pig came to worship. Accordingly, the pig was cursed, and that is why the pig cannot lift his head to look up.

For the Christmas mass people bring the image of Baby Jesus, and sometimes their whole nativity scene, to be blessed by the priest. He sprinkles holy water on the Baby Jesus. After mass they return home to eat *picaña*, which is beef, lamb, and chicken cooked with carrots, potatoes, and corn along with *aji amarillo*, a yellow, slightly hot sauce.

One year Marisol gave the following testimony: "We used to celebrate Christmas according to the beliefs of another religion. For us the birth of Jesus was very sacred. The images of Jesus, Mary, and Joseph were handled with reverence and respect. We really believed Jesus was born on that night, and that each year He is born again on Christmas Eve.

"After we came to know Jesus, our beliefs underwent a radical change. We no longer believe that Jesus is born every December 24. We stopped decorating the manger scene. Our Christmas is different now. We remember the birth of God as man, but we await His return as our sovereign King."

Furlough Time and Shoes

One day in early December Irene said to me, "Your father is getting up in years. Why don't you plan a short furlough during summer vacation from Bible school?" South of the equator summer vacation comes during the Christmas season. I contacted the home office and received permission for a brief furlough.

I had been serving as pastor of the church in Bolognia. In preparation for my leaving, it was decided that the congregation would elect a Bolivian to serve as pastor. They chose Fernando, more often called Nano, who had married Marisol. Nano and Marisol had been some of the mission's first converts when the Bolognia church was started by Frank and Leah Klassen. Those two young people had served as Sunday school teachers and youth leaders, and now they would lead that congregation.

Late in December of 1991, I left Bolivia for another three-month furlough. The end of January my stepmother entered the hospital and passed away on February 12. God then worked it out for me to take my father with me on deputation services for a week. We had a wonderful time traveling together. On February 23 at the Wesleyan

Nano, first national pastor of our church in Bosque de Bolognia, with his wife, Marisol, and their daughter, Sara

Holiness Church in St. Louis, Michigan, Fred Starr asked me, "Faith, when are you going back to Bolivia?"

"Well, I am scheduled to go on March 17 and I have my ticket, but I will go when Jesus wills. I cannot leave until I have my father well cared for."

Fred continued, "I am lonely. I live alone and I have room." After talking more with him and discussing it with his married daughter on whose property his mobile home was parked, it was agreed that Papa would go and live there. Since my father had a place to stay, I continued with my plans to return to Bolivia on March 17. Later Papa left Michigan and went to live with my brother in Windsor, Indiana.

Shortly before I left for furlough, Irene admonished me, "Faith, your shoes are getting to look rather shabby. Be sure to get yourself another pair while you are home." Something prevented me from getting them, and I returned to the field without new shoes.

Irene inquired, "Did you get new shoes?"

"No."

"Now what are you going to do?"

"I don't know. Pray, I guess." So I prayed, "Lord, would you please give me a pair of new shoes?"

Later Carrie Boyer wrote, "Faith, you must really need shoes. People keep giving me shoes for you."

Lyndal and Rebecca Black with their girls Alecia and Leah came to Bolivia as new missionaries in June 1992. Lyndal told me he had shoes for me but thought he would not give them to me until Christmas.

"OK," I replied.

On Christmas Day I was given five pair of shoes: one black pair, one gray pair, one blue pair, one maroon pair, and one tan pair. "I would never have thought of buying blue shoes," I acknowledged, "but I did have blue outfits." My God had once again answered in His abundant manner!

Chapter 16

Church Advancements
1992-1996

Light in the Darkness

Shortly after I returned to Bolivia in March 1992, Florentino, Irene, and I went to Huarcamarca for special weekend services. When we arrived at the beginning of the trail that led to Huarcamarca, Florentino and Irene started walking down the mountain before darkness came. Carlos, a village boy, went with them, and Irene planned to send their two flashlights back with him. I waited in the Toyota for men to come and get the large baskets of food we had, which included baked meat, potatoes, and bananas for our noon meal the next day. A group of at least one hundred people would be eating together.

For a long time I sat alone in the mission Toyota. Daylight had vanished, and I peered into the darkness searching for Carlos with the two flashlights and praying for our church men to come. At last to my great relief, I saw two tiny lights coming up the mountain. However, it was not Carlos, but the men carrying kerosene lanterns and coming for the food. How happy I was to accompany them down the mountain. Surely Carlos would meet us along the way.

The meal served in Huarcamarca at the time of the special services. The food was in baskets placed on the ground.

Enrique, a boy of thirteen, took my hand while in his right hand he carried one of the lanterns. The men followed behind single file with loads on their backs, and the other lantern was carried by the last man.

Pastor Florentino's stepfather was with us, and as the night grew darker, he called out, "To the right," and we stepped right. Later, "To the left," and we went left. "Now straight ahead." We followed his every command, stepping in the small circle of light from the lantern.

"Enrique, this reminds me that Jesus is the Light of the World. Have you given your heart and life to Him?" I asked.

"Yes," he replied.

"We must let Him lead us along life's path just as you are leading me now."

I was happy to reach Enrique's home. I noticed that his mother stood by the stone wall watching our approach. Just then Carlos appeared from the other direction carrying the two flashlights, so I told Enrique he could stay home, and Carlos would help me the rest of the way.

"No, son," Enrique's mother replied. "You go and help the *señorita* down the mountain." Enrique continued to hold my right hand, and Carlos took my left. Finally, we reached Irene and learned that she, too, had been caught in the darkness, but Florentino's mother had come and thrown pieces of burning straw on the bare ground to lighten the path for them for the last part of the way.

The next morning we had a baby dedication, and Enrique's parents wanted him to be dedicated also since he had not been dedicated as an

Dedication of Enrique

225

infant. What a thrill it was for me to present Enrique to the Great Shepherd, the One who is the Light of the World! I prayed that Enrique might always walk in step with Jesus.

Lucio's Death

Nestor and Lucio's mother had passed away just a few weeks before the brothers were severely burned in a house fire. Early on a Sunday morning Nestor's father called to tell us of seven-year-old Lucio's death. Irene and I had a wedding planned for that day as well as the regular services at Alto San Antonio. We decided that Irene would take care of the wedding, and I would take care of the funeral. Marjorie Hall, a visiting missionary from another mission group in Tarija, Bolivia, kindly accepted responsibility in my place for the services in Alto San Antonio. The Richard Smiths were also visiting from the same mission work as Marjorie. The Smiths took me to the Children's Hospital in La Paz where we met Nestor's father, got Lucio's body, and then went to the community of Belén.

Heartrending cries broke out as we entered the one-room house with the body of Lucio. Fifteen-year-old Nestor cried especially hard. I put my arms around him as he lay on a bed nursing his badly burned leg.

"Oh, Lucio wasn't bad!" Nestor cried. "He was a good little boy! Why did he die?"

Jesus came to my rescue as I began to tell him that Lucio was now in heaven enjoying eternal life. I told him about Jesus, the streets of gold, the river of life, the tree of life, and the love and joy in heaven.

"Is Lucio happy then?" Nestor asked.

"Oh, yes, he is very happy, and he is not suffering anymore," I replied. Nestor smiled broadly and dried his tears.

I then went to the Jocopampa church property to get wood for them to make a coffin. The family had so little in their house, and I did not want them trying to make a coffin from their furniture. After we returned with the wood, the men built a small coffin. During the service I explained the way of salvation and told them that anyone could see Lucio again if he yielded to Christ. God met with us, and Nestor, his father, and another man gave their hearts to Jesus.

TLC Team in 1992

Joy Budensiek was the leader of the TLC team that came from Hobe Sound, Florida, in the summer of 1992. A few days later four of the team members—Tom McCall, Jason Martain, Rebecca Patterson, and Julie Budensiek, the daughter of Joy—joined me in the Toyota for a trip to Sixilla Baja for DVBS and revival services. I anticipated the thrill of showing them the beautiful, snow-capped Mount Illimani, and I was not disappointed in their reaction as we rounded the curve and saw that awesome sight.

Road to Sixilla Baja with Mount Illimani in the background

Unfortunately, we arrived in Sixilla Baja after dark. Pastor Francisco met us, and he and several others were anxious to show us the new road they were making on the ascent to the mission property. I saw immediately that more work needed to be done before we could drive to the top.

Ruben, a young married man from our Bolognia church, had joined us. We unloaded the supplies from the Toyota and put up Ruben's tent for the young men. Then we checked the mission house where the ladies would be staying and found it had been swept clean.

Boys and girls came early the next morning for DVBS. They knew what to expect since that would be our fourth DVBS in Sixilla Baja. That year's theme was "The Creation Story."

"Si yo fuera una mariposa, Te daria grascias por mis alas!" meaning "If I were a butterfly, I'd give You thanks for my wings!" rang out over the thin air as the children sang. As I looked over the group, I noticed there were few tiny tots and mentioned it to the pastor. "They are growing up," Francisco said. Then I thought of the past years and how many of the children had prayed, and God had changed their lives.

Each evening the light from the pressure lantern scattered the darkness on the patio. After a rousing song service Tom McCall preached. I enjoyed interpreting the messages into Spanish and then listening to Francisco interpreting them into Aymara. During the day Tom and Jason worked on a section of the road that the men were building.

Joy Budensiek and the other six members of the TLC team remained with Irene in Bolognia to help at the Gran Poder church with a DVBS during the day and anniversary revival services in the evening. Seventy children attended that DVBS. Lyndal and Rebecca Black with their daughters, Alecia and Leah, had just arrived a few weeks previously, and Lyndal was scheduled to do the preaching. However, he was ill, and Irene had to get substitutes for the first few nights. Thankfully, by the weekend he was able to preach. For the closing service on Sunday, the church was packed with people from most of our *altiplano* or high plateau churches. We were thankful that there were seekers in most services.

Easter Convention

The day before Easter in 1993, I was walking across the compound in Jocopampa when I heard the sound of a big bus like a Greyhound called a *flota*. I hurried to see if it was the Cochabamba people, and sure enough, the Lyndal Black family and fifty-eight Quechua Indians disembarked. They had been riding for six and one-half hours.

Earlier in the day the people from Sixilla Baja had arrived and had been given the Bible Institute classrooms for their domain for the weekend. Irene and a few pastors had gone to Chacoma to get wooden planks and sheepskins. The planks were to be used for seating the large crowd, and the sheepskins were for the *Cochabambinos* to put under their bedrolls on the cold, cement floor of the church.

228

Pastor Pedro and his church people had been very busy preparing for the convention. One woman who herded sheep donated several for the meals. On Saturday morning I went into the church to wash the windows, and when I looked outside, I saw some sheep being butchered on the patio. I quickly went to the other side of the church to wash those windows instead! Once the sheep are butchered and cooked, I can enjoy eating them, but I cannot watch them being killed. The Saturday evening meal was soup made from the intestines and stomachs of the sheep. Sunday morning the *micros*, which are small buses, arrived from the churches in El Alto, Bosque de Bolognia, and from faraway Huarcamarca. About four hundred representatives from all the churches of EFM in Bolivia gathered for another celebration of our Lord's resurrection.

Lyndal Black preached in the morning and Pastor Florentino in the afternoon. Each church group presented a special song in the afternoon, and in the middle of those specials, a young man from Cochabamba wanted to give his heart to Jesus. That afternoon we had a message, two altar services, a healing service, an exhortation from another pastor, and a number of specials.

The Jocopampa people served refreshments to the Quechuas and the Blacks before they boarded the bus and started home. Lyndal thought his people would be "sung out" by then, but they continued singing until they arrived in Cochabamba at 12:45 a.m.

The morning following the convention Pastor Francisco came to La Paz. The Food for the Hungry organization had given our Mission food to distribute to the needy, and we were able to supply him with flour, cornmeal, soy mix, cracked wheat, sugar, and salt. He took those supplies with him when he returned to Sixilla Baja by bus.

A month later when Irene and I went to Sixilla Baja, the people were having their fruit harvest. They shared their peaches and pears with us and thanked us for all the food we had helped to provide for them.

Cholera had been sweeping through Bolivia for nearly two years. In the early part of 1993, it reached Sixilla Baja. We prayed that it would not affect any of the Christians. Many in the community contracted cholera and several died, but not one of the Christians even got sick!

Reports on Churches and Pastors

Irene and I rejoiced to see the churches growing and the people going deeper spiritually. I was happy that the church in Bolognia was giving fifty percent of their tithes to support Pastor Fernando, Marisol, and little Sara. The rest of their tithes was being saved for building a church.

* * * * *

When I first went to Bolivia, David Mamani was living with his parents in Collana. His father pastored our church there for a number of years, and Frank Klassen used to say he hoped that some day David would be a pastor. Now David and his wife, Manuela, were pastoring our church in Gran Poder. Their home had been blessed with a little daughter named María Eojenia. The Gran Poder church was near several housing projects, and the church conducted Daily Vacation Bible Schools for children living in the area.

Gran Poder church

* * * * *

In May 1993 Irene and I again made the seven-hour trip from La Paz to Huarcamarca. After we traveled all day, we were happy to unpack our supplies and get settled for the night. Stepping outside in the darkness, I was thrilled to see the sky thickly peppered with the most beautiful stars. They looked like diamonds. As I gazed into the sky, I saw I was right under the Milky Way. Truly the heavens declare the glory of God and the earth shows forth His handiwork!

The next morning as I was sitting on a high rock overlooking the adobe church, I held my breath as four alpaca ran and slid down some steep rocks, landing far below without mishap. I was thrilled to see all that had been accomplished on the mission property since our

Church and visitors' residence in Huarcamarca with Florentino's mother's house on the right

last visit. The building near the church was completed, and we now had a room of our own. A social organization had piped water into the area and installed a faucet near our buildings.

* * * * *

On a cold July evening, winter in the southern hemisphere, Irene and I taught our Bible Institute classes. We then visited the home of Angel and Victoria, young newlyweds. Angel had gone to a fiesta where he had been drinking, and as he was going home, he felt he was being chased by demons. He lay under the covers on his bed with his wife sitting beside him.

A number of Christians gathered in the home, played musical instruments, and sang songs about the blood of Jesus. We then had prayer during which time Angel prayed and was reclaimed. When we were preparing to leave, Angel's father asked us to stay for refreshments. He served everyone hot tea and bread. Angel never had a problem with demons after that night.

231

* * * * *

The last weekend of September Irene and I with some of our believers made the long trip to Huarcamarca, that time through fog so dense that we had to look out our side windows to see the road. Since we could not visit that work in the summer during the rainy season when the roads are nearly impassable, we needed to visit now to hold church elections and install officers for the new year. While we were there, I held a short DVBS for the children. Two of the sessions had to be held outside in the churchyard because other services were being conducted in the church. The fog was so dense that it was like a drizzle, but the children still enjoyed the DVBS.

* * * * *

Ceferino, assistant pastor of the church at Cosmo 79, asked EFM to start a church in his home village of Sullcavi. Within a few weeks Irene and I accompanied him and his wife to Sullcavi. Eight families expressed their interest in having a church started, and Ceferino's mother was among the eight.

"I am so thrilled at the prospect of having a church in my village," said that widowed mother. "My children and I used to walk nine miles to attend a church, but now I am too old to walk that far!" Many lives have been touched in that area through the church that was built by EFM.

Visiting Huarcamarca

We were preparing for another trip to Huarcamarca in 1994. On a bright fall day Irene and I traveled to El Alto to meet Pastor Pascual and several others who would be going with us. Before we left the city, we stopped to buy bread and fruit for our trip. Irene remained in the car while I went with the others to buy food. She had given me money, so I left my purse in the car.

It is a common practice for the nationals to distract someone's attention and then steal from that person. While we were shopping, vandals started throwing stones at the Toyota, so Irene took the keys out of the ignition and locked her door as she got out of the car to check for damage. Immediately someone reached in the door on the driver's side that I had left unlocked and grabbed my purse.

The crowd began screaming at the thief, who was already in a minibus headed for La Paz, and he dropped the purse out the window into the middle of the street. Someone from the crowd retrieved it, and to our amazement, nothing had been taken. The people clamored for recompense for their part in getting my purse back, so I gave each of them a small reward. We were reminded once again how we constantly need God's protection.

During that visit we conducted a DVBS. Irene and I asked the public school teachers Martha and Celia to bring their students on Friday. We were pleased when they brought sixty children and stayed the entire day. Martha, the head teacher, took notes as she listened to the program. Both teachers came back to revival services on Saturday and Sunday.

Public school children from Huarcamarca with their teachers Martha and Celia who attended a one-day DVBS

"The Word of God is wonderful!" Martha exclaimed. We came to realize that she was hearing it for the first time. What a thrill it was for me to preach the Word to first-time hearers! How I longed for the salvation of Martha and Celia.

Later that year two nationals, Irene, and I endeavored to visit Huarcamarca again but failed to reach our destination because of two flat tires and a loose screw in the alternator that caused our battery to discharge. After we spent a frightening night in the area where highway robbers hide out, we were happy when daylight came. Anxiously we waited for help from a passing vehicle. Praise God, one stopped and the driver helped us get the Toyota turned around and headed back to La Paz. Our hopes of reaching Huarcamarca on that trip had vanished.

We had the car pushed several times, but each time the motor ran for only a short distance. It finally became clear that the Toyota would not make it back to La Paz. Two men offered to take one or two of our group back toward La Paz to a public phone. Pastor Pascual from our Huarcamarca church and I were chosen to go.

Irene and a Bible Institute student stayed with the vehicle. Irene's fears for Pascual and me were aroused when the student asked, "Did you notice that that truck did not have a license plate either on the front or on the back?" So they prayed earnestly for our protection.

Pascual climbed in the back of the truck while I rode up front with the two strangers. In my heart I pled with God for His hand of protection. On the way those two men heard the story of redemption thickly sprinkled with verses from God's Word.

As we passed through each community, I looked anxiously for the promised telephone. None appeared. They had said it was not far away, but we were on the road for two hours before one came into sight. When we finally saw the sign indicating a public phone, how my heart rejoiced! As we climbed out of the pickup truck and said our good-byes, I offered to pay for our ride. However, the men graciously declined.

F. Tropical

The Lyndal Black family started visiting our work in the town of F. Tropical in the province of Chapare in early 1993. Shortly thereafter the congregation, which was meeting on the front porch of a house, wanted to have a church building. The Mission purchased land, and with financial help from the States they were able to build a church on the property. Since it was located in the hot, steamy jungle, the church had iron bars on the windows instead of glass.

Aurelio Choqui, the main builder of the F. Tropical church, had been saved as a result of his contact with EFM in that area. He and

Felix Vargas, a faithful lay preacher, pastored the flock. Aurelio and his family lived on the open back porch of the house that had been used for services. He owned a piece of property in another place in the province of Chapare, but instead of developing the land he owned, he chose to live in F. Tropical so he could pastor those for whom he was burdened. He and his family experienced hard tropical rains, heat, and at times cold air from the South Pole.

By October 1994 the F. Tropical church was ready to be dedicated, and Irene and I accompanied the Blacks to the special service. During our visits to that area, we became well acquainted with Aurelio and appreciated the great sacrifice he was making. At that time he did not know how much his sacrifice was going to cost him, for later the local authorities confiscated his property and sold it to someone else because he had not built on it. That sometimes happened in the developing areas of Bolivia.

With Irene in the mission apartment in Bolognia in 1995

Events Following My Return

I returned from a three-month furlough in March 1995 in time for the Easter services. Some of our believers traveled many miles to be present at Jocopampa. J. Stevan Manley, the new president and director of EFM, had come for his first visit to Bolivia, and he preached the Easter morning message.

The noon meal consisted of Bolivian-style potatoes and mutton stew. Lyndal Black spoke in the afternoon service, and then representatives from each of the fourteen churches sang specials. President Manley later commented about how the people love to sing and how difficult it was for each congregation to limit itself to one song.

* * * * *

During the heavy rains in 1995, ground began shifting in the La Paz suburb of Tupac Amaru. Our congregation there was renting a small room in the house of Juan, one of the believers. Soon his house began to crack because of the shifting ground. Thankfully, he was able to salvage the building materials from the part of his house that was damaged. The small room where services were conducted was not affected. However, since he lacked the funds to rebuild his living quarters, he negotiated with EFM to advance him rent money so that he could build a new addition to his house.

Roofings are special occasions in Bolivia, and Pastor Atanacio invited Irene and me to join them for their roofing celebration. The pastor came down the mudslide and aided me as I climbed to Juan's house. Then he retraced his steps and helped Irene climb the mudslide. Though the climb was difficult, the descent afterwards was even more difficult!

* * * * *

In 1996 we had our first Sunday school in Sacaba in the Cochabamba district. We who have attended Sunday school all our lives can hardly imagine the anticipation of attending for the first time. How excited the children were! A lady in our Bolognia church contributed money to buy crayons, and I photocopied pictures for the children to color. They eagerly took their colored pictures home and put them on the walls. Within a short time we purchased Sunday school quarterlies for three age groups and sent them to Sacaba.

Irene's Dedication

Irene and I had been fervently praying for the Lord to send someone to come and help me since Irene was retiring from service overseas. God answered those prayers by sending Lloyd and Ruth (Franklin) Gordon who arrived in May 1996. They came to help us for a year. Previously, Ruth had worked with EFM in Egypt and Eritrea. After she left Eritrea, she trained as a teacher and then taught in Christian day schools. Eventually she married Lloyd, a skilled carpenter and mechanic. After the Gordons arrived, I flew with them to Cochabamba and stayed with them over Sunday. They remained there for about another six weeks because Cochabamba is at a lower altitude than La Paz, and they needed time to adjust before moving to the higher altitude. Since the Lyndal Blacks were no longer in Bolivia, the people of Cochabamba pled with the Gordons to stay there, but they were needed in La Paz. At that time EFM had at least twenty congregations worshiping in different areas of the province of La Paz.

On a Sunday afternoon in July, Irene and I took the Gordons with us to an anniversary service at Gran Poder on the high plains of Bolivia. Most of the crowd of nearly two hundred had not come inside yet, so we were able to get a good seat near the front. The west windows were catching the afternoon sun and warmed us for which we were thankful.

Lloyd and Ruth were amused by all the special songs. Even though the nine singing groups were told the service needed to end by 5:00, some could not limit themselves to one special. It was 5:20 when the special singing ended, and then the pastor announced they would have three more congregational songs before they closed. They had five instead. How those people love to sing!

The Gordons joined Irene and me in attending two more anniversary services before Irene left Bolivia. The first one was at Villa Tunari where the newly organized church band was playing outside the church when we arrived. That band was composed of seven men who traveled to our various churches for special occasions. In that service I spoke on "The Way That Leads to Heaven" using Isaiah 35:8 and Matthew 7:14-15. Many came to the altar to pray just as they had at Gran Poder.

A few Sundays later we attended the fourth anniversary service at Chapari in the province of Cochabamba. There I officiated at a baby dedication in the morning service. After a good meal we went to the river where six candidates were baptized.

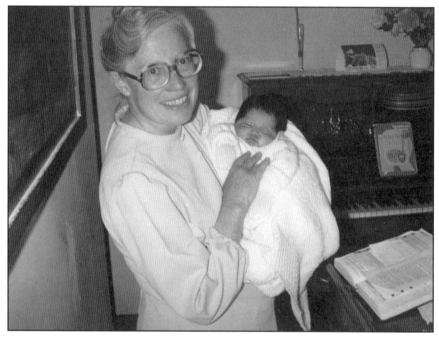

Holding one of the many babies I dedicated in Bolivia

In April 1997 it was necessary for me to take another three-month sick leave. At the same time Lloyd and Ruth Gordon returned to the States leaving no missionary in Bolivia during my absence. I returned in July. Irene Maurer, realizing that there was too much work for me to do by myself, offered to return to help me. The EFM Board of Directors accepted her offer, and she returned to Bolivia in September of that year.

Chapter 17

Concluding My Overseas Missionary Labors 1997-2001

First EFM Camp Meeting in Bolivia

Our first Faith Mission indoor camp meeting in Bolivia was to be held at the Santiago II church in El Alto. For some time I had been praying, "Lord, couldn't you send us a good pianist like the Central Friends have?" The Lord saw fit to answer that prayer by sending Sandra Miller. She came to help us for a short time and arrived just in time for our first camp meeting!

For months our people had been looking forward to the first service. Leonard Sankey from Bedford, Indiana, was scheduled to be our guest speaker. When he arrived in October 1997, his first reaction while looking out the plane window was that Bolivia looked more like a "moonscape than a landscape." He had been accustomed to the lush countryside of Central America where he had worked for a number of years as a missionary with EFM.

Leonard had asked the Faith Mission Church where he pastored in Bedford to pray that he would be able to speak upon his arrival without having to take days to adjust to the high altitude. After resting for a few hours, he was able to preach in the Tuesday evening prayer meeting on the day he arrived.

Leonard knew Spanish well, and it was a blessing not to need to interpret for him. Wednesday was a day of rest. The camp meeting started on Thursday and continued until Sunday with two services each day. The people worked during the day, so not many were able to attend the morning services. However, the evening services were much better attended with seekers each evening.

On Monday following the camp meeting, Leonard, Sandra, Cici our house girl, Irene, and I picnicked beside Lake Titicaca, and on Tuesday we went down to the Cochabamba area with its typical Latin American ambience. Leonard's immediate response was, "I could live here!" On Wednesday he preached in our Sacaba church and Thursday in the F. Tropical church in the lush, green jungle area

Leonard Sankey preaching in the Santiago II church during our first indoor camp meeting in Bolivia

of Bolivia. On Friday we waved good-bye from the Cochabamba airport as he returned home.

My Needs Abundantly Supplied

Irene and I had ministered in our church in Sixilla Baja, and while there I lost the filling from a tooth. As we were climbing the steep ascent out of the valley on our way home to Bosque de Bolognia, I was concerned. I had no money to pay a dentist to fix the tooth and was fearful that before I would have the necessary funds, the tooth would completely crumble.

There was another concern that was even more pressing. My father was now an elderly man who had served as a holiness preacher for many years and had no money saved for his funeral expenses. Repeatedly, he and my mother had sold out to follow God. Soon I would need money to pay for his funeral. All I knew to do was to cry to my heavenly Father who promised to supply all my needs. That is what I did with tears. I knew I was not trusting as I should, but admitting that to my heavenly Father, I turned it all over to Him.

A few days later when I went to the post office in La Paz to get our mail, I had a surprise awaiting me. Among my letters was a long white envelope with a return address unknown to me. When I got home, I opened the envelope, and to my shock discovered a check for $10,000! It had been sent as regular mail instead of registered mail. I showed the check to Irene and asked, "Irene, does this check say what I think it says?"

"Why, yes! It's $10,000!" Irene replied.

James and Grace Fulton of the Central Friends Mission happened to be visiting us at the time. I showed it to them and asked the same question. In amazement they also assured me that indeed it was a check for $10,000.

While reading the enclosed letter, I learned that the writer was the pastor of my Aunt Lillian Hemmeter, the wife of my father's only brother, Virgil. Uncle Virgil had died some time before, and Aunt Lillian had asked her pastor to send the money to me as a gift from them.

The money was enough to have my tooth fixed and to purchase a prepaid funeral for my father from the Miller Mortuary in Farmland, Indiana. It included the expenses of having his body transported after the funeral in Indiana to Cedar Crest Cemetery near Gladwin, Michigan, to be buried beside Mama. In addition, my heavenly Father knew I desired to have a couple of suitcases with wheels on them. There was enough money left to cover that expense also.

Daddy's Home Going

On June 29, 1998, I received a phone call from Charity Faith Hemmeter Davis, my niece, telling me that my father had gone to be with Jesus. The evening before, my brother, John, and his wife, Margey, and all their family had gathered in the nursing home in Muncie, Indiana, to visit Daddy. John's son, Walter, later told me that it was almost like a camp meeting. He said that my father spoke to everyone and asked if they were going to be ready to meet him in heaven. No one realized then that Jesus would take him home the next day.

Later that evening Daddy asked for ice cream and Coke. They gave him diet Coke, which he refused and said he wanted the same kind they drank. The next afternoon Daddy laid down to take a nap, and the Lord took him to heaven while he slept.

I left La Paz on June 30 to return to the States for Daddy's funeral. It was such a relief to know that the arrangements for his funeral were already made. Roy Norton had been so helpful in getting that business done ahead of time. The funeral was held in Farmland, Indiana, on July 2. Daddy looked like a statesman in his casket.

One of the administrators from the nursing home came to the viewing, and I thanked her for all she had done for my father. She responded, "Thank you for letting us have him. He read the Bible to us." She also said that my father had told her that God had revealed to him that he would not live to see July 1.

Daddy had attended the Dunkirk Friends Church when he was able, and Wayne Covert, his pastor, conducted the funeral. It was a rather small funeral, but a number of well-known ministers attended, including J. Stevan Manley. The next day Carrie Boyer took me to Michigan for the burial where Daddy was buried beside Mama. Nathan D. Shockley, pastor of the Wesleyan Holiness Church in St. Louis, Michigan, conducted the graveside service. Gertrude Campbell read a lovely poem she had written in honor of my father, Walter Nelson Hemmeter. He had lived a godly life and was ready to meet his Maker.

Carrie and I returned to Bedford, and I stayed with her until I went back to Bolivia on July 21. We enjoyed reminiscing about our missionary labors not realizing that would be our last time together.

Second Bolivian Camp Meeting

Glen and Helen Reiff arrived in September 1998 to help in our second, indoor camp meeting, which was held in our Santiago II church. We certainly appreciated their labors among us. One day Helen conducted a teacher-training seminar for our Sunday school workers. I was happy to have Glen teach one of my classes in the Bible Institute. In the evening services he shared a series of illustrated lessons called "God's X-rays of People's Hearts" with seekers each evening. The Reiffs also attended an anniversary service at our Quillcoma church during which time Glen dedicated the new church building and ordained Lorenzo Salinas.

Carrie Boyer's Funeral

During February 1999 we were attending a three-day seminar on soul winning in our Villa Tunari church. On Friday afternoon of the seminar, I went to La Paz to transact some business. When I returned home and entered the backdoor of our house, Irene's first words were, "Faith, sit down."

I thought, *Why is she telling me to sit down? She never tells me that.* However, I sat down. Then she told me that Geneva Ramsey had just called from the home office and said that Carrie Boyer had passed away. My first response was, "Oh, I want to go, too!" I meant that if she had gone to heaven, and I knew she had, I wanted to go also.

Irene responded, "Oh, Faith, don't talk that way." Realizing the close friendship that I had with Carrie, Irene suggested that I call the home office and talk to President Manley. When I called, he thought I should come home for the funeral.

I left La Paz on Saturday morning, February 13, and arrived in Indianapolis, Indiana, the following day. Russtom Gebremichael and Salas, his wife, along with Aroda Idris and Elisha Awate were at the airport to meet me. What a joy it was to see those Eritreans again who were now living in Indianapolis. Together we rode to Bedford and went directly to the Day and Carter Mortuary arriving in time for the viewing. The funeral was held the next day in Bedford, and then Carrie's body was taken to Pennsylvania for burial.

Stifanos Almedom, Mesgun Tedla, and I traveled to Pennsylvania with J. Stevan Manley and his wife to be present for the committal service. On Wednesday, February 17, we gathered at the Evangelical Methodist Cemetery near Richfield where Carrie's body was laid to rest. As we returned to Bedford, we reminisced about the wonderful, selfless missionary she had been.

Soon it was time for me to return to my labors in Bolivia. I arrived in La Paz on February 26.

Arrival of Gaynell Thacker and the Budensieks

Twelve grandchildren and their parents gathered at the Indianapolis airport on August 2, 1999, to bid Gaynell Thacker farewell. She was coming to help us in Bolivia as a short-term missionary secretary. Irene and I met her night flight at the El Alto airport. She had been traveling for 26 hours and was so weary that she had difficulty locating her passport.

Gaynell arrived on August 3, my birthday, and I felt she was a **wonderful** birthday gift. She came to help me since Irene Maurer was retiring from the work in Bolivia. On the way to the mission house, Gaynell saw the many steps leading up to the various houses. "Is our house on level ground where we can get to it without going up a hundred steps?" she asked.

"Yes," was the glad reply.

Shortly after Gaynell arrived, Irene returned to the States after serving for more than fifty years with EFM. She had faithfully labored in Egypt, Eritrea, and Bolivia. She would do some traveling in deputation for the Mission but be considered semiretired.

* * * * *

Mark and Nancy Budensiek had contacted EFM in 1997 and inquired about returning to Eritrea. However, a year later a border war between Eritrea and Ethiopia was still continuing. The

Budensieks then asked if there was another field where they might labor. About that time I was in my room praying and asking God to send a missionary man to be over the churches. Without any premeditation the words came out of my mouth, "Couldn't you send us Mark Budensiek?"

Not long afterward the phone rang. President Manley was on the line. "Guess what, Faith? Mark and Nancy Budensiek want to work with EFM again. Since the door to Eritrea has

Mark and Nancy Budensiek who helped in Bolivia during their retirement years

244

not opened for them, they are willing to help us in Bolivia." What a direct answer to my prayer!

Glenda Kempa accompanied the Budensieks to Bolivia on October 18. She was a senior at the Wesleyan Holiness Bible College in Point Pleasant, West Virginia, and was coming to do her eight-week mission internship. Gaynell and I gave them a hearty welcome at the airport in El Alto, after waiting for them for four hours because their plane had been diverted to Santa Cruz. We had brought both mission vehicles to the airport to get them and their luggage. Glenda rode with Gaynell and the Budensieks rode with me.

A group was protesting against the government and blocking the main highway, so Gaynell and I drove on back roads hoping to avoid blockades. We came to a place where stones were across the road. While we pondered what to do, a taxi came to the blockade and turned around. We decided to follow, and the taxi driver led us to a very steep road that took us into La Paz. Later we encountered another group of protestors but were able to find another way to the mission compound. How happy the Budensieks and Glenda were to arrive safely in Bolognia!

After enjoying a meal together, Gaynell and I took the Budensieks to the house where they would be living. The Central Friends missionaries were allowing the Budensieks to rent their house that was just three blocks from ours. Glenda would be staying with us. That evening in the local church the three newcomers were asked to stand at the front of the church while the congregation sang a welcome song. Then each person greeted them with a handshake and often a hug.

Two New Churches

It is necessary for all our churches to have guards to keep thieves from stealing musical instruments and sound systems. Severo, our guard at the Villa Tunari church, moved with his wife to Bautista Saavedra, another part of El Alto, and asked EFM to start a church in that area. Services were started under a canvas that was draped over a wall. Later, in August 1995 we held a tent meeting and several sought the Lord. In January 1996 I held our first DVBS in Bautista Saavedra. For that DVBS the Severos vacated one room of their

DVBS children in the Saavedra church

house. The children filled it to overflowing. The Severos then vacated part of a second room. Soon both rooms were filled. The Bible story, scripture memorization, and singing were conducted with wall-to-wall children. My helper and I hardly had a place to stand. The little ones sat on backless benches as they worked in their workbooks and then knelt on the cold floor and used their benches as tables on which to do their crafts.

Later the congregation rented a building for its services, and we used that for our second DVBS, but it also was crowded with children. A neighbor offered the use of his garage for the classes for the little ones. That year it again was wall-to-wall boys and girls. I did my best to keep the children from stampeding as they raced to get a place to sit on the backless benches.

How thrilled I was to see the members of the Saavedra congregation working on the foundation for their church building when I visited in May 2001. They had made bricks of mud and straw and now had enough to begin building. Later, donations from the States helped to purchase rafters, roofing, window frames, and doors. When Irene and I returned in April 2003 for a visit, we had the privilege of worshiping in the newly completed church although it still had a dirt floor.

* * * * *

In early 1997 a new church was opened in the community of 25 de Julio. Those people had been attending the Villa Tunari church, but their numbers had increased to the point that there was a problem with them staying in Tunari between services on Sunday. Also at night it was hard for those with little ones to ford the river between Villa Tunari and 25 de Julio. They asked if they could start a church in their community. I consulted with the Villa Tunari congregation, and it was agreed that starting a work in 25 de Julio would be a wise thing to do.

Our people in 25 de Julio started their services in a room that belonged to Luciano Lopez. The room was so narrow that the benches had to be put in sideways. Often people had to stand in the street to listen because the room could not accommodate them. Eventually the group purchased a store building that faced a street and there was enough land behind it on which to build a church. The congregation decided not to put a floor in the store building though they had the money to do so. They thought it best to wait and use that money to help build a church, which they did later.

Events During 2000

The first full week of January 2000 Mark and Nancy Budensiek, Gaynell Thacker, and I went to Jocopampa for a week of DVBS and special evening services. Each morning Gaynell and I went to the Sullcavi church to hold a DVBS. Thirty children from that farming area attended. They were well behaved and showed their enjoyment for the Bible stories and activities. In the afternoon we had a DVBS in Jocopampa where approximately fifty children attended.

For almost a week we lived without electricity or running water and cooked on a gas hot plate. Gaynell fixed breakfast, and Mark and Nancy prepared the noon meal. Nancy said it was quite an interesting experience. When she was asked to help with the singing, she searched for a song she could sing in Spanish. "Hal-le-lu" was the perfect solution, and the children enjoyed the motions, but Nancy found them exhausting at that altitude. Mark preached for the evening services and on Sunday morning. I interpreted for him from English to Spanish and another person from Spanish to Aymara.

The second week of January my helpers and I conducted Daily Vacation Bible Schools in the Villa Adela and 25 de Julio churches. That year the lessons were on the judges of Israel.

The Christians of Bolivia were desirous to see God move in their country. Pastor Florentino, field committee president, called for fasting services the first Saturday of each month. On February 5, God met with us and gave us spiritual feasting during our time of fasting.

Pastor Mariano Apaza decided to go a step further and called his people to a day of prayer and fasting on the following Sunday. His people were not content to stay at their church, but they walked more than five miles out onto the high plains to a desert place to pray and fast. Florentino and the other missionaries rode with me in the Toyota. The roads were so bad that it took us two hours to get there. When we arrived, we were surprised to see more than forty people in attendance!

The service began with prayer and singing. Then it started to storm. It rained and sleeted. The wind blew and it was **cold**! However, the Bolivians did not let those things dampen their spirits! They were accustomed to that type of weather and were prepared. They pulled out a big sheet of plastic and fastened it to the Toyota; everyone got under the plastic, and the service continued. We knelt on the wet, cold ground as we prayed, and then we stood to sing and praise God for meeting with us and for the answers He was going to give. There were times of preaching in which the speakers admonished the congregation to continue to seek God until He came in revival.

During July I returned to the States for another three-month furlough. Much of my time at home was spent traveling with Glenda Kempa to camp meetings for missionary services and visiting with my family.

After returning to Bolivia in October, I began making preparations for Daily Vacation Bible Schools for the coming summer. While conducting the DVBS at Bolognia in December, I became concerned that there was no fruit. One morning I poured out my heart to the Lord asking Him to speak to the hearts of our boys and girls. At the end of class that day, I entreated, "Is there any boy or girl here who would like to ask Jesus to come into your heart and forgive you for your sins?"

"I do! I want to give my heart to Jesus!" said a little girl about nine years of age. She left her seat and came forward to pray. Immediately other children followed. It was a joyful privilege to pray with them.

Training DVBS Teachers

Glenda Kempa returned to Bolivia in January 2001, this time as a missionary. Shortly thereafter Glenda and I went to the Villa Tunari church to hold a training session for those who were willing to take charge of Daily Vacation Bible Schools and other children's work for their churches. Children's work was the burden on my heart. I was not well physically and was facing the possibility of returning to the States permanently. Pastors, Sunday school teachers, and any youth who had an interest in such work had been invited. I wondered how many would come and if there were people with whom I could share my burden. Were there other shoulders broad enough and other hearts willing to get into the yoke and pull together for the salvation of children?

When I arrived at the church on Monday, I was thrilled to find a Sunday school room overflowing with pastors, Sunday school teachers, and youth who were eager to learn. I was happy to take the class upstairs to the sanctuary for the extra space needed to train that many people!

As I started the class, I said, "Part of the time I will be teaching you as though you were children. Part of the time you will be participating as teachers." I took the lessons for the Daily Vacation Bible Schools that year from the book of Ruth. With joy I taught them to sing the "Gospel Train" song and "What Can Wash Away My Sins?" Glenda had helped me make enough illustrated songs so that every church could have their own copy of each song. They also received a folder containing a program of activities for every day of the DVBS. Instructions stated the goal for the lesson, the Scripture to be studied by the teacher, and a schedule of crafts they could make. On the inside cover of the folder was an outline showing how to win a child to Christ, and I emphasized that as the goal for the entire project. We continued our classes on Tuesday morning.

Previously, I had purchased a large roll of white flannel material and cut it into pieces. Each church was given a piece, and I showed them how they could place it over the pulpit and use it to hold their flannelgraph figures while they told the Bible stories. Glenda and I had sorted figures from the flannelgraph material I had collected over the years and gave each church a package and taught them how to find the figures for the stories. Afterward I told the story for the first day as an example of how to do it.

I also gave each church a chart of the Bible verses to be memorized. Pretending that they were children, I taught the first verse explaining the meaning of the pictures interspersed throughout the chart. Finally I gave them the needed supplies—scissors, paste, crayons, pencils, books for each age group, and the materials for the crafts. The next week I drove to several of the churches to give them supplies I had lacked on the days of training.

In late January the Daily Vacation Bible Schools were held in the city of El Alto. Each day I drove to the various churches to observe how the schools were progressing. It was thrilling to see how well the youth were doing. I praised God for allowing me to see my long-time dream fulfilled in such an exciting manner.

The following week the Daily Vacation Bible Schools were held in the country churches, and I visited those in Tuquiriri, Collana, and Quillcoma. In each place I found the teachers encouraged and enthusiastic and the children delighted to be attending.

Easter Convention and Physical Problems

The Tuesday before Easter of 2001, Steven Hight and Ronald Cook landed at the airport in Bolivia after a night flight from Miami. They came for our annual Easter convention. Later in the day we missionaries went to La Paz to the immigration office to get our papers renewed to stay in the country. We were standing in line hoping to get our pictures taken for our ID cards when we heard shouting. Outside a group of people were protesting in the street, some of them sitting on the street and stopping traffic. That was nothing new to us. We had seen it many times.

Suddenly we heard a shout from a police officer in the building, and the other officers rushed toward the doors to shut them. Glenda was on the balcony looking down and saw a cloud of tear gas enter the building before the doors were shut. Everybody tried to cover his nose and mouth. The people on the main floor ran upstairs and tried to get behind a barrier on the other side of the room. We were not quick enough. The gas burned our faces, noses, mouths, throats, and lungs. Everyone was crying, coughing, gasping, and choking.

When the air cleared, we hurried to the main street and decided not to wait for a bus. We were uncomfortable, badly shaken, and eager to get home, so we hailed a taxi. That experience made us extra thankful for the clean air that we had to breathe.

On Friday evening of the convention, Steven Hight preached on holiness. That night Benancia, the wife of Florentino Paco who was then the president of our work in Bolivia, and Jesusa, the wife of Lorenzo Salinas, our vice president, both sought and claimed holiness.

Easter Sunday morning Steven preached again. It was a real blessing because he knows Spanish well and could express himself freely, thus contributing to the liberty of the Spirit to move among the people. Ronald Cook, who had come to visit our work, preached. I interpreted for him since Steven was not feeling well. It was good to fellowship with our people and to have God move in our midst.

* * * * *

I was suffering with digestive problems that caused me to have very high blood pressure, and my weight had dropped to 100 pounds by May 10. After spending several days in the German clinic in La Paz, it was decided that I should return to the States on May 21. Because I was quite weak, Glenda Kempa accompanied me on my flight. It was humiliating to submit to wheelchair rides in the airports at Miami and Indianapolis. As my "chariot" was wheeled down the corridor of the Indianapolis airport, I was greeted by J. Stevan Manley and his wife who took me to their home in Bedford. Glenda went to visit relatives for a few days and then returned to Bolivia.

Chapter 18

Ministry During My Semiretirement Years
2001-2007

Getting Settled in Bedford, Indiana

When Irene Maurer retired from work on the foreign field, she returned to Pennsylvania and planned to live near her relatives. However, when she learned that I was returning to the States and needed care, she readily agreed to come to Bedford, Indiana, to help me. She arrived a few days after I did. It was arranged that temporarily we would stay in the house on the property where our International Headquarters is located in Bedford. I appreciated **very much** all that Irene did for me since I could not have coped without her help.

One day President Manley informed me that the Mission had decided not to send me back to Bolivia except for perhaps short visits. He reminded me that I had come home ill several times, and this time I was only "running on fumes."

All was in the divine plan. Had I come home just a little later, Irene's niece and nephews would have already purchased a place for her to live in Pennsylvania. Eventually, it worked out for Irene to move to Bedford and for us to live together in the mission house. We would be considered semiretired and do deputation work for the Mission from March to November of each year as long as we were able.

On June 5, 2001, as I was walking slowly through our dining room and feeling very weak, suddenly new strength flowed through my body. I was so remarkably strengthened that I spoke audibly, "Something has happened to me!" That evening Anita Brechbill, leader of a prayer band called Rope Holders, telephoned to tell me that they had a special prayer meeting on my behalf that day and felt that they had touched God. Then I told her what had happened to me. Praise the Lord, He still touches bodies! Throughout the summer months my strength gradually increased, and it was also a time of drawing closer to the Lord.

About that time Irene's sister Helen Bump needed help, and Irene had promised that she would go to Colorado Springs, Colorado, for the winter months to help her. Before she went, she returned to Shamokin, Pennsylvania, to get ready to move to Bedford.

Irene left on Wednesday, September 12, and that evening Helen Manley took me to prayer meeting with her at the Faith Mission Church in Bedford. I was really missing Irene and was not looking forward to staying by myself while she was gone. After service Helen took me home, and just as I stepped into our living room, I felt Jesus' presence **very near**! It was such a blessing that I walked through the house praising Him.

Esther Norton, a widow, had invited me to spend a few days with her in Parker City, Indiana, while Irene was away. We greatly enjoyed our time together, and I returned to Bedford before Irene came from Pennsylvania.

J. Stevan Manley and his wife traveled to Pennsylvania for a missions convention in October and rented a U-Haul truck and brought Irene's things to Bedford. Irene returned a few days later after being gone for five weeks, and it was good to see her again. She kept busy getting settled, and before long it was time for her to fly to Colorado.

Just before Thanksgiving the sewer line in the mission house malfunctioned, so I took my clothes to a Laundromat. While there I met a young man named Robbie. When I looked at him, I did not know if I could trust him. Cautiously, I asked him if he had lived in Bedford all his life.

"No," he said. "To tell you the truth, I just got out of the pen."

"Do you go to church?" I asked.

"No, I am an atheist, because there is no Santa Claus."

For a moment I did not know what to say. Then the Holy Spirit came to my rescue. "Robbie," I said, "you make me think of what happened to my Grandfather Hemmeter. Both of his parents died by the time he was nine years old. Some relatives took him, not because they loved him, but because they wanted his inheritance. When Christmas came, they told him there was no Santa Claus. He then thought about how his parents had told him that there was a God and there was a Santa Claus. He reasoned that since there was no Santa Claus, there must not be a God either. If there were a God, he also reasoned, He would not have taken both of his parents when he was very young.

"My grandfather ran away and lived as a hobo. One day when he returned to Cleveland, Ohio, he saw a mission in an old store building. He went inside, ascended some stairs, and entered a room. When he heard the people downstairs singing, he picked up a chair and pounded it on the floor to disturb them. At the close of the service, he went downstairs and found a godly woman waiting for him. She kindly placed her hand on his shoulder and said to him, 'Sonny, I love you and Jesus loves you, too!' It touched his heart, and he gave his heart to Jesus that evening. Later he was called of God to preach."

Robbie responded, "Maybe someday I, too, will give my heart to Jesus."

I asked him to wait for me while I went to the car and got a tract for him. I told him where our church was located and invited him to come. He accepted my invitation and came one Wednesday evening.

On Thanksgiving Day my brother, John, and his wife, Margey, and their children and families came to my home. The fifteen of us had a lovely time together. A few days later I returned to Parker City to spend the winter with Esther Norton.

Later that winter I made a trip to Michigan to meet Linda Kelley who was helping me with the early stages of this book. While there I stayed with Gertrude Campbell who had cared for my mother. During my visit in Michigan, Esther Norton's son Donald moved his mother to a house in Muncie, Indiana, that belonged to their family. After returning from Michigan, I helped Esther unpack and get her house in order. I also had a few deputation services while staying in Muncie.

I returned to Bedford in February, and Irene arrived a few days later from Colorado Springs. The next day we left with the Manleys to drive to St. Louis, Michigan, where we attended the celebration of Gertrude Campbell's eightieth birthday.

Gertrude Campbell celebrating her 80th birthday

254

Visiting the Dominican Republic

During early April 2002 I was busy preparing messages about holiness for the convention in the Dominican Republic where I would be the speaker. I was excited and at the same time concerned. Would their Spanish be too different from the Spanish we used in Bolivia? I found that it was not.

I flew from Indianapolis to Miami and on to Puerto Rico. Then I took a flight in a prop plane to the Dominican Republic, and from my

Congregation worshiping in the Dominican Republic

Children in the Dominican Republic

window I viewed the beautiful blue waters of the Caribbean Sea. David and Marilyn Middleton met me at the airport. Linda Kelley arrived on a later flight, and we went to the Middletons' home in Los Prados. We had the joy of spending some good times in prayer each day for the services.

God met with us time and again throughout the convention. I thank Him for the individuals who received help during that time.

Working with Youth

One thing the devil told me when I knew I was not going to return to Bolivia was that I would never again work with children and young people. Well, as we know, he is a liar. In March of 2002, Irene and I held a missions seminar at the Wesleyan Holiness Bible College in Point Pleasant, West Virginia. The topics for the three days were "Understanding God's Call," "Reacting to the Call," and "Keeping Focused on the Call." Each topic was broken into four parts with Irene and me each giving two sessions every day. There also were services each evening. What a joy it was to work with those precious young people!

In July Irene and I went to Candy Run Youth Camp near Lucasville, Ohio, to be the missionary speakers. It was a delight to challenge those young people to serve Jesus wherever He wanted them to go.

I especially remember wondering what I would do to keep their attention on the last day. I knew the young people had been up late the night before and would be sleepy. The Holy Spirit gave me the idea to have some of the youth act out one of the trips Irene and I had made to a distant church in the Andes Mountains of Bolivia. After the skit I invited the youth who wanted to dedicate their lives to Jesus to come and pray, and most of them came. Praise God for His help during that last session of the youth camp!

In May of the following year, Irene and I held a children's revival at Freedom Chapel in Hamilton, Ohio. On another occasion we helped in a DVBS there. We gave instructions regarding missionary work to four different groups of children. It was a delight to work with boys and girls on both of those occasions.

Thank God He has given me wonderful opportunities to work with children and youth!

Visiting Bolivia in 2003

Early in 2003, President Manley asked Irene and me if we would consider going back to Bolivia to participate in their annual Easter Convention. When I left Bolivia in 2001, my departure was quite abrupt. I was very sick and unable even to pack many of my things to bring home. When it was decided that I could not return as a full-time missionary, Glenda Kempa and Mark and Nancy Budensiek packed my things, and the Mission paid for them to be sent to Bedford. It was a dark hour for me, and it looked like I would never return to Bolivia. Now I was being offered an opportunity to go back with Irene. "Yes," was our happy answer.

My heart bubbled over with joy as Irene and I walked from the customs area into the entrance hall at the airport in El Alto, Bolivia, and saw the crowd waiting to welcome us. Along with Mark and Nancy Budensiek were fifteen Bolivians. I was thrilled when five-year-old Veronica and six-year-old Elias, two of my godchildren, presented me with kisses and baskets of flowers. Then I greeted Celia Ormachea. Oh, how happy I was to see that faithful servant of the Lord! When I had been the only EFM missionary in Bolivia, she often called me on the phone and quoted Scripture to encourage me. She even stayed with me at the mission house as often as she could.

The city of La Paz that sits in a bowl between the mountains. Notice the homes built on the steep mountainside in the foreground.

I then greeted the others in the group. The committee presented both Irene and me with a large basket of flowers, and Celia gave each of us a vase of beautiful red roses.

After loading the suitcases into the Toyota, Mark Budensiek took all of us to Burger King in the airport for breakfast. What a wonderful time we had visiting together while we ate. I told everyone that it was **one of the happiest days of my life!**

How good to see all the familiar sights again. We passed through La Paz with snow-covered Mt. Illimani in the background and climbed to another mountain pass and then down into Bosque de Bolognia.

That evening was the regular time for Bible study at our Bolognia church. We were invited to the front while they sang the welcome song, and the congregation came and greeted us Bolivian fashion with hugs. It was wonderful to be back!

After breakfast Wednesday morning Mark and Nancy took us to the nearby community of Calacota where we changed our Traveler's Checks into *bolivianos* and visited the local market. The rest of the day was spent resting and preparing for the revival services that were to begin the next evening.

About 5:00 p.m. on Thursday, the people were invited to have tea in the mission house. Our church people came with baked goods and salty snacks. We enjoyed a good time of fellowship together. After tea we went to the chapel behind the house for our first service. Irene and I took turns preaching in the services that weekend. God graciously met with us in each service and gave good altar services. Praise His name!

Shortly after Irene and I arrived, we were surprised to learn that our pastors were requesting lessons on prophecy, hermeneutics, homiletics, and Christian perfection. What a surprise! I had sent e-mails twice asking if they wanted us to preach or teach on any special subject while we were there. Alberto Abán said he e-mailed the home office to request those subjects, but somehow the message never got to us. We had taught those subjects to our Bible Institute students for years but were not prepared to teach them at that time. Consequently, we were up late at night and up early in the morning preparing for those lessons for the next week. I was grateful when

Irene located some prophecy charts I had made for my students in the past. She also borrowed a large chart on prophecy from a pastor. I was thankful for all the help I could get. Irene realized she could use some of her message outlines for lessons about sanctification. She found the Bible Institute textbook on homiletics, and I found books on Wiley's theology.

Monday morning I went with the Budensieks to a hospital in Mira Flores to interpret for them. They needed physicals because the Bolivian government required such before renewing their residency

Some of the pastors who attended special classes at Easter time in 2003.
Irene Maurer is in the back.

More pastors who attended the same classes. Mark Budensiek is in the back.

papers. We returned to Bolognia for dinner and to get Irene and then proceeded to our Villa Tunari church to begin the pastors' retreat. That evening several gathered together for a time of prayer, and then classes began on Tuesday morning.

Monday through Friday our pastors stayed in one of the downstairs classrooms where they put mattresses on the floor. The missionaries commuted each day. We taught classes during the day from Tuesday to Friday and had evening services on Wednesday through Friday.

Also on Friday morning we held our annual conference before we had class. That afternoon Mark Budensiek preached for the communion service, and I interpreted into Spanish. First Mark called our field committee to the front and served them; then he opened it to all who were present and asked the committee members to help serve those who came. Again God met with us. Praise His name! On Saturday we prepared for Easter Sunday.

Five hundred people braved the early morning temperatures and met in El Alto at 5:00 on Easter Sunday to begin a march to commemorate the resurrection of Jesus. Mark joined with our believers in that

Villa Tunari church where we held our Easter services in 2003

procession and drove the mission vehicle leading the group. With the sound of beating drums and voices raised in praise to God, the group rejoiced because of Jesus' resurrection. Nancy, Irene, and I felt it best not to join the march. Mark returned to Bolognia after the march to get us and take us to the Villa Tunari church in El Alto.

Bolivians love to sing! Florentino Paco had informed our pastors that their people could sing three or four special songs. They started their specials immediately following the march; however, with three songs from at least twenty churches, there would be sixty specials! Some churches had special instrumental numbers. We had a wonderful time praising our risen Savior.

It was my privilege to give the morning message on the resurrection of Jesus using Hebrews 13:20-21 as my text. I focused on the blood being the basis of the new covenant. All glory to Jesus, several people found Christ as their Savior that Easter morning. In the afternoon Florentino Paco preached an excellent message.

During the next several days we enjoyed visiting with our people and being in their homes for tea or a meal. One time we had my favorite Bolivian meal, *sajta de pollo*, a hot, spicy chicken dish made with freeze-dried potatoes, chicken, onions, and sliced tomatoes. At a farewell tea the field committee presented Irene and me with pewter plates that had the word "Bolivia" around the rim. The Bolivian flag and coat of arms were in the center. Engraved on the plates were the names of all the members of the committee. Mariano's family presented each of us with a miniature set of the various Bolivian musical instruments and a plush llama. Friday evening we attended a tea with the people of the Bolognia church. They also presented each of us with a gold-rimmed pewter plate that had the names of the people of the congregation engraved on it.

On Sunday we drove to the 25 de Julio church in El Alto where Tomas was the pastor. He is a widower with three precious little boys and an older daughter. He had been working diligently in his community and was influential in bringing some new people to the service on Easter Sunday. Several of them gave their hearts to Jesus that day.

After opening prayer and a good song service, Irene and I were asked to come down from the platform to accept a *chuspa*, a woven wool book bag in which to carry a Bible and songbook. Each bag had the figure of a llama woven on the front. The congregation came and gave us the traditional Aymara greeting, shaking one hand and putting the other hand on your shoulder. I had the privilege of preaching that morning.

Irene and I went to the home of Patricio and Agustina Chambi for dinner. They served *timpu*, which is mutton, rice, freeze-dried potatoes, and a yellow hot sauce. We enjoyed it greatly! In the afternoon Patricio and his family accompanied us to Bautista Saavedra where the believers were enjoying their recently built church. It was our first time to see their new building, and we rejoiced with them. That congregation had been moving from one rented place to another, but at last they had a lovely building of their own with the only drawback being a dirt floor. When we arrived, we were surprised to find the band from the 25 de Julio church already playing outside the church.

Monday was our last day in Bolivia because we had a 6:50 a.m. flight on Tuesday, April 29. We were at the airport in plenty of time to have breakfast with Mark and Nancy at Burger King. Going down the stairs for departure, we found five Bolivians waiting to say farewell. How we do praise God for His goodness in allowing us to visit Bolivia!

Visiting Bolivia in 2004

When Mark and Nancy Budensiek left Bolivia in October 2004 and retired from mission work, there were no other EFM missionaries available to take their place. After much prayer the Mission decided to send a national leader from Guatemala to Bolivia to help with the work. Elmer Sánchez, who had just finished his second term of leadership of the EFM work in Guatemala, was chosen.

When Irene and I were informed of the plans to send Elmer Sánchez, his wife, and their two young children to Bolivia, we realized that perhaps someone should be there to introduce them to our Bolivian pastors, so we began to pray accordingly. We were very desirous to go but left the matter in God's hands and went about our work. One morning President Manley asked if we would be willing to go to Bolivia and prepare the way for the Elmer Sánchez family. We were **delighted** and quickly agreed to go.

The Lorenzo Salinas family

On Monday, November 16, 2004, we had the joy of flying to Bolivia. Lorenzo Salinas, who was our national president at that time, and most of the national committee met us at the airport. We cleared customs and Lorenzo took us to Bosque de Bolognia where we had lived for many years. After he unloaded our suitcases, he took us to a Burger King for dinner, and then we purchased needed supplies before returning to the mission house.

I had wondered how we would get around during the time we were in Bolivia. To my surprise Lorenzo handed me the keys to the mission Mitsubishi. We surely did appreciate his kindness!

The day after we arrived, we received a phone call from the family of our close friend Celia Ormachea whose birthday is November 18. They were inviting us to the home of one of her daughters for a birthday gathering.

Celia Ormachea

263

The family served us *sajta de pollo* and also had a lovely birthday cake for Celia. As the custom is, they pushed her face into the cake frosting even though she was well up in years. We sang "Happy Birthday" in English and then in Spanish. It was so delightful to be back with our people again!

That evening was the regular prayer meeting for our Bosque de Bolognia church. When we got to church, they asked me to speak. Thankfully, I had some notes in my Bible that I had taken while listening to someone else preach. God helped me to minister using those notes.

Later that week we communicated by e-mail with Elmer Sánchez in Guatemala regarding the Bolivian government requirements for his family to enter the country. We learned that there is no Bolivian embassy in Guatemala. Immigration in La Paz told me that he would need to go to another country that had a Bolivian embassy, and Costa Rica was the nearest country. Eventually, all the paperwork was completed for them to come.

Before the arrival of the Sánchez family, we met with our national committee and explained to them that the Mission was sending that family to be their missionaries. One major advantage for that Guate-malan family was that they spoke Spanish as their first language.

The field committee had scheduled visits to a number of our churches for Irene and me while we were in Bolivia. The first one was the church at Jocopampa. However, I had developed a severe cold, and since our churches are not heated, Irene and I decided it would be wise for us not to go. Alberto Abán, the pastor of our Bolognia church at that time, asked Irene and me to speak in their services whenever we were present. We enjoyed sharing the Word with that congregation a number of times.

Early in December we visited our San Roque church. I had the privilege of giving a Christmas message and spoke from John 12:20-27 about the magnificent plan of God the Father. The presence of the Lord was in our midst and a number prayed at the close of the service. Later we ate our packed lunch in the mission vehicle and then drove to our Santiago II church where Irene preached.

It is customary to have the main holiday celebration on Christmas Eve, and we were honored to be invited to the home of

Sebastian Abán who attends our Bosque de Bolognia church. However, after we arrived, we went with Sebastian's family to the home of Carmen, one of his married nieces. We greatly enjoyed her two little children, Natalia and Ray, although we missed Carmen's husband who was working.

After the children opened their gifts, Carmen's father-in-law invited us to come downstairs for the special Christmas Eve supper that is always served about midnight. The meal is called *picaña*, which is beef, lamb, and chicken cooked with carrots, potatoes, and corn on the cob with a yellow, slightly hot sauce.

Before we ate, we were ushered into another room where they had a lovely Christmas tree, a large manger scene, and other Christmas decorations. We sang "Silent Night" in Spanish, and then Damian read the Christmas story from the Bible, and we all prayed the Lord's Prayer together.

From there we entered the dining room where the *picaña* was served along with some Christmas desserts made by Lourdes. Even though I could not eat the *picaña* at that hour of the night and feel well, I did have a little piece of dessert with a cup of hot tea.

Sunday, December 26, I drove with Irene to El Alto where we got Mariano and his wife, Juana. Together we traveled to our church in Cosmos 79 where I had the joy of preaching another Christmas message to our people. Christmas treats were given to the children of the congregation. After the morning service we shared a Bolivian potluck dinner on the patio of the church and had a pleasant time of fellowship.

That afternoon I asked Mariano to drive the Mitsubishi to our church in Villa Adela. We knew that property had been bought for a new church in that zone of El Alto, and we wanted to see it. More than seeing the property, we wanted to see our precious people. Irene was scheduled to preach at Villa Adela, but the congregation was having its elections, so that was not possible. After service we drove over to see the new property.

Next we went to the home of Lorenzo, our national president, but he and his family were not there, so we then headed toward the four-lane highway in El Alto. When we came to the intersection, the light was green and Mariano started through the intersection. Horrified, I saw a minibus headed toward us. The driver had the red light but did not stop. Soon we heard and felt the crash. Mariano, Irene, and I were thrown up against the roof of the vehicle in spite of wearing our seat belts, and we all had sore heads. I was in the back seat and had my window open a little. Glass from the minibus came through my window and landed **under** Irene and me! After we examined ourselves, I found that I had a slight scratch over my eyebrow, and the frame of my eyeglasses was greatly bent out of shape. At first Irene did not think that she had been hurt. However, both her legs had minor cuts that later became badly infected, and she went to a doctor for antibiotics for the infection. Mariano's wife, Juana, had been thrown up against the gearshift and injured her face, which swelled immediately. Our vehicle was severely damaged and could not be driven.

The people in the minibus were more seriously injured. The whole windshield of their vehicle was shattered, and when they got out of the minibus, blood was running down their faces. The wife of the driver was shouting accusations at Mariano. Soon the policemen arrived. The wife told them that Mariano must have been drinking. I told the policemen that was not the case and explained that he is a pastor and had been with us all day. One of the policemen asked me if perhaps he had been drinking the night before. Quickly I said, "No." The policemen then took Mariano and the driver of the minibus to the police station.

At that same time the pastor of our San Roque church, Martin Huanca, was returning to his home using public transportation. When he saw the crowd at the accident and recognized the mission Mitsubishi, he came to see if he could help us. Martin offered to call Lorenzo Salinas, but he was still not home, so he called Florentino Paco, our vice president, who came immediately.

Juana was being taken to a hospital just as Mariano returned from the police station. When he saw where his wife was going, he quickly ran and accompanied her.

The police came and towed our Mitsubishi to the police station. Florentino, Irene, and I rode inside the vehicle to the station, and then Florentino hailed a taxi and took us to Bosque de Bolognia. When we arrived at the mission house, Florentino called our insurance agent, the brother of one of the ladies in our Bolognia church, and reported the accident to him. Eventually the police learned from observers that the minibus driver had run a red light.

The next day Mariano took his wife to her own doctor and got the help she needed. In a few days she recovered from her injuries. We thanked God for His mercy to each of us.

The Elmer Sánchez family arrived from Guatemala in January 2005. I presented them to our pastors at a preachers' meeting. They gladly accepted Elmer as their missionary advisor.

The Elmer Sánchez family

While in Bolivia those three months, I was busy with government paperwork for the Mission. Irene busied herself in seeing that repairs were made on the mission property in Bolognia. We enjoyed being in the service of the King of kings again in Bolivia.

All too soon Irene and I found ourselves flying back to the States on February 22. We thanked God for a profitable trip to Bolivia and for His protection upon us.

Finding Another Hungry Soul

Back in Bedford, Indiana, Irene and I resumed our deputation travels for the Mission. We were always happy for an opportunity to share the gospel with needy souls, wherever we found them. On a bright July day in 2006, Irene and I were traveling to attend the wedding of James Rickenbach and Rachel Arndt.

As I drove, I became sleepy and decided I needed to eat some pretzels or wintergreen hard candy. To my dismay I found that I had failed to bring either of those with me. While discussing if we had time to stop and buy some, we saw the sign for a Marathon gas station.

As I pulled into the gas station, I noticed that they had a convenience store and found both pretzels and hard candy. When I walked to the counter, I observed that the young woman at the cash register looked to be either Hispanic or an Indian from India. While paying for my items, I asked her if she spoke Spanish. She replied, "No, I am an Indian from India." I told her she was a beautiful young woman.

I then went into the ladies' room, and Irene stepped to the counter and began talking with her. When I returned, I handed the young lady a tract. Irene asked about her religion, and she said she was Hindu. That opened the opportunity for Irene to tell her of our contact with Hindu teachers in the government school in Eritrea when we were there. She became very interested as we told of our work as teachers with our Mission in that country. We learned her name is Amisha. Finally we bid her good-bye and left the store.

Suddenly, to our surprise Amisha appeared beside our car. She told us that if we ever had a service near or in Indianapolis to let her know so she could attend. I asked her to write her name, address, and phone number on a piece of paper, which she did.

Irene and I talked about Amisha's spiritual interest as we continued our journey. I really feel that God allowed me to forget my candy and pretzels so that we might come in contact with her, a precious Hindu young lady who has a spiritual hunger. We added Amisha to our prayer list.

When we got back to Bedford after the wedding, I called Tim Stuart, pastor of the Wesleyan Holiness Church in Indianapolis, and told him about Amisha and her interest in spiritual things. I asked him and his wife to try to contact her.

At Thanksgiving while traveling through Indianapolis again, I took Amisha a Gideon New Testament that Carrie Boyer had left here in the house. She readily accepted it, and I encouraged her to begin reading in the Gospel of John.

Eventually Tim Stuart and his wife, Mary, were able to make contact with Amisha. Whenever possible, Irene and I endeavor to stop and see her. She told us that Pastor Stuart had told her about their services on Sundays and on Wednesday evenings. She has to work each Sunday but said she was thinking of attending some Wednesday evening service.

In December we were able to take Amisha a lovely new Bible. She was not working then, but her uncle was there. He told us she had just gone home but that he would give her the Bible. In fact, he called her on his cell phone and told her two ladies were there to see her and that we had a gift for her. He also allowed us to talk with her. I am praying that she will read the Bible, and as she does, God will speak to her.

With Irene at a recent Christmas party in the home office

To This Present Hour

God has gloriously guided my life unto this present hour. I am confident that He will continue to lead me until I behold His glory in heaven. Jesus, who first loved me, saved and sanctified me, called me, and led me, is worthy of **all the glory** I can possibly give to Him who died that I might have eternal life! Truly I have found the words of the song "It Is Glory Just to Walk with Him" true in my life. Verse two best expresses my walk with Him:

> It is glory when the shadows fall to know that He is near.
> Oh! what joy to simply trust and pray!
> It is glory to abide in Him when skies above are clear.
> Yes, with Him, it's glory all the way!

The chorus says,

> It is glory just to walk with Him.
> It is glory just to walk with Him.
> He will guide my steps aright,
> Thro' the vale and o'er the height.
> It is glory just to walk with Him.

"O give thanks unto the LORD; call upon his name: make known his deeds among the people. Sing unto him, sing psalms unto him: talk ye of all his wondrous works. Glory ye in his holy name: let the heart of them rejoice that seek the LORD. Seek the LORD, and his strength: seek his face evermore. Remember his marvellous works that he hath done; his wonders, and the judgments of his mouth" (Psalms 105:1-5).

Epilogue

I have been privileged to serve all of my missionary years in association with Evangelistic Faith Missions. During these years it has been my delight to work under the leadership of three EFM presidents—Victor Glenn, J.B. "Juddie" Peyton, and J. Stevan Manley.

While my father was pastoring the Church of the Nazarene in Roseville, Ohio, we often exchanged visits with the people of Fairview Mission near Glouster, Ohio. In 1959 I first heard about EFM and Victor Glenn from Dorothy Jago, pastor of the Fairview Mission. At that time I wrote to the Mission and inquired about missionary work. They sent me an application, but I did not complete it until some time later when the Lord prompted me to do so.

Rev. Victor Glenn

In the summer of 1960, Glenn Griffith introduced me to Victor Glenn at the Tri-State Holiness Association Camp at Clinton, Pennsylvania. I did not realize then what a plus that would be for me. Later I learned that Victor Glenn had promised Glenn Griffith that any young person he recommended to him as having a missionary call, he would see that he got to the mission field. The sixteen years I served in Ethiopia, East Africa, were under the leadership of Victor Glenn.

After coming home on furlough from Ethiopia in 1977, I heard Victor Glenn speak about starting a new work in Bolivia, South America. Just months before that God had reminded me about my call to Bolivia. After hearing Victor Glenn speak, I told him about my call to Bolivia. Later the Board approved my going to Bolivia, and in the summer of 1978, I went to Spanish language school in Costa Rica and then to Bolivia.

Rev. J.B. "Juddie" Peyton

J.B. "Juddie" Peyton became president and director of EFM in 1982. At that time I was working with EFM in Bolivia. I first met the Peytons when they came with Victor and Jennie Glenn to visit our work in Ethiopia in 1963. While home on furlough during 1977-1978, I sometimes worked in the home office with Eunice Peyton. Several times during that year I traveled with the Peytons in deputation work. It was a joy to serve under Juddie Peyton's leadership and to work with his wife, Eunice.

I first met J. Stevan Manley when I went as a missionary speaker to the church he was pastoring in Peoria, Illinois, in 1972. At that time I was on furlough from Ethiopia. In 1985 he became the General Superintendent of the Wesleyan Holiness Association of Churches of which I am a member. I was serving as a missionary with Evangelistic Faith Missions in Bolivia when he became president and director of EFM in 1994. It is a privilege to work under this man of God and with his precious wife, Helen.

Rev. J. Stevan Manley